DIY GUIDE TO

Ponds,
Fountains,

REVISED EDITION

Rain Gardens & Water Features

T0274063

Kathleen Fisher

Technical Editor for Current Edition: Nina Koziol

CREATIVE HOMEOWNER®

DIY Guide to Ponds, Fountains, Rain Gardens & Water Features
SENIOR EDITOR Kathie Robitz
PRINCIPAL AUTHOR Kathleen Fisher
CONTENT EDITOR Nancy T. Engel
CONSULTING HORTICULTURAL EDITOR Elizabeth P. Stell
INTERIOR DESIGN CONCEPT Glee Barre
GRAPHIC DESIGNER Kathryn Wityk
DIGITAL IMAGING SPECIALIST Mary Dolan
TECHNICAL REVIEWERS Ken Badgley, Carole Ottessen,
Mike Stoll, Brian Trimble
INDEXER Schroeder Indexing Services
COVER DESIGN CONCEPT Kathryn Wityk
FRONT COVER PHOTOGRAPHY left Photos Horticultural, design: Paul
Dyer/The Very Interesting Landscape
Co.; top right Bluestock/Dreamstime;
bottom right Lisa Turay/Dreamstime
BACK COVER PHOTOGRAPHY top right Jerry Pavia; bottom left Photo
Horticultural, design: Ash Parish
Garden Club

Updated Edition
Managing Editor: Gretchen Bacon
Editors: Joseph Borden and Christa Oestreich
Technical Editor: Nina Koziol
Designer: Chris Morrison
Indexer: Jay Kreider
Proofreader: Jean Bissell

DIY Guide to Ponds, Fountains, Rain Gardens & Water Features, Revised Edition
ISBN 978-1-58011-584-1

Library of Congress Control Number: 2022949271

We are always looking for talented authors. To submit an idea, please send a brief inquiry to acquisitions@foxchapelpublishing.com.

Printed in China

Second Printing

Creative Homeowner® is distributed by Fox Chapel Publishing Company, Inc., 800-457-9112, 903 Square Street, Mount Joy, PA 17552.

Dedication

In memory of Kathleen Fisher.

Many people were generous with inspiration and images. Thank you to the following for their help updating this version of the book: Lora Lee Gelles, Publisher, *POND Trade Magazine*; landscape architects Bob Hursthouse, Hursthouse, Inc., and Mary Allen, Plandscape, Inc.; Larry Carnes, president, Reflections Water Gardens; Jason Lenox, Ponds Inc. of Illinois; Dean MacMorris, Night Light, Inc.; Ashley Marrin, Bret-Mar Landscape; John Magyar, biologist and owner of Universal Aquatics LLC; and Tim Wood, owner of Aquatic Edge Ponds & Landscaping.

Safety First

Though all concepts and methods in this book have been reviewed for safety, it is not possible to overstate the importance of using the safest working methods possible. What follows are reminders—do's and don'ts for yard work and landscaping. They are not substitutes for your own common sense.

▮ Always use caution, care, and good judgment when following the procedures described in this book.

▮ Before you dig, determine if there are underground utility lines—gas, electric, water, cable, or phone—in the area. Call 811, the national call-before-you-dig phone number. Your state may have an 811 center website where you can request that the approximate location of buried utilities be marked so they are not accidentally hit while digging. Note: previous owners may have installed underground drainage, sprinkler, or lighting lines without mapping them.

▮ Always read and heed the manufacturer's instructions for using a tool, especially the warnings.

▮ Always ensure that the electrical setup is safe; be sure that no circuit is overloaded and that all power tools and electrical outlets are properly grounded and protected by a ground-fault circuit interrupter (GFCI). Do not use power tools in wet locations.

▮ Always wear eye protection when using chemicals, sawing wood, pruning trees and shrubs, using power tools, and striking metal onto metal or concrete.

▮ Always read labels on chemicals, solvents, and other products; provide ventilation; heed warnings.

▮ Always wear heavy rubber gloves rated for chemicals, not mere household rubber gloves, when handling toxins.

▮ Always wear appropriate gloves in situations in which your hands could be injured by rough surfaces, sharp edges, thorns, or poisonous plants.

▮ Wear safety glasses, a disposable face mask, or a special filtering respirator, when creating sawdust or working with toxic substances.

▮ Keep your hands, other body parts, and clothing away from the business ends of blades, cutters, bits, and other sharp tools.

▮ Always obtain approval from local building officials before undertaking construction of permanent structures.

▮ Never work with power tools when you are tired or under the influence of alcohol or drugs.

▮ Never carry sharp or pointed tools, such as knives or saws, in your pockets. If you carry such tools, use special-purpose tool scabbards.

Metric Equivalents

All measurements in this book are given in U.S. Customary units. If you wish to find metric equivalents, use the following tables and conversion factors.

Inches to Millimeters and Centimeters

1 in = 25.4 mm = 2.54 cm

in	mm	cm
1/16	1.5875	0.1588
1/8	3.1750	0.3175
1/4	6.3500	0.6350
3/8	9.5250	0.9525
1/2	12.7000	1.2700
5/8	15.8750	1.5875
3/4	19.0500	1.9050
7/8	22.2250	2.2225
1	25.4000	2.5400

Inches to Centimeters and Meters

1 in = 2.54 cm = 0.0254 m

in	cm	m
1	2.54	0.0254
2	5.08	0.0508
3	7.62	0.0762
4	10.16	0.1016
5	12.70	0.1270
6	15.24	0.1524
7	17.78	0.1778
8	20.32	0.2032
9	22.86	0.2286
10	25.40	0.2540
11	27.94	0.2794
12	30.48	0.3048

Feet to Meters

1 ft = 0.3048 m

ft	m
1	0.3048
5	1.5240
10	3.0480
25	7.6200
50	15.2400
100	30.4800

Square Feet to Square Meters

1 ft² = 0.092 903 04 m²

Acres to Square Meters

1 acre = 4046.85642 m²

Cubic Yards to Cubic Meters

1 yd³ = 0.764 555 m³

Ounces and Pounds (Avoirdupois) to Grams

1 oz = 28.349 523 g

1 lb = 453.5924 g

Pounds to Kilograms

1 lb = 0.453 592 37 kg.

Ounces and Quarts to Liters

1 oz = 0.029 573 53 L

1 qt = 0.9463 L

Gallons to Liters

1 gal = 3.785 411 784 L

Fahrenheit to Celsius (Centigrade)

$°C = °F - 32 \times 5/9$

°F	°C
-30	-34.45
-20	-28.89
-10	-23.34
-5	-20.56
0	-17.78
10	-12.22
20	-6.67
30	-1.11
32 (freezing)	0.00
40	4.44
50	10.00
60	15.56
70	21.11
80	26.67
90	32.22
100	37.78
212 (boiling)	100

Contents

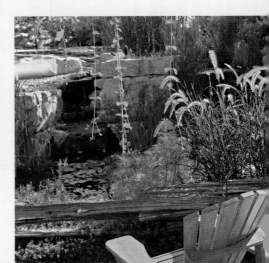

Introduction

Earth. Fire. Wind. Water. Our ancestors were fascinated by those elements, and they continue to captivate us in gardens today. Water is often an overlooked feature for residential gardens, but the sound of trickling or cascading water can be very relaxing. It can also mask some of the street noise in urban areas. This book will help lead the way as you create a beautiful water feature of your own.

An ornamental water feature can be as simple as a fountain, a birdbath, or a contemporary pondless waterfall. It can be a deeper, koi-filled pond, fed by water that cascades gently over large boulders and flows slowly down a meandering stream. Or it could be an elegant fountain or formal pool (or both) in front of your home. Whatever form it takes, water adds tranquility, provides pleasant reflections of the sky and clouds, and adds ambiance to a garden. This book is organized to inspire you and provide practical, hands-on information.

Join me as we tour historical water gardens through the centuries—all inspiration from the past. Discover ways to plan and design your water feature, and how you can make it an integral part of your home landscape. A good, basic plan helps ensure that your pond, fountain, or other water element will bring you, your family, and your visitors delight for years to come. We cover the nuts and bolts of installing a pond, beginning with how to sketch your ideas on paper. Proper installation is the key to long-lasting enjoyment of a pond. The sections on moving water—fountains and sprays—as well as lighting, stonework, and bridges offer tempting ideas in the pages ahead. And for something completely different, we've included a section on "natural" swimming pools—without chlorine or other chemicals.

Rain gardens show how to capture water runoff so it replenishes the groundwater without spilling into a pond. We'll also tackle attracting (or discouraging) critters, routine maintenance, and plant selection for inside and around your pond.

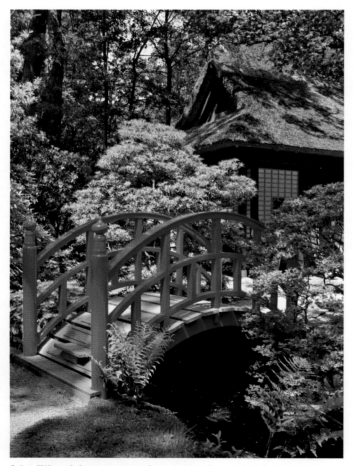

A traditional Japanese garden may inspire you to adapt one or two elements and incorporate them into your own design.

There's no better inspiration than nature. You can create a naturalistic look for your pond using freeform shapes, plantings, and stones.

Hardiness Zone Map

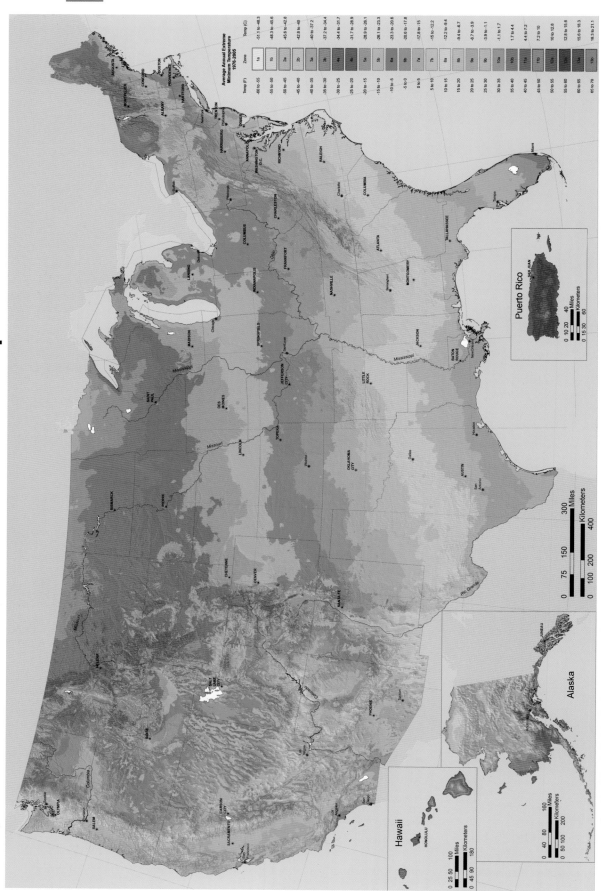

Temp (F)	Zone	Temp (C)
-60 to -55	1a	-51.1 to -48.3
-55 to -50	1b	-48.3 to -45.6
-50 to -45	2a	-45.6 to -42.8
-45 to -40	2b	-42.8 to -40
-40 to -35	3a	-40 to -37.2
-35 to -30	3b	-37.2 to -34.4
-30 to -25	4a	-34.4 to -31.7
-25 to -20	4b	-31.7 to -28.9
-20 to -15	5a	-28.9 to -26.1
-15 to -10	5b	-26.1 to -23.3
-10 to -5	6a	-23.3 to -20.6
-5 to 0	6b	-20.6 to -17.8
0 to 5	7a	-17.8 to -15
5 to 10	7b	-15 to -12.2
10 to 15	8a	-12.2 to -9.4
15 to 20	8b	-9.4 to -6.7
20 to 25	9a	-6.7 to -3.9
25 to 30	9b	-3.9 to -1.1
30 to 35	10a	-1.1 to 1.7
35 to 40	10b	1.7 to 4.4
40 to 45	11a	4.4 to 7.2
45 to 50	11b	7.2 to 10
50 to 55	12a	10 to 12.8
55 to 60	12b	12.8 to 15.6
60 to 65	13a	15.6 to 18.3
65 to 70	13b	18.3 to 21.1

Average Annual Extreme Minimum Temperature 1976-2005

The Hardiness-Zone Map developed by the Agricultural Research Service of the USDA divides the country into 13 zones according to average minimum winter temperatures. Hardiness zones are used to identify regions to which plants are suited based on their cold tolerance, which is what "hardiness" means. Many factors, such as elevation and moisture level, come into play when determining whether a plant is suitable for your region. Local climates may vary from what is shown on this map. Contact your local Cooperative Extension Service for recommendations for your area. Or go to www.planthardiness.ars.usda.gov to find your hardiness zone based on your zip code. Mapping by the PRISM Climate Group, Oregon State University.

AHS Heat-Zone Map

AMERICAN HORTICULTURAL SOCIETY
7931 East Boulevard Drive
Alexandria, VA 22308 U.S.A.
(703) 768-5700 Fax (703) 768-8700

Coordinated by:
Dr. H. Marc Cathey, President Emeritus

Compiled by:
Meteorological Evaluation Services Co., Inc.

Underwriting by:
American Horticultural Society
Goldsmith Seed Company
Horticultural Research Institute of the
American Nursery and Landscape Association
Monrovia
Time Life Inc.

Copyright © 1997 by the American Horticultural Society

The American Horticultural Society Heat-Zone Map divides the United States into 12 zones based on the average annual number of days a region's temperatures climb above 86°F (30°C), the temperature at which the cellular proteins of plants begin to experience injury. Introduced in 1998, the AHS Heat-Zone Map holds significance, especially for gardeners in southern and transitional zones. Nurseries, growers, and other plant sources will gradually begin listing both cold hardiness and heat tolerance zones for plants, including grass plants. Using the USDA Plant Hardiness map, which can help determine a plant's cold tolerance, and the AHS Heat-Zone Map, gardeners will be able to safely choose plants that tolerate their region's lowest and highest temperatures.

Canada's Plant Hardiness Zone Map

Canada's Plant Hardiness Zone Map outlines the different zones in Canada where various types of trees, shrubs, and flowers will most likely survive. It is based on the average climatic conditions of each area. The hardiness map is divided into nine major zones: the harshest is 0 and the mildest is 8. Relatively few plants are suited to zone 0. Subzones (e.g., 4a or 4b, 5a or 5b) are also noted in the map legend. These subzones are most familiar to Canadian gardeners. Some significant local factors, such as micro-topography, amount of shelter, and subtle local variations in snow cover, are too small to be captured on the map. Year-to-year variations in weather and gardening techniques can also have a significant impact on plant survival in any particular location.

Plant Hardiness Zones

0a	4a
0b	4b
1a	5a
1b	5b
2a	6a
2b	6b
3a	7a
3b	7b
	8a

PART 1

A World of Inspiration

A garden is an invitation to a wonderful sensory experience. Colorful flowers, fragrant herbs, and the sound of birds draw us outdoors. A water feature adds a different, unexpected dimension. It reflects the sky and clouds. It may be a bubbling fountain, a cascading waterfall, or the flash of a golden-yellow fish in a pond that excites us. Large or small, liquid assets can enhance the garden. But first, you need a plan.

CHAPTER 1

Inspiring Ideas: Past and Present

Humans have long valued water. We know it as the sustainer of life and sense it as a source of our origins. The earliest recorded water gardens reflect these things: the need for water to drink and bathe, the necessity to irrigate life-sustaining crops, the desire for a sense of coolness and for comforting sounds in harsh surroundings, a need to control nature, and in many religious traditions, a connection with the Creator.

This is where water gardens began—in the Cradle of Civilization, located between the Taurus Moutains of eastern Asia Minor and the Persian Gulf.

Fountains Abbey, in North Yorkshire, England, is the remains of a medieval Cistercian monastery.

Early Civilizations

Ancient Egyptians drew water from the Nile with a simple device called a shadoof.

The Cradle of Civilization was the birthplace of water gardens. The inhabitants of ancient Mesopotamia (which corresponds to modern-day Iraq and parts of Iran, Syria, and Turkey) owed their success to their ability to control the Tigris and Euphrates rivers. They developed a complex system of canals and waterworks for irrigation. Evidence of ornamental water gardens from this period is limited to a few artifacts—a carved water basin from 3000 BCE and a stone fountain from about 1,000 years later.

The Assyrians, who inhabited the southern half of the Tigris and east, built vast hunting parks, and lifted water at least three stories high to plant the temple towers called ziggurats, the most famous of which were the Hanging Gardens of Babylon.

The Egyptians harnessed the Nile River with a device called the "shadoof" or "shaduf," consisting of a horizontal pole attached to a pivot with a bucket on one end and a counterweight on the other. Carvings and relics in Egyptian tombs show us that they had elaborate pleasure gardens, where these desert dwellers could escape the heat.

In a tomb built in Thebes around 1400 BCE, archeologists found plans for a garden divided into four main areas with a rectangular pond in each. This cross-shaped motif often featured lotus plantings. Egyptians revered the lotus as medicine and a religious symbol. Another early water garden plant was the bulrush, famous for hiding the abandoned infant Moses in the Bible, but also used to fashion ropes, mats, sails, and to construct rafts solid enough to transport stone obelisks.

In the middle of the eighteenth century, the Landscape Movement in Great Britain inspired a naturalistic style that emphasized water rather than heavy planting. Here, the reflection of the house in the water enhances the overall landscape.

PERSIA

The citizens of Persia (now Iran) also divided their gardens with cross-shaped channels, a form they called "chahar-bagh." Cyrus the Great, in the sixth century BCE, watered his garden through underground channels called "qanats," made by drilling a shaft to the source of water, then sloping a channel to its destination.

About a century later a descendant, Cyrus the Younger, is credited with coining the word "paradise" (although certainly not the concept) for a garden. He named his garden "Pairidaeza," from the Persian words meaning "around" and "wall." Persians loved their gardens so much that they wove their designs into rugs to enjoy them in winter.

When Islamic Arabs invaded Persia in 637 CE, it launched the spread of this garden throughout the Islamic world for at least a millennium. These road-and-dust-weary nomads were enchanted by the walled gardens and further inspired by the Koran, in which Mohammed described paradise as a garden complete with fountains.

The Generalife. In the thirteenth century, the Moors—descendants of Arabs and Berbers who invaded Spain in 711 CE—built two exemplary gardens in existence today in the hills overlooking Granada, Spain. The Generalife Palace and Gardens was the leisure summer residence for the kings of Granada. The garden is romantic, intimate, and sensual. The Generalife Gardens include the Patio de la Acequia (Court of the Water Channel).

Alhambra. Gardens of the Alhambra (Red Castle) are massive and expansive as befits a fortress, which it was. In the Court of the Lions, a dozen carved King of Beasts spout water into a hexagonal pool and hold aloft a 12-sided fountain basin. Around the edges of this court, alabaster columns support ornate arcades.

India. Some 7,000 miles away in Mogol India (captured by Asian warlords such as Tamberlane and Genghis Khan in the thirteenth and fourteenth centuries), gardens reflected the Persian influence in their canals and geometric shapes. They harnessed rivers to fuel water features, notably the chute called the "chadar."

In the late 1500s, hundreds of Mogul gardens were built at the foot of the Himalayas in Kashmir, where water flowed down the mountains and into Lake Dal. One of those surviving is Shalamar Bagh, as famous for its name, meaning "place of love," as for its series of pavilions surrounded by water. The nearby Nishat Bagh is made breathtaking by a central canal descending over 12 levels, each linked by a broad chadar. Over these falls, water plays over indentations in the rocks, which are angled to capture sunlight.

Taj Mahal. The Moguls are also famous for their tomb gardens, particularly The Taj Mahal, built between 1632 and 1654 by the last Mogul emperor, Shah Jahan, in memory of his favorite wife, Mumtaz Mahal. He broke tradition by positioning the tomb at one end of the cross-shaped canal, rather than in the center, so that the entire structure is reflected.

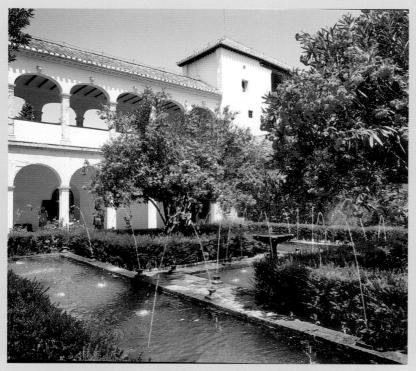

Moorish water garden. The Generalife is a sensual garden near Granada and was a summer residence for Spanish rulers.

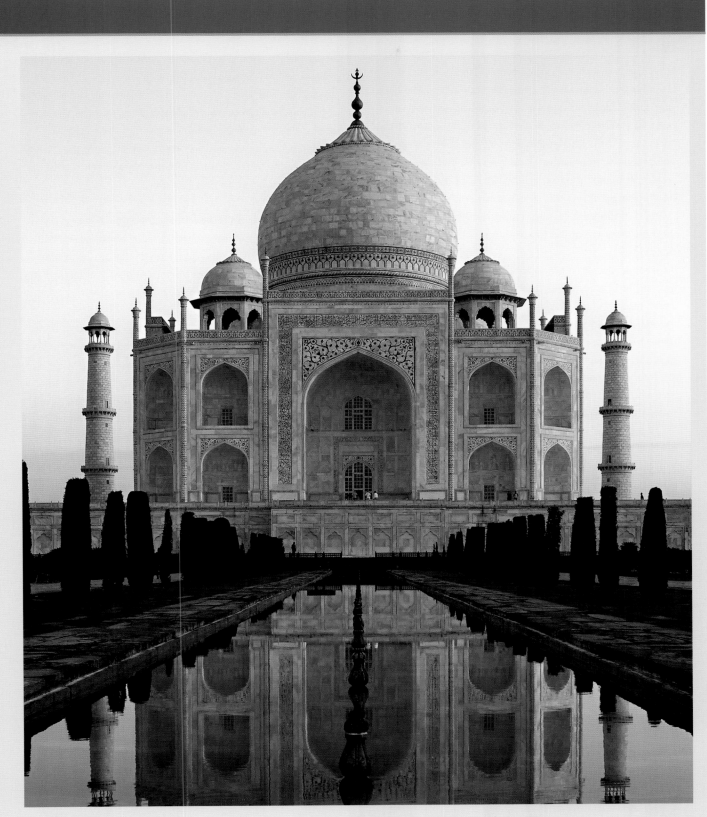

The Taj Mahal, the most famous of the Indian tomb gardens, honors the memory of a Mogul emperor's favorite wife.

ASIA

The earliest Chinese gardens, like those of the Assyrians, were sprawling hunting parks. Their emperors, beginning at least with the Han dynasty (20 to 220 CE), built lakes covering hundreds of acres as centers for boating and socializing. But even though most of these lakes were artificial—and in winter, sometimes the flowers were, too—nature was the ideal in these as well as in small private gardens. Many of the latter have been reconstructed in Suzhou, sometimes called the "Venice of the East," where canals and enclosed courtyard gardens lap at the foundations of homes and other buildings.

Confucius set the tone for Chinese gardens in 500 BCE, with the axiom that "the wise find joy in water, the benevolent find joy in mountains." These two elements—the water representing the female, or *yin*, and rocks the male, or *yang*—have been central to Asian gardens ever since. Just as *feng shui* is the art of creating interior spaces with positive energy, the goal of shanshui (the word for landscaping that means mountains and water) is to bring energy to gardens.

Western gardeners often remark that plants play a secondary role in Asian gardens, although this is less true than it was for the Islamic or Italian Renaissance gardens, where the majority of plantings were evergreens. In China, the favored plants were the three friends of water (plum, bamboo, and pine), and peonies, chrysanthemums, and of course, lotuses. Lotuses were especially sacred to Buddhists, who believed that Buddha was born in the heart of a lotus.

In 612 AD a missionary from Japan described the Chinese imperial gardens to his own empress, who adapted the lake-and-island motif for her gardens. Although the basics of Asian gardening have changed little over the centuries, as they have in the West, there are some distinct periods of influence that changed garden design:

■ **The Heian period (795–1195),** which further emphasized reproducing natural beauty in small landscapes, with specific suggestions for the diversion of streams and placement of rocks. Ponds were to be shaped like a crane in flight and islands like a turtle, both symbolizing eternity.

■ **Momoyamam (1573–1603),** when the tea garden came to the forefront, with the introduction of water basins for that ceremony and stepping-stones across lakes.

■ **Edo (1603–1867).** Edo was the name for Tokyo until 1869, and this burgeoning city saw the development of wealthy estates with attendant large lakes.

Some Japanese gardens are stroll gardens, intended to take visitors on a contemplative journey, while true contemplation gardens are to be viewed from indoors or a terrace. When bringing water to a garden is impossible, the Japanese suggest water with the placement of rounded stones.

Egyptians and Chinese revered the lotus flower, here depicted by Yum Shou-Ping (1633–1690) in Album of Flowers.

Garden design is an artform that has existed in Japan for centuries. This traditional design is located in Kyoto.

ANCIENT GREECE, ROME, AND THE RENAISSANCE

The ancient **Greeks** did not create artificial water gardens around their homes, but rather, revered natural areas endowed with springs, which they believed were homes of gods and nymphs. Later, these were embellished with statuary, and in time evolved into elaborate nymphaea, or water theaters.

Romans. The Romans were considerably more ambitious. Pliny the Younger (62 to 113 CE) left detailed records of his hillside garden, where a pool with a tall water jet alternately filled and emptied and water gushed from a stone cistern under a semicircular marble bench into a marble basin below. Pliny's villa also featured a hippodrome—a structure for horse races—as did that of Hadrian, emperor from 117 to 138 CE. Hadrian's, at Tivoli, contained a central canal longer than 5 football fields. His circular Marine Theater contained a pool with an island, on which stood a pavilion large enough to have its own garden and several rooms. Surviving still is the Canopus, a curving colonnaded canal in an excavated valley. That more modest private gardens did exist we know courtesy of Mount Vesuvius' eruption in 79 CE. It preserved for all time the city of Pompeii, where small open spaces, surrounded by colonnades, often contained basins with fountains. It was during the Renaissance in the sixteenth century that Italy and then France developed the ornate classical-style water gardens and fountains.

The Greeks believed springs were home to gods and embellished them as elaborate water theaters.

Italian Renaissance. Many Italian Renaissance water features evoked scholarly subjects. There were the massive stone fountains carved by great artists of the time such as Andrea del Verrocchio (Boy with a Dolphin), frequently depicting goddesses such as Venus or January shivering in the cold. But these artisans had an equally playful side. They devised grottos to frighten visitors, whimsical beings animated by water (automata) to amaze them, and water games (giochi d'acqua) to play tricks on them.

Tivoli. Considered the ultimate example of this creativity is the Villa d'Este at Tivoli. Designed by Pirro Ligorio for the Cardinal Ippolito d'Este, it was sited at the top of a steep slope with views to Rome and the Sabine Hills. The fountains are powered by diverting water—over 300 gallons a second—from a nearby river. Its most famous feature is the Terrace of One Hundred Fountains, where terraces hold three rows of spouts punctuated with carvings of eagles and obelisks.

The towering geysers of its Organ Fountain are indeed reminiscent of a mighty organ's pipes, but in fact the fountain was named for its sound, as were the Owl and Dragon fountains. Elsewhere, stair rails are also water chutes, and water spurts from the breasts of a sphinxlike creature.

Villa Lante. At the Villa Lante, the sides of a narrow canal called a catena d'acqua are scrolled to look like a chain. While the more reverential Muslims raised the sides of water channels as an invitation to sit and contemplate the heavens, here architect Giacomo Vignola built a long table with a trough in the center with more earthly intent—cooling wine.

Grottoes. These water features had their origins in the nymphaea of ancient Greece. In the classical world, they evolved into ornate terraces or rooms with statues, columns, and balustrades. The grotto, on the other hand, retained a pretense of being a rough-hewn cave while becoming ever more elaborate and fanciful. Like the Haunted House at an amusement park, grottoes combined bits of lore with special effects, with the same results—squeals and nervous laughter. Some went for glitter, with crystal stalactites and high ceilings encrusted with semiprecious stones and imported seashells. One that Bernardo Buontalenti created for the Medicis at Boboli featured a sculpture of slaves by Michelangelo and was lit by a crystal fish bowl inserted in its roof.

At the Villa Pratolino, a Medici garden that no longer exists, he gave free reign to his playful side, in some cases combining automation with classical figures such as the Apennine (January), pressing his hand on the head of a sea creature to squeeze water from its mouth. A washerwoman appeared to wring water from a marble cloth. Guests who weren't soaked by squirting benches were drenched by jets on staircases. Water-activated whistles imitated numerous bird species.

On a purely grand scale were the baroque water theaters, most notably the one built at Villa Aldobrandini for Pope Clement VIII. Created as a semicircular amphitheater behind the villa, its balustraded wall is punctuated with huge niches inhabited by statues. In the central cove, Atlas stands atop a hill of stones hoisting on his shoulders a globe that releases a curtain of water. But the show continues above him, where a steep water staircase, flanked by two spiral-dominated pillars, is cut into the wooded hillside.

The most famous feature of this Tivoli garden is the Terrace of One Hundred Fountains, with three rows of water spouts.

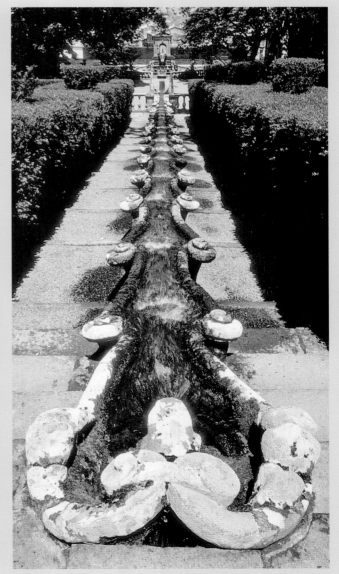

This scroll-sided canal, the Catena d'Acqua (chain of water), was designed for Cardinal Giovanni Francesco.

FRANCE

As the Italian influence flowed to France, its style was first copied and then adapted, with the baroque flourishes and aquatic playfulness displaced by emphasis on tying architecture to the formal landscape on a sweeping scale. In many cases, these grand gardens were extensions of the moat-surrounded French chateau. Because the landscape sites were often much flatter than in Italy, cascades gave way to reflecting pools and parterres, gardens with paths between features. Italian Renaissance style moved most literally across international lines via the Francinis. One of them, Thomas, had been at Pratolino before he and two brothers came to France to work for King Henry IV (whose wife was Marie de Medici) in the 1590s. (Thomas's sons would eventually work for Louis XIV at Versailles.)

At Saint-Germain-en-Laye, the Francinis filled the royal garden with fountains, grottoes, and automata. But it was the garden of Cardinal Richilieu at Rueil, begun in 1610, where the brothers made their biggest

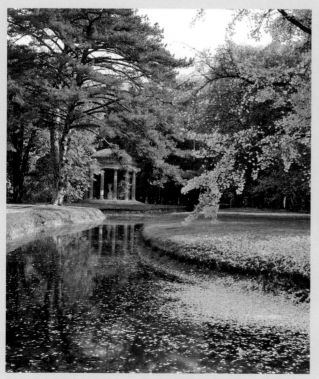

Temple of Venus. Le Notre used water to bring life to the Temple of Venus and the sprawling landscape of Versailles in France.

splash (so to speak). Bringing water a mile and a quarter by aqueduct, they powered among other things an immense cascade and two grottoes. In one grotto, satyrs and nymphs spouted water from their genitals, and visitors could manipulate a water spout to form flowers, umbrellas, stars, and other shapes.

Seventeenth-Century France. Another hallmark of this period was converting shallow muddy areas into lakes or canals by giving them a new artificial edge. At the royal gardens at Fontainebleu southeast of Paris, for instance, a marsh was shaped into a triangular lake. The chateau was further surrounded by moats on other sides. Later, Thomas Francini's brother Alexandre would add his famous Tiber fountain. But it was Andre Le Notre who, after putting the finishing touches on Fountainebleu, created the three gardens considered to be exemplary of seventeenth-century France: Chantilly, Vaux-le-Vicomte, and Versailles.

Chantilly. A relatively small chateau, Chantilly was surrounded by large moats but positioned so that Le Notre chose to open vistas in two directions. Andre Le Notre edged an existing river to form the Grand Canal more than 100 yards across and extending a mile before turning a half mile in a second direction. Chantilly also is characterized by a water parterre, long vistas, and a series of rectangular, round, and oval reflecting basins. The chateau there was destroyed during the Revolution 200 years after its constuction, but has been rebuilt.

Vaux-le-Vicomte. Owned by Louis XIV's finance minister, Vaux-le-Vicomte is an example of the moated chateau. The garden, surrounded by woods, descends slowly past an immense parterre of swirling greenery. The main canal, some 1,100 yards long, is concealed from visitors by a terrace, but far in the distance they can see a grotto with seven immense arched niches, topped by a balustraded terrace, then a hillside sweeping up toward a statue of Hercules. Between the house and main canal is the Grand Miroir d'Eau, a square pool that reflects the entire water-surrounded chateau. The effect has been compared to that of the Taj Mahal, which was completed two years before Le Notre began work here. A buttressed cascade tumbles down from the platform on which the chateau seems to float, but there are few fountains. Instead, this garden is famous for the exquisite proportions and perfect relationship of its elements.

Peterhof. At the palace of Russia's Peter the Great in Peterhof, a canal flows to the sea between jets of water.

rounding mountains. That garden in turn inspired the Palazzo Reale near Naples, the home of Philip's son Charles III and site of what is considered the grandest of all cascades, stretching almost two miles up a hillside and fed by an aqueduct almost 25 miles long.

Peterhof. In St. Petersburg, Russia, the palace and park at Peterhof (also known as Petrodvorets) are often referred to as the Russian Versailles. The Emperor of Russia, Peter I (the Great), founded Peterhof in 1709 as a country estate. After visiting France in 1717, he decided to make Peterhof into an imperial residence that would rival Versailles. The Grand Cascade has 64 fountains and more than 200 statues, bas-reliefs, and other decorations.

Versailles. One of the most famous gardens in Europe, Versailles was the playground of the Sun King, Louis XIV. While the major design of the garden was carried out in the mid-1660s, both structure and landscape saw expansion over several decades.

Individual features may sound like echoes of other Le Notre designs—a cross-shaped canal (5,900 by 4,920 feet), a water parterre, numerous reflecting basins—but what sets it apart are both the sprawling site and the skillful way he used water to make it vibrant, rather than an outdoor museum. Like many Renaissance gardens, its sculpture focused on a classical theme, in this case Apollo the sun god. In one of Versailles's most photographed images, Apollo rises from a pool on his horse-drawn chariot. In the water parterre are two pools that reflect the palace façade; beyond the vast orange grove is a lake 765 yards long. On cross axes with the grand canal are bosquets—groves of trees—each framing a fountain that continues the Apollo legend. Unlike Chantilly, water resources were not up to the task, and it was a constant struggle to pressurize the 1,400 water jets.

The Sun King's grandson Philip V was more fortunate in this regard when, as King of Spain, he tried to copy Versailles at La Granja, where two reservoirs collected water from sur-

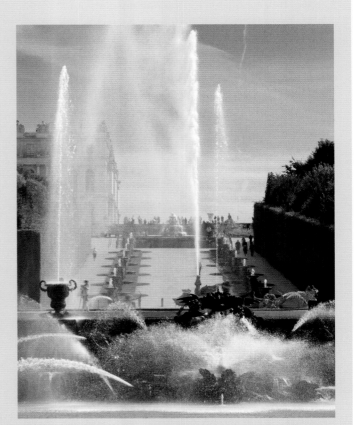

Neptune fountain in Versailles. The fountain represents Neptune, the ancient god of seas and oceans.

ENGLAND

Elsewhere in Europe, gardens were relatively austere. The Dutch and Germans preferred formal canals, jets rather than fountains, and relatively little sculpture. An example is Herrenhausen in Germany, begun in 1680, where water adds movement to rectangular patterns of tall trees and hedges.

Chatsworth. A notable exception to this restraint is Chatsworth, developed over two centuries beginning with the first Duke of Glouchester in the late seventeenth century. From a domed "cascade" house built by baroque architect Thomas Archer, a 24-foot-wide water stair tumbles down a hill toward the house. A pupil of Le Notre designed other waterworks. In the eighteenth century, the grounds would take a step toward the future with the work of Capability Brown, who altered the course of the nearby Derwent River to give the home a more picturesque approach.

Beginning in 1826, under the sixth Duke of Devonshire, head gardener Joseph Paxton attempted to link artifice and nature, shaping rocky cascades and woodland water features. The Duke, wanting to impress Russia's Czar Nicholas I on a planned visit, had Paxton build the single-jet Emperor Fountain. Powered by gravity from a lake 381 feet higher, it was then the tallest jet in the world at 290 feet. (The czar became ill and never saw it.) Paxton also designed the famed Crystal Palace, built to house the temperate world's first giant waterlily, *Victoria amizonica*, with pads more than six feet across.

Landscape Movement. Beginning with the first half of the eighteenth century, the Landscape Movement led a trend away from enclosed outdoor rooms and toward gardens that linked architecture to the world beyond. As in Asia, nature was the model to emulate. Fountains and jets were considered gauche. "Only the vulgar citizen...squirts up his rivulets in jettaux," wrote one critic. Instead, designers created waterfalls, bubbling streams, rocky ravines, or rills—narrow channels that wound among trees or hillocks. By 1819, even the ingenious design at Villa Pratolino in Italy would be replaced by an English-style garden. Somewhat ironically, those who espoused the natural landscape often altered both wetlands and historic gardens in ways that would be unthinkable or even illegal today.

Blenheim Palace. This French-influenced water parterre was built for the Duke of Marlborough at Blenheim, his Oxfordshire, England, estate, in the 1920s.

Monet's Garden. The artist Monet broke from tradition by damming a stream to create his romantic and heavily planted pond.

Mid-to-Late 1800s

By the mid-1800s, there were fewer grand private estates where landscape architects could move even miniature mountains or streams. Public parks became a more frequent subject for water-garden designers. Joseph Paxton's design for Birkenhead Park near Liverpool, with two labyrinthine lakes and an island, inspired American Frederick Law Olmsted's work in New York's Central Park, Brooklyn's Prospect Park, and Boston's Back Bay.

Monet's Garden. In the 1890s, artist Claude Monet made a radical move at Giverny by damming a stream to create his famous pond. Divorced from any reference to the surrounding architecture, it was lushly and sensuously planted, inspiring most of his late work—and many romantically inclined gardeners today. In the early twentieth century, architect Edwin Lutyens and plantswoman Gertrude Jekyll were a famous pair, billed as collaborators but often disagreeing about whether structure or plantings should get top billing. One of Lutyens's favorite water features was the dipping well: an arched alcove where a basin was fed by a spout. Adapted from Renaissance designs, it nevertheless fit beautifully in small landscapes.

Jekyll, known for her lavish perennial borders and use of flower color, recommended restraint in the number of species planted adjacent to a pond. She recommended planting the garden leading away from the pond to segue into natural areas beyond with spring wildflowers, then larger perennials and shrubs leading toward water-loving trees.

Modern Water Gardens

We can thank modern technology for making water gardens available to anyone with a shovel and an electrical supply, rather than just to royalty and others who could afford teams of engineers, architects, and artisans.

In Victorian times, the steam pump brought water to some gardens, but even then, most relied on gravity. When soil wouldn't hold water, it had to be "puddled" by stomping straw into clay. The first rubber liners came along in the late nineteenth century, and have steadily become both more durable and less expensive, as have pumps and filters.

Modern Perspective. What hasn't changed much are our motivations for creating water gardens. More imperative for many of us now, perhaps, is the recognition that our natural environment is shrinking.

Longwood Gardens. The fountain garden is a famous feature of this Pennsylvania estate built by Pierre du Pont in the early 1900s.

Seattle Center. The Dandelion Fountain, at Seattle Center, an entertainment complex, exemplifies modern public water features.

CHAPTER 2

Planning Your Water Feature

Water is one of life's vital elements—it's no surprise that we find ourselves attracted to it. What better place to enjoy water but in your own garden? A well-designed landscape with a water feature requires thoughtful consideration and preparation. Careful planning helps prevent first-time mistakes. Adding a water feature to the garden deserves thoughtful placement and installation. Will it be a focal point in your garden? Will it be enjoyed from indoors when you can't be outside? Will it be lit at night? Determine what feature is right for you—from the style and size to where it is located—before you start.

Consider Your Lifestyle

When professional landscape designers begin a project, they ask about the client's lifestyle and goals for their property. Consider how you use your outdoor space. Do you spend a lot of time outside enjoying your property? Do you want your pond or fountain to beautify the view from inside the house or to enhance your entryway for the pleasure of your guests? Your budget is also a consideration before you make a selection.

When your time outdoors is limited to relaxing on the patio or deck, a pondless waterfall or fountain may be all you want or need. If you enjoy entertaining in your garden, a small water feature softly bubbling in a corner can be relaxing and prompt quiet conversation. A pond provides endless entertainment especially if it contains colorful fish. An informal pond placed near a deck or patio allows you and your guests to admire the fish and unusual plants, as well as birds, dragonflies, and other wildlife that are attracted to water.

If you have a patio that looks out over a long, narrow garden, you can make the space look even deeper by installing a long formal pool or placing a pond at the far end to create a focal point. Keep the lines of a more remote water feature clean and bold so that the design can speak from a distance.

If you enjoy gardening, a new water feature can be as simple or as demanding as you like. As with any other part of a landscape, a pond offers endless possibilities. You can add plants or rearrange your existing plants. There are many colorful aquatic plants that can sit in or around a pond. There's the added enticement of adding fish and other creatures like turtles.

Or perhaps the pond will be a secondary feature to existing flower beds and borders. For example, one gardener used a backhoe to dig a half-acre pond as the centerpiece of a collection of unusual trees and shrubs. The beautiful colors and shapes are reflected in the water, which can be viewed from his sunroom. Another gardener placed a three-tiered fountain as a focal point off the patio. Because she lives in an area that has very cold winters, the fountain is turned off and covered for the season. Your climate will also help you determine what type of water feature works best. Good planning results in a water feature that requires minimal maintenance and provides enjoyment for years to come.

The hardy water lily's beauty, above, and the colors and fragrance of some varities, can be the inspiration for creating a lush water garden. They bloom by day and by night, so you can enjoy their pleasure for hours.

Including a relaxing, low-maintenance water feature can add value to your home.

Choosing a Site

Whether you live in an urban setting with a small yard or a sweeping suburban lot, there may be spots for a water feature or two. But where will it give you the most pleasure while being practical? In a large garden, the water feature can be a pleasant destination tucked among the plants. Any water element should look as though it belongs where it is placed.

AESTHETIC CONSIDERATIONS

Your view of a pond, fountain or pondless waterfall is critical. Ideally, it would be nice to watch a pond change throughout the seasons from as many vantage points as possible. From indoors, you can enjoy your pond even in inclement weather: the reflection of the clouds, the splash of raindrops, the formation of ice. If your region has long winters or if you spend relatively little time outdoors, think about where you might be able to see the pond from one or more windows.

Before you dig, consider whether you'll be able to see the water feature from your intended viewing location. For example, if you want to view the pond outside a breakfast nook, will you be able to see it when you are sitting down? You can "test drive" your pond by placing a blue plastic drop cloth or a blanket or sheets in various spots to experiment with positioning and size of a pond. If it's a fountain you are after, use large cardboard boxes for placement and size.

One other consideration is whether or not your local building codes will require fencing depending on a pond's depth. In some communities, fencing is required to keep children from entering the pond.

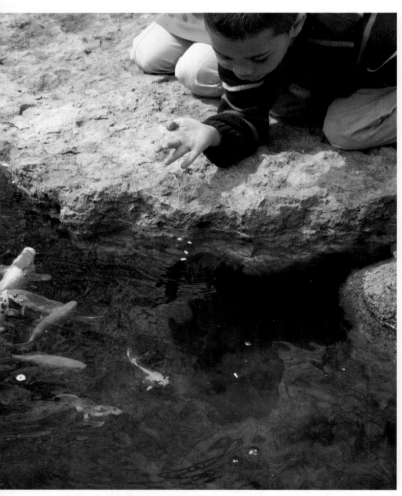

A pond with fish is a delightful way to engage children with nature.

If positioned near a window, a water feature will give you year-round enjoyment.

HIDDEN WATER FEATURE

You can employ a landscape-design trick known as evoking a sense of mystery. Instead of putting the pond in full view, hide it so that just a teasing glimpse beckons and invites strollers to investigate. Between the path and the pond, plant tall grasses or a hedge of lacy conifers—or erect a bamboo screen or vine-covered trellis—allowing just a shimmer of water to hint at what lies beyond.

A completely hidden water feature offers other advantages. You can still create a sense of mystery by beckoning a viewer toward a camouflaged pond with a curving path. Such a concealed pond can be a welcome retreat where you can be alone with your thoughts, enjoy the sights and sounds of nature, and forget the chores that await you in the study or laundry room for a while.

To make this area even more of an outdoor "room," add decking (or a flagstone or gravel floor), a dining table, and lighting so that you can enjoy it at night. Total enclosure of a water feature is especially appealing if you are surrounded on all sides by sights and sounds that you want to block out: heavy traffic, nearby neighbors, or a less-than-beautiful toolshed, for example.

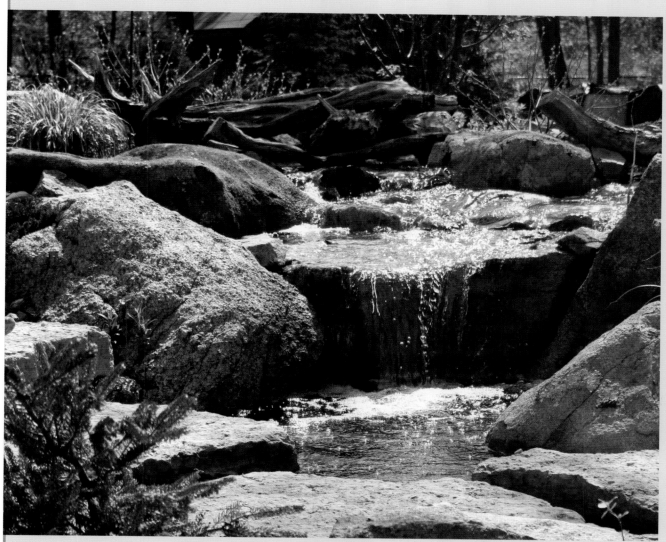

Tucked out of sight, a pond offers an element of surprise while strolling the garden.

This beautiful tropical garden contains a decorative bridge over a waterfall that empties into a large pond.

Reflections. In considering views from your pond, remember that you will want to look not only across it but also into it. What will be reflected in the pond, and how will those reflections change throughout the day and throughout the seasons? Can you capture sunrises or sunsets? The full moon in June? What about azaleas in spring or maple leaves in autumn? Some experts suggest placing a large mirror on the prospective pond site to give you some idea of how water might reflect light and color. If you're a photographer, you know it's easier to see the image well if you keep the sun behind you, and this is true of ponds as well. If you're staring straight across at the sun, all you'll see is glare.

Existing Features. Another important aesthetic consideration when choosing a site is how easily the water feature can be integrated into the existing landscape. Determine which existing yard features will complement the pond and which will detract from it. Before deciding

BORROW VIEWS

When picking a spot for your pond, see whether there are any views worth "borrowing" for your design. Borrowing a pleasing but more distant view is like adding a window to your garden room. It makes a small enclosure seem larger without sacrificing privacy. Decide which elements of the wider world to allow into your cozy spot. Consider the potential view from each side of the pond to see what pleasant vista you could incorporate—the corner of a neighbor's lot with a perennial bed or expanse of green lawn, or a view back toward your own house where you have plantings you enjoy. A hedge of just the right height can capture the top of a church steeple or tall trees while blocking out less-attractive lower views. If there is a nice view from only one side of the pond, draw attention to it with a small area of stone, brick, or wood decking. A bench or a lantern will suggest a place of welcome. It doesn't need to be functional; the bench can be a rustic child-size seat, and the lantern can be stone or a battered antique.

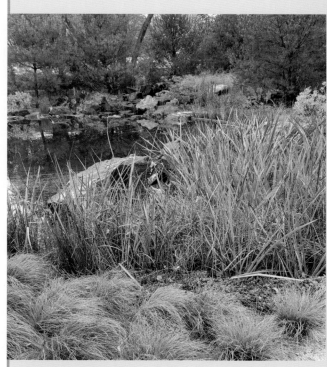

To soften a pond's edge, plant evergreens, grasses, and perennials.

Ample seating provides a place to relax, entertain, and enjoy this formal pool.

on a site, examine the views from all angles. For example, siting the pond in one area of the yard may mean that you would need to remove one or more large trees or shrubs to allow you to see the pond from the house. Or you may find eyesores such as an old shed that will need to be razed or a bare house wall that should be disguised with vines.

If you have decided on a particular size for your pond, you'll need to take that into consideration when choosing the site. For example, a small pond can get lost next to an

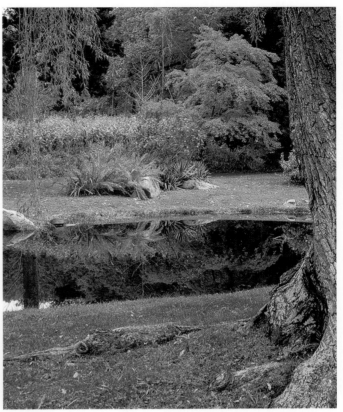

Factor in reflections when siting your pond. Water lets you double your visual enjoyment of the landscape's existing features such as trees and rocks.

immense deck. A large pond stuffed into a small side yard may look out of proportion.

Many ponds look like a hole in the ground with a necklace of stones, and gardeners don't solve the problem by adding a starched collar of plants. Ponds look more natural anchored to an existing feature such as a large boulder or a small specimen tree or tucked into the curve of a perennial or shrub border.

If you don't have such an existing feature, you may need to create one. Or you can connect the pond to the rest of the garden by echoing other elements in the landscape. Incorporate bricks in the pond's design to complement a brick house, a deck surround to mimic the deck on the house, a shape similar to that of the planting beds, or plants of the same species (or shape) as planted elsewhere.

Paths. Paths are another way to tie your pond to the rest of your landscape and to your home. (See the sidebar "Pond Surrounds and Paths," on page 43, for more information.)

For a small pond, a little shade reduces algae and evaporation, and keeps visitors cool.

PRACTICAL CONSIDERATIONS

Other elements will determine where to place your water feature. Will you be able to view the water from indoors or from a patio or deck? Existing structures, trees and shrubs, and the general lay of the land must be considered.

Sun and Shade. If you want flowering plants to be an important part of your water garden, you need to place the pond where it will get at least six hours of sunlight a day. Water lilies, in particular, don't bloom well with less sun (although there are a few varieties that will perform in partial shade). If you've recently moved to your property, keep records through each season the first year on how much sunlight lands and where. This can help you decide whether a site will meet the needs for your water feature.

Depending on where you live, there is a downside to too much sun, however. Water will evaporate quickly from a pond in full sun in hot climates. Sun encourages algae, and if the pond is small, can heat the water too much for fish. For this reason, small water features—and especially tub gardens—need shadier sites. For larger ponds, provide shade with floating plants or situate small trees to give dappled shade across at least part of the pond's surface. Use rocks to create shade under which fish can cool off, as well as hide from predators. Nature creates inviting pools even in the heart of heavily shaded woodlands, and you can, too, by choosing appropriate plants.

Wind. Ponds should have some degree of protection from wind, which, like sunlight, will hasten the rate of evaporation. Wind can also blow leaves and other debris into the pond, spoil the grace of fountains, and knock over tall plants in containers. If possible, choose a sheltered site, one protected from wind by a hill, woods, building, or fence.

If your site is open and has no sheltered spot, you'll need to create some type of a windbreak. Surprisingly, a barrier that lets some wind through is more effective than a solid windbreak such as a close-board fence, which allows wind to blow across its top and resume full force a few feet beyond it. Depending on the style of your pond, you can create an effective windbreak by installing an open-board fence, a screen of native evergreens, or an attractive flowering hedge.

Trees can be used to create shade or as a windbreak. Careful selection and placement is important. Many fast-growing trees are inexpensive, but their branches may be brittle and messy. When adding new trees near your pond, choose species that will stay small or are slow growing.

Trees can add to your cleanup chores by dropping twigs, berries, nuts, and leaves into the pond, where this debris may decompose and change the water's chemistry. Some plants that otherwise make attractive windbreaks—such as yews, hollies, rhododendrons, and mountain laurels—have toxic leaves that can harm fish if allowed to accumulate. Pine needles contain tannins that can turn water brown and sicken fish. A willow or maple tree's roots can punch through pond liners that have even the tiniest of leaks.

This pond's location, opposite, offers a perfect view and just the right amount of sun and shade.

COMPLYING WITH LOCAL REGULATIONS

Make sure your plans comply with local building codes. Depending on where you live, regulations may deem a pond beyond a certain depth a safety hazard and, just as they do with swimming pools, require that you fence it. Fencing may be required for ponds as shallow as 2 feet. Most zoning boards consider a pond a structure, and as such there may also be rules pertaining to its placement and size.

If you intend to redesign a natural water feature, such as a pond or stream, you would be altering a wetland. In that case, find out if you need to apply for a permit, usually with your local conservation commission, department of natural resources, or other environmental review agency. But keep in mind, this process usually involves preparing a complex and legally demanding environmental impact statement.

Before you lift a shovel, check with your municipality to see if permits are required and contact utility companies to mark underground cables, pipes, and electrical lines.

Microclimates

Trees, shrubs, fences, the house, garage, or shed can all create "microclimates." It may be a sheltered site between a fence and the house. It can be cool and shady on the north side of house and warm and sunny on the south. A west-facing site receives the hot afternoon sunlight while the east side may have only gentle morning sunlight.

Driveways, patios, and sidewalks absorb and reflect the heat. If a pond is nearby, it may experience faster evaporation, or the surrounding plants may need more frequent watering. If you live in an area with cold winters, cold air will settle in low areas of the garden first, and they will thaw later in the spring than higher spots.

Where summers are short, you can extend your pond experience by choosing a site on your property that receives the greatest sun exposure. In regions where the summers are long and hot, reduce evaporation and protect fish and plants by siting the pond where it receives some protection from the midday sun.

Many factors have an impact on your pond's water, plants, and fish. Study your property's little idiosyncrasies to maximize success.

A large paved area is pleasant near a pond but can create a hot spot that will speed evaporation.

A retaining wall can protect a pond that is located downhill from being polluted with dirt and debris.

Because trees slow the wind, they are better wind breaks than solid structures, which let wind resume full force beyond them.

If you want to grow water plants in a container on your patio, give it some shade, or the water will become too hot.

The south side of a structure can protect borderline hardy plantings, while the north side may be too shady and cool for many plants.

Locating the pond in full sun will help water lilies and other plants bloom.

Water plants temper the sun's heat, giving cover to fish and other water creatures.

Slopes and Runoff. Slopes create an array of possibilities as well as challenges for siting water features. A steep slope lends itself easily to waterfalls and natural-looking rock terraces. A gentle slope presents an opportunity to create a stream. Even though nature creates ponds at the bottoms of slopes, this can be the worst place for an artificial pond. Runoff from a slope can wash dirt and debris into the water, as well as pollutants such as lawn chemicals from your property or from a neighboring site.

It's possible to divert runoff with retaining walls or ditches on either side of the pond. A microclimate may be present at the bottom of a slope where it can be several degrees cooler than other parts of the garden. And the bottom of a slope is also where you are most likely to encounter problems with the water table.

Convenience. While you don't want your pond on top of your electrical line, you do need access to power. Pumps for a waterfall, aeration, or cleaning, mechanical filters, fountains, and lighting require electricity.

The water feature should be located near a water source because midsummer droughts, leaks, and natural evaporation will require that you occasionally replenish the water. Tools needed to clean the pond and tend plants should be handy as well. Will you store delicate tropical water plants in a garage, a shed, or a basement? Think about ways you can make it easy on yourself.

Underground Surprises

If you dig a pond below the water table, flexible pond liners can balloon up and rigid liners can heave out of the ground, or the soil around them can erode. Determine the depth of the water table under your potential pond site by digging some test holes.

These test holes will also tell you about the composition of your soil—an important factor when you are planning. Soil texture can vary from one area of your property to another. Good garden loam is easiest to

work. Other soil types require a bit more work. Clay soil is heavy, making it harder to excavate, whereas sandy or pebbly soil can collapse along the edges.

Rocks and a high water table may not be the only surprises you'll hit with your shovel. Hitting underground utilities can be a nasty shock, literally. Most areas now have a single agency with a memorable name such as "Miss Utility" that will come out to your home and mark any underground lines.

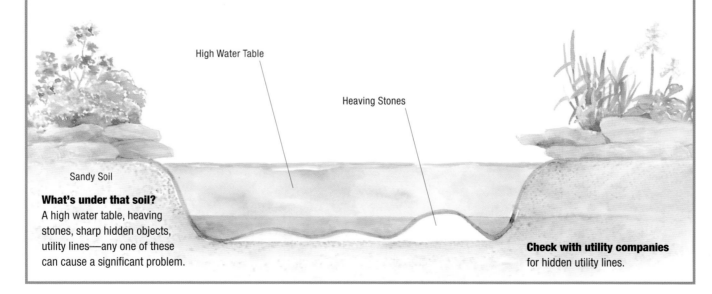

High Water Table

Heaving Stones

Sandy Soil

What's under that soil?
A high water table, heaving stones, sharp hidden objects, utility lines—any one of these can cause a significant problem.

Check with utility companies for hidden utility lines.

WATER GARDENS IN CONTAINERS

One of the easiest ways to try your hand at water gardening is to create a miniature pond in a container. You can use something as elegant as a ceramic planter or as rustic as an old horse trough, kettle, or half a whiskey barrel. Choose a container at least 18 inches in diameter—24 inches is better.

Locate your container garden where you can enjoy it often, such as on a deck or a patio. Because it will overheat more quickly than a pond in the ground, situate the container so that it gets some shade during the hottest part of the day. It will also need frequent topping off and cleaning, so consider how you will drain the container and refill it; a spot within reach of a hose works best. Keep in mind that the planter will be heavy when filled.

To keep your container from rusting or leaking and to deter any toxins it might contain from harming plants or fish, you should line it. There are now fiberglass shells specially made for half barrels. For other containers, use a piece of PVC liner.

Although you shouldn't cram the container with plants, it's possible to enjoy a half dozen species in even a small one. Try to include an upright plant or two, as well as one that will hang gracefully over the side. If the container is too deep for a marginal species, grow one in a pot set on one or more bricks.

A few small goldfish or mosquito fish will help keep your minipond free of mosquito larvae. Unless you live in a warm-winter climate or can sink the container into the ground for the winter, you'll need to transfer the fish to an indoor aquarium for a few months each year. Plan on replacing most of the plants. If you have a sunroom with a tile floor, you may be able to move the whole display indoors. (In the case of a particularly large container, you may want to have a contractor do an inspection and verify that your floor will support its weight when filled with water.)

A more complex pool design could include a fountain and container plantings.

Water lilies in a container enhance a perennial planting.

Size and Styles

Once you've picked a spot that's breathtaking and not backbreaking, you need to think about the size and style of pond that you want. You need to give these decisions a lot of long and careful consideration. Although you may easily reshape and replant a flower bed, you'll find it difficult to reshape or move a water garden.

Your best bet is to visit as many other ponds as possible before finalizing your plans. Some water-garden suppliers have demonstration ponds, as do public gardens. Although many public water features will seem too huge and expensive to relate to your home garden, focus on the details: the overall shape and setting, the plants, and the material used for the edge and the surround. If nothing else, you will gain a sense of what you like.

Traditionally, ponds have been divided into formal and informal styles. The style you choose will guide your choice not only of pond shape but also of plants, decorations such as fountains and statues, and other materials that you use around your pond. The design guidelines for a formal style are not as flexible as those for an informal style. The style tips that follow are merely suggestions. In the end, you'll need to make the choices that please you.

With an informal water garden, you have the greatest design latitude and the opportunity to create something truly unique.

POND SIZE

Most people err with a pond that is too small. A small pond in the middle of an open lawn can look lost. In a typical, sparsely planted suburban backyard, a pond up to one-third the area can be pleasingly balanced. The more heavily your garden is planted, the more charming a tiny pond can be as an element in a busy bed or along a landscaped path. Use a rope or a hose to mark the pond outline, and live with the layout for a few days.

Consider 18 inches the minimum depth for an inground pond. The colder your climate, the deeper your pond will need to be to keep the roots of water lilies and other hardy water garden perennials from freezing in winter. A local water-garden supplier or an Extension Agent can advise you on your area's frost line, the depth at which your soil freezes in the average winter.

Even in relatively warm climates, koi ponds are an exception to the usual depth recommendations. These large fish need water at least 3 and preferably 4 feet deep. Ponds designed to attract wildlife should have variation in depth, including some shallow ledges or a tapering beach area, inviting different aquatic creatures, birds, and mammals.

Visit as many ponds as possible to get a feel for what you like. This one would probably excite a plant lover.

Bubbling water enhances this formal pool.

FORMAL STYLES

Generally, formal pools are geometric—square, rectangular, circular, triangular, or some combination—and have a clearly defined edge. They typically include features such as fountains or statues but rarely bridges or stepping-stones. Plantings are minimal. Surrounding plants are often those commonly used in formal gardens, such as pruned boxwood hedges, topiaries, or rose standards. But today there is a trend toward more relaxed-looking plants (especially ornamental grasses) in the landscape surrounding formal water features. Some designers believe that only formal pools are appropriate in urban gardens and even most suburban yards. Formal pools can be dug into the ground, be of a raised or semiraised style, or be sunken into a patio. Raised pools may be less of a safety hazard for small children. They are also easier to tend without bending and stooping, and they can be built with a wide edge that allows you to admire goldfish without having to drop down to your knees.

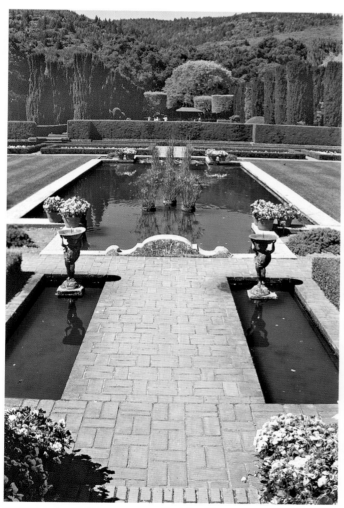

Formal water features are generally defined by their geometric shapes, above. They needn't be big to be elegant.

A formal water feature complements this home's contemporary architecture.

Choose a design that will coordinate with the architecture of your house, opposite. Classical motifs and ornaments are consistent with formal designs.

Statuary and ornamental furniture complement formal water garden design, below.

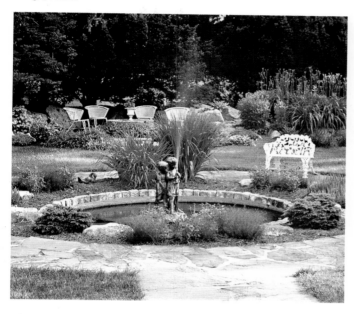

Hardscape and Ornaments. The lines of a formal pool need to be kept plain and simple. The crisp edges are built with regularly shaped materials such as bricks, machine-cut stones, tiles, or landscaping ties. If you want to create a patio or a path beside the pool, consider using a material similar to that used for the edging. Within or adjacent to a deck, the same wood decking can be used to create a pool that is formal in shape yet relaxed in feel. For benches, look to classic designs such as stone or park benches; to create shade, consider a wisteria arbor of white columns or something similarly elegant.

A fountain can serve a practical purpose: if you have fish and don't have a waterfall, a fountain will aerate the water for them. In a small pool, though, a fountain may disturb the water too much for water lilies.

Some statues are designed to highlight water by appearing to walk on it or to chase fish. Others double as fountains by pouring or spraying water. Remember that one such arresting figure is generally enough for a pool.

Bridges and stepping-stones can work in a formal design if they are geometric. Waterfalls and streams for a formal pool are normally highly stylized with water falling in a curtain over a sheet of acrylic, or down a series of stone steps.

Softscape. As for plantings in and around a formal pool, the species of plants are less important than the manner in which they are employed. Formal pools are usually planted with restraint so that the clean outline of the pool and its edging remain apparent. Some small formal pools with fountains are not planted at all. A single dramatic tree—such as a weeping pear or a bonsai on a pedestal—or a matched pair of containers holding rosemary will complement the emphasis on hard materials.

Around the pool, consider using conifers and other plants that lend themselves to pruning. Some of the most famous formal pools are surrounded on three sides only by a clipped, U-shaped hedge. Some contemporary pools in country settings have what amounts to a "hedge" of ornamental grasses. Adjacent flower beds, when present, are often geometric in shape, like the pool, and are planted with a limited selection of species.

Within the pool, water lilies and lotuses will look beautiful if they aren't disturbed by the splashing of a fountain. Restricting yourself to water lilies and other low, horizontal plants can make the garden seem larger. But if you find this effect too static, consider adding individual clumps of ornamental grasses, a tub of cattails, or margins of irises, lilies, or daylilies. Their more vertical shapes will add visual interest.

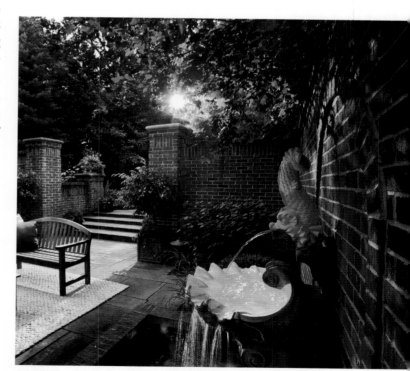

A formal water feature is integrated with the home's architecture and materials.

Informal pond designs use nature as a model.

INFORMAL STYLES

An informal pond can range from one that is a bit more playful in shape to one that mimics nature with a carefully planned mini-ecosystem of native plants and adjacent bogs. In addition to being irregular in outline, most informal water gardens are built into the ground with their edges concealed by natural-shaped stones, pebble beaches, or tall native grasses. They are unlikely to include fountains and more likely to be complemented by waterfalls or streams. You can keep plants to a minimum and employ rather traditional cultivated annuals and perennials, or you can surround the pond with so many subtropicals or wetland species that the water surface almost disappears under such a vast assortment of floaters, creepers, and waving grasses.

Informal ponds can be appropriate for many styles of homes and gardens, from old farmhouses to ultramodern designs, rich with natural woods and windows. If your home is in a natural setting of fields or woods or if you can picture it in such a setting, it probably deserves an informal pond.

Hardscape and Ornaments. The edging of informal ponds is usually quarried or hand-cut stone intended to mimic nature. Similar stones may be arranged in tiers to serve as the foundation of waterfalls. Islands are sometimes included in large ponds; boulders serve that purpose in smaller ponds. Paths and surrounding areas are of natural materials, such as bark, pine needles, or gravel.

Architectural elements are kept to a minimum, but they might include arbors of grapevines or bent willow. Seating can be of almost any style that beckons the viewer to stop awhile and relax. For accents, possibilities could include a simple birdhouse, boulders, or sculptures. Wood is the most appropriate material for bridges. In keeping with the level of informality you choose, options range from a span of decking to weathered planks to a single fallen tree across a stream. (Flatten the undersides of the ends so that it doesn't roll, and cover the top with hardly noticeable chicken wire to provide traction for walking.) Handrails of rustic timber with bark still attached will add to the informality and safety of these choices.

Stepping-stones, like edging, should be natural shapes rather than cut, and arranged in an uneven line. A single slab of weathered stone may do for a small pond or a narrow stream. The most informal ponds are not a place for fountains, except those that bubble just above the surface like a natural spring. A simple spray or geyser is good for slightly more formal ponds.

Softscape. Even though there are fewer guidelines for planting informal water gardens than for formal pools, resist the urge to plant one of every variety you can get your hands on. Strive for a minimum of three plants of each variety. An uneven number of plants in clusters or masses will keep your design from looking stiff and formal. The edges of your planting areas should be big bold curves, not little squiggles or straight lines.

In addition to taking design cues from your home's architecture, you might want to choose a planting style that is regionally appropriate both in terms of style and plant material. For example, rock gardens often become an adjunct to water features through serendipity, when gardeners with a mound of leftover dirt or rocks put two and two together. Gardens such as these look right at home in arid mountain climates because many traditional rock-garden plants flourish in the bright sun and dry climate there.

If you live surrounded by deciduous woodlands, fill your rock garden with plants that grow naturally in this environment. Good bets include ferns, native ground covers, or ornamentals such as creeping bellflower that droop gracefully over embankments.

If you live in the subtropics, an appealing option is to strive for the jungle look, cramming your pond with tropical water lilies, parrot's-feather, and giant papyrus, and planting the surrounding area with huge-leaved green taro, hibiscus, and giant chain fern. But if you have a Zone 7 garden with a warmer Zone 9 spirit, capture a tropical feel with lush-leaved perennials such as ligularia and hosta, evergreen shrubs such as acuba, and a hardier species of papyrus.

When hardscaping, combine natural elements, such as stone slabs and boulders, with ornament. Arrange elements in tiers.

POND SURROUNDS AND PATHS

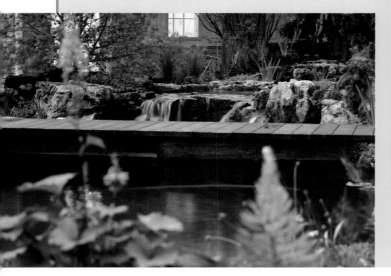

The style of the walkways and paths around your water feature should match the style of the pond. For informal ponds, create paths of loose materials such as gravel or bark chips; you can install edging to keep the material in place. Try large, irregular stepping-stones or wooden rounds around the pond edge to provide access. Formal pools may incorporate walks of brick, patio tiles, wood blocks, concrete, cut stone, or similar paving materials.

Extend the path around the perimeter of the pond to encourage strollers to view the pond from different vantage points. If the pond is large enough, extend the path or stepping-stones into or even across the pond itself.

Pondside seating areas can be as simple as a wooden garden bench or as elaborate as a wood deck or a masonry patio with table and chairs to accommodate a sit-down dinner for 20. Be careful, though, not to let features overwhelm the pond itself. They should be in scale with the size of the pond. Regular trimming and pruning activity may be needed to retain the look.

JAPANESE GARDENS

The Japanese garden is by far the most popular non-European style imitated by North American gardeners, and water—sometimes actual, other times only suggested by stones—plays an integral part in such a garden.

The Japanese style may be appealing because it contains both formal (stylized) and informal elements. Its goal is to echo nature with rocks, water, and plants, but in a controlled way. A Japanese pond may be accented with a formal stone lantern, but the pond itself is irregular in shape. Landscaping may include carefully pruned topiary along with softly waving grasses and bamboos. The arrangement of elements is more dynamic than in other formal styles, while still creating a relaxed and peaceful feeling.

Hardscape and Ornaments. A water feature in a Japanese garden doesn't need to be big. It could be as simple as a stone basin. Basins are valued for both form and function—for instance, as a place where you can wash your hands or birds can bathe. In Japanese culture, a *tsukubai* is a basin where guests wash before tea; the water is fed into the basin through a bamboo pipe, called a *kakehi*. A more specialized variation is the *shishi odoshi*, or "stag scarer," in which water flows into one end of a bamboo pipe that is suspended in a seesaw fashion. When the pipe is full of water, it tilts and dumps its water into a basin or pond (or stream), and then it swings back to its original position.

The pipe makes a hollow clack at one or both ends and is sometimes sold in catalogs as a "deer chaser."

Often, a Japanese pond is edged with boulders of different shapes and interesting textures. Islands are a common feature in larger ponds; they can consist of a single large boulder or a berm of earth for a small Japanese maple. Koi, the beautifully colored carp, are classic additions, but they require more attention and deeper water than do other fish.

Softscape. One reason Japanese-style gardens are so popular is that the plants they employ are well suited to North American gardens. Many plants native to Japan—including ferns and dogwoods—have close relatives in North America and are easily adaptable to the region's growing conditions. A lot of the favored plants—mosses, camellias, azaleas—are shade lovers, which makes this style ideal for a gardener who wants a water feature but doesn't want to give up beautiful old trees. You can have a wonderful Japanese garden in the sun as well, by leaning toward a collection of unusual conifers.

Foliage plays a more important role in this garden style than do flowers. Evergreens are essential and generally make up a majority of the plants. Boxwoods and conifers are often meticulously pruned, although broad-leaved flowering shrubs may be allowed a more natural form. Simplicity, balance, and calm are hallmarks of Japanese garden design.

A stone pagoda, opposite, is a feature that often graces a Japanese garden.

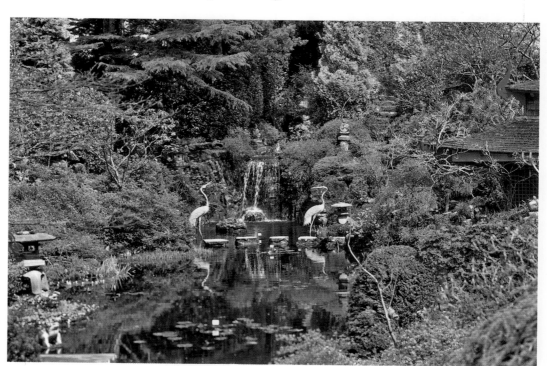

Meticulous manicuring imparts formality, but materials are chosen with the goal of echoing nature. The resulting mood is both dynamic and peaceful, right.

Japanese maples are one of the most popular plant choices. A single specimen may be used as a focal point, or several may be planted in a grove to create a small-scale echo of a large woodland. There are Japanese maples with red or variegated leaves; most have brilliant fall color. Shapes and sizes range from ground huggers to those that will grow 30 feet high and wide.

Plants included for flowers should also provide interest at other times of the year. A weeping cherry offers eye-catching form even when not in bloom; classic shrubs such as azaleas, rhododendrons, and camellias contribute both an elaborate burst of spring bloom and handsome evergreen leaves. Because their foliage provides interesting shapes and textures when they are not in bloom, good perennials include Japanese or Siberian irises, astilbes, and daylilies.

Texture. Create interest by using foliage that is ribbed or variegated. Hostas and lungwort (*Pulmonaria*) are just two perennials with interesting leaf colors and shapes. Rather than plant them in a row, use them as specimens—plant one next to a boulder or at the bend of a path. Taller native grasses like big bluestem and switchgrass (*Panicum*) provide vertical interest and the leaves rustle with the breeze.

Large gardens may employ an elaborate footbridge design. Smaller gardens may do with something less sophisticated.

Bamboo is a popular plant for water gardens. However, if you grow bamboo, keep in mind that they can be very aggressive, spreading by runners that are difficult to corral. You will want to restrain them. One method is to plant them in culvert pipes 2 or 3 feet deep in the ground.

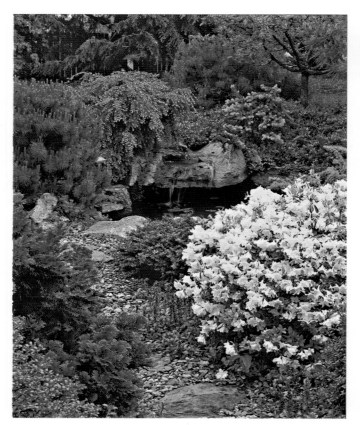

A MOSS MILKSHAKE

Moss needs shade and humus-rich, moist soil with a low pH to thrive. If you're lucky enough to have moss growing in your yard, you can transplant it. Dig up a tuft of moss with soil attached, and crumble it into a blender. Add equal amounts of water and buttermilk, and process the mixture until completely blended. Add water, if necessary, until the finished product is the consistency of a cream soup. Spread the resulting moss shake where you want a new colony of moss. Keep the area constantly moist until the new moss is established.

In choosing plants for Japanese gardens, left, foliage and form are as important as bloom color.

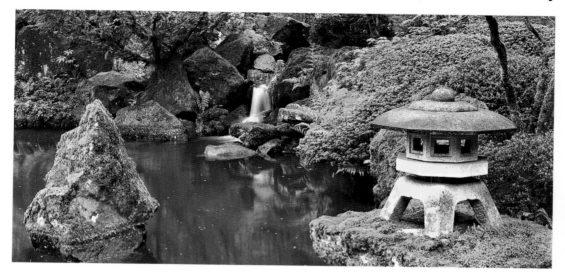

Rocks have an important role in Japanese ponds, sometimes serving as islands. All are carefully chosen and placed.

ENHANCE YOUR DESIGN WITH LIGHTING

Lighting can extend the hours you enjoy your pond or water garden and add entirely new dimensions. Lights can give star status to plants or features that have only supporting roles during the day. You might focus a spotlight onto a contorted willow on a well-planted berm, use uplighting to exaggerate the rough texture of tree bark, or highlight a small statue partly concealed by pondside growth. Or use a spotlight to

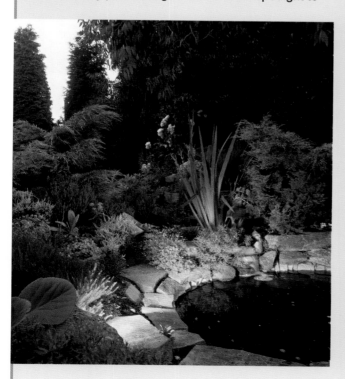

emphasize a waterfall or the branches of a tree. (To get the best effect, hide the lamp behind a clump of grasses; tuck it behind stones; or place it high in a tree.) If you have a fountain, an underwater light at its base will allow you to admire its play from a window after dark.

Lighting is easily overdone. Harsh spotlights may deter burglars, but they detract from the magic of nightfall. A bright light directly on the pond can cast everything in an artificial glare or—even worse—let you see nothing beyond the reflection of the light fixture. When in doubt, start with fewer lights. A strictly utilitarian design might use low downlights to outline the path to the pond, position a low-wattage yard lantern near a bench, or directly illuminate a dining area with a light pointed away from the pond. Carefully positioned lights will allow you to feel safe while still catching the moon and stars in the water's surface or marveling as a night-blooming water lily unfolds.

If your pond is situated some distance from your house, consider a system that will let you turn on the lights from the house and then turn them off when you arrive at the pond. That way, you can enjoy the natural darkness when the mood strikes you. This is particularly important if you have a wildlife pond. Keep lighting dim, and turn it off when you go to bed to reduce energy consumption and avoid scaring off creatures of the night. Also consider using solar light fixtures.

CHAPTER 3

Choosing a Pond Liner and Edging

O you've decided whether your pond will be formal or informal, it's time to think about choosing a flexible or pre-formed pond liner. Do you need a site plan before you begin? How will you create the pond's edging? Will it be boulders, plants, or a combination? Before installing a pond you must decide on some preliminary issues.

Liners

There's more to creating a pond than just digging a hole. You'll need to provide a watertight foundation. Most ponds today are built using flexible liners or preformed shells. Either material can be used to create a formal pool or an informal pond. You'll also need to provide an edging to mask the rim of the liner.

FLEXIBLE POND LINERS

Although they're called flexible because of their physical malleability, the big selling point of these liners is their design flexibility. From a small and shallow splash pool for toddlers to a raised koi pond for fish hobbyists, or a multiacre fishing hole to a winding creek, you can make a flexible liner adapt to your design. Flexible liners are also relatively inexpensive and easy for do-it-yourselfers to install. You lay the liner in the hole, fill the pond with water, trim the liner, and install the edging.

Polyethylene liners resemble the black plastic sheeting sold in hardware stores, but they're much thicker. Polyethylene sheeting isn't particularly durable, though, so don't

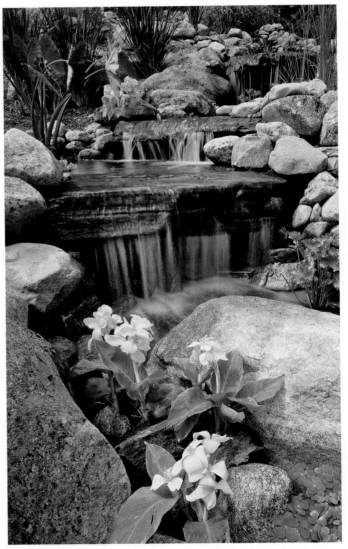

If you want to create a naturalistic water feature such as this one, above, a flexible liner may be the best choice.

Flexible pond liners (right) can be cushioned with an underlayment to make them more resistant to punctures or tears.

use it for a pond unless you want just a small, temporary one with which to try your hand at water gardening for a couple of years. You can, however, use it successfully for a wetland or bog garden, because in such situations it doesn't need to be watertight.

Liners made especially for ponds are either PVC (polyvinyl chloride) or synthetic rubber—either butyl rubber or EPDM (ethylene propylene diene monomer). English gardening books usually talk about butyl, which is made only in Sweden, but EPDM is more readily available in North America. Be sure you get a liner made for ponds; EPDM rubber sheeting that is intended for use on roofs and other purposes can contain toxins harmful to plants and fish.

Naturally, the best liners cost more. Rubber liners last longer than the best of the less-expensive PVC liners because they are stretchable and more resistant to ultraviolet light. Thicker liners of any type generally last longer, too. Butyl or EPDM rubber liners are available in thicknesses from 30 to 45 mil and will typically last from 20 to 30 years. PVC liners are available in thicknesses from 20 to 32 mil.

At the bottom end of the scale, a 20-mil PVC liner can be expected to last from 5 to 7 years; a 32-mil PVC liner will last from 10 to 15 years.

Flexible pond liners come in stock sizes ranging from about 5 x 5 feet to 30 x 50 feet. Some manufacturers offer custom sizes. By joining the edges of the sheets with seam sealer, you can create any size or shape.

Because flexible liners are susceptible to punctures from rocks, gravel, broken tree roots, or other sharp objects, cushion it with an underlayment. A carpet pad is one choice. Other options include 2 to 3 inches of sand, fiberglass insulation material, or layers of newspaper. Sand won't pack well onto steep sidewalls, however, and it can be heavy to transport, and newspapers tend to deteriorate over time. (Even carpet padding deteriorates eventually.) So most water-garden suppliers offer a tough, flexible underlayment material; you can also buy liners with underlayment material bonded to the liner material.

If your soil is especially rocky, full of roots, or subject to excessive shifting during winter months, install both a layer of sand and of underlayment fabric.

PREFORMED POND SHELLS

Rigid or semirigid pond shells are sometimes referred to as liners, but they are a specific molded shape and are often non-flexible. They are sold in many sizes, shapes, and depths, but the dimensions and size of the shell cannot be changed on site.

Preformed pond shells are generally made from high density polyethylene (HDPE) or fiberglass and resin. They must be placed completely in the ground to prevent the liner from flexing, and as a result, cracking. Fiberglass liners need no confinement and can remain freestanding on the ground while filled with water. Fiberglass can handle more abuse before damage and leaks occur. However, fiberglass liners are more expensive because they tend to be heavy and large. Rigid fiberglass shells are easy to repair and durable, but may discolor if exposed to sunlight. Semirigid plastic shells are more difficult to repair, aren't sturdy enough to be used aboveground, and become brittle. Look for materials that resist ultraviolet light.

Depending on their composition, thickness, quality,

and installation, the shells may last from five to 50 years. The thickest shells (1/4 inch or more) can be installed above ground with little support around the sides, provided the bottom rests on a firm, level base.

Preformed pond liners typically range in depth from 9 to 24 inches. (If you want to grow water lilies, the shell should be a minimum of 18 inches deep. Unless you live in a subtropical climate, shallower ponds are likely to freeze solid in winter, so you'll need to bring fish indoors.) Many preformed shells have ledges on the side walls for shallow-water (marginal) plants. Some models have depressions around the perimeter for wetland plants.

The perimeter of a preformed pond can be more difficult to disguise with edging and offers less "give" to heavy rocks, as well as less support. Use the exact measurements of the preformed liner when you dig the soil. If there's a mismatch in the measurements the pond liner will not fit properly.

Pond with Waterfall Dip

Pond with Full Shelf

Deep Pond with Partial Shelf

Pond with Stream

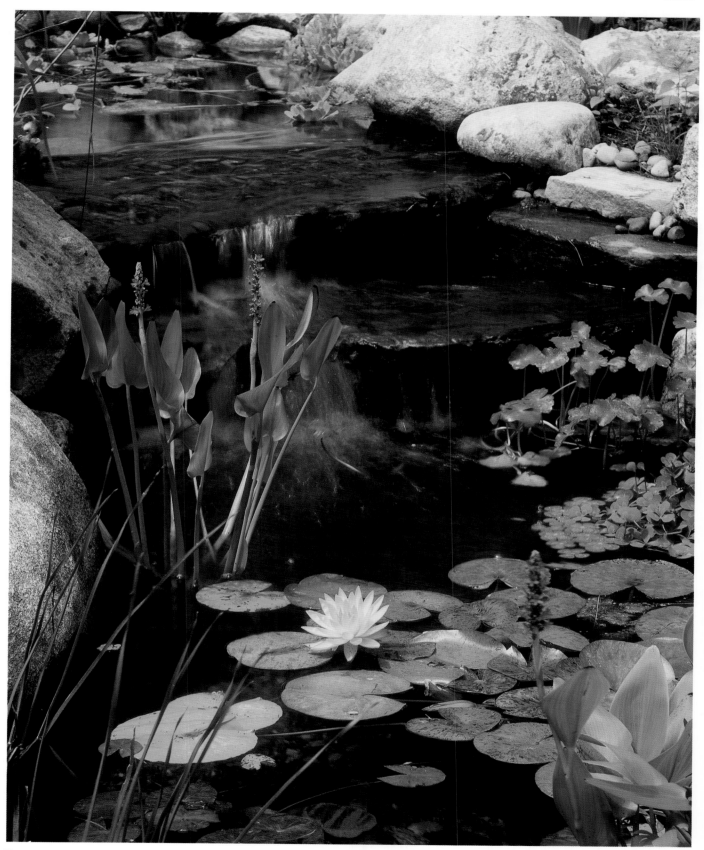

You can use separate overlapping pieces of flexible liner to create a stepped-down design.

The rocks positioned around the pond's edges conceal the liner.

A GUIDE TO FOUNDATIONS

You need to decide between a flexible liner and a preformed shell. Each offers benefits and drawbacks. Whichever you choose, specify quality material for durability.

CHOOSING MATERIALS

MATERIAL	ADVANTAGES	DISADVANTAGES
Flexible Liner	■ Unlimited shapes, sizes ■ Less expensive than preformed shell ■ Inexpensive to ship ■ Folds small enough to transport in car ■ Easy to customize for wetland, marginal plants ■ Easier to conceal edges	■ Less durable ■ Punctures easily ■ Degrades in sunlight ■ Any exposed material must be covered
Preformed Shell	■ Lasts longer ■ Resists punctures ■ Small units easy to install ■ Relatively quick to install ■ Poses no design concerns ■ Easier to clean	■ Limited sizes, shapes ■ Hard to customize ■ More expensive than flexible liner ■ Hard to conceal edges ■ Needs to be perfectly level ■ Requires firm foundation to prevent buckling

OTHER OPTIONS

Concrete Ponds. Years ago, practically all garden ponds were made of poured concrete, concrete block, or a combination of the two. But the popularity of these materials waned with the advent of flexible pond liners and pre-molded pond shells, which are easier to install and can even be dug up and moved if you relocate. Not only does pouring a concrete pond require a great deal of skill and backbreaking work, it is also more expensive than other options, even if you do the work. A concrete pond can last a lifetime if properly installed but will crack and leak almost immediately if it is not. Once a crack opens, there's usually no way to permanently repair it. The best fix is to cover the concrete with a flexible pond liner.

If you decide to use concrete, have the pond installed by a masonry contractor familiar with this sort of construction in your particular climate (and familiar with local building codes). In cold climates, the concrete shell must be at least 6 inches thick and adequately reinforced with ½-inch (No. 2) reinforcing bar ("rebar") or wire mesh to ensure that the pond will survive alternate freezing and thawing. In milder climates, the shell should still be 3 to 4 inches thick.

New concrete can leach lime into the pond water, so you must neutralize the lime with acidic chemicals—or seal the concrete with a coat of paint—before adding fish and plants to the pond. You can paint concrete with a rubber-based pool paint to create various effects: use earth tones for a natural look, white or blue for a more formal appearance, or dark colors for a "bottomless" look.

Clay and Bentonite. To create the most natural wildlife or farm ponds, where edging is minimal and punctures unheard of, it's possible to construct a clay-bottomed pond. For very large ponds, where handling a liner becomes unwieldy, this is often the preferred approach. Where the soil is already heavy clay, you can make the pond bottom watertight by stomping it, pounding it with a post, or renting a tamper to compact it. You can also make the soil more watertight by mixing in bentonite, a powdered clay made from volcanic ash. In addition, you can buy flexible liners made of bentonite granules sandwiched between layers of landscape fabric; you may be able to order them through your water-gardening supplier under the brand name Bentomat or Bentofix. The bentonite swells when it gets wet and forms a tight seal. The downside of a clay pond is that the bottom and sides will crack if allowed to go dry, and it's easily damaged by roots or tunneling animals.

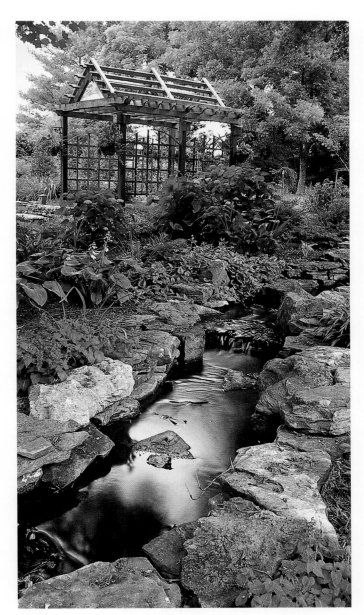

Unless the site's soil is fine-grained and rock-free, it's best to provide protection for the liner with an underlayment fabric and a layer of sand.

Pond Kits. Some manufacturers offer complete pond kits. These include a rigid shell or flexible liner with a matched pump, filter, and in some cases a fountainhead or self-contained waterfall, planting containers, and pond-treatment chemicals for the initial start-up. If you find a design you like, the kits are much easier to install than separate components. Such kits are usually limited to smaller ponds, however.

A pond with a rock bottom looks more natural than one with an exposed liner.

Edging

Pond edgings are typically rock, other masonry materials, or wood. The edging serves to hide the rim, visually define the pond perimeter, and keep surrounding soil from washing into the water. The material you choose can complement nearby landscape features; the edging for a formal pond might also be decorative in its own right. Or the edging can blend into the surroundings, as is the case with an informal pond edged with lawn or native stone. Plan for the edging (also called coping) to overhang the pond by a few inches so that it hides the liner.

At least one section of the edging should be wide and flat enough to allow easy access to the pond for maintenance tasks. (An overhang of a deck or patio could also serve this purpose.) Because stepping on edging could dislodge it, be sure that the area intended for maintenance access is secure; you may wish to mortar at least a por-

tion. Design the edging so that it rises slightly above the surrounding ground to direct runoff away from the pond.

Solid Edging. Formal pools usually have the same edging all the way around, typically poured concrete, brick, pavers, patio tiles, or cut stone. The most common edging for an informal pond is one line of natural stones, either boulders or flagstones. But you may stack flagstones in several vertical layers or arrange boulders and round stones several feet from the pond, decreasing in size as they get closer to the water. Or you can edge an informal pond with a mix of plantings and different types of stone.

Wood Edging. In the unlikely event that you use wood as an edging material, make sure it's labeled for marine or seawall use. Avoid pressure-treated wood because it is treated with chemicals that are toxic to fish and plants.

Informal ponds (left) are typically edged with boulders, rocks, and smaller stones.

Lawn Edging

Lawn grass can make a handsome edging, but you'll have to trim it by hand, taking care not to drop grass clippings in the water. The high nitrogen content in grass will disturb the chemical balance of the pond. If you use lawn for edging, you can make a solid edge for it by embedding stones or bricks in mortar on a ledge along the edge of the pond and bringing sod to the edge on a thin layer of topsoil.

A turf edging can give a pond a clean, open look and easy access for maintenance, but can be difficult to maintain.

Lawn Edging

Layer of Topsoil

Concrete-Block Support

Mortar

Backfill

Grass and Stone Edges

Pebble Beach

For a wildlife pond, a pebble beach is a popular edging option because it allows birds and mammals to bathe or to wash their food in the shallow water. To create a beach, dig a gradual slope into your pond on one side, and surface it with pebbles. Unless you want pebbles on the bottom of your pond—which is not advisable because the plant debris that gets trapped between them makes the pond hard to clean—you need to create a lip, or stone stop 4 to 6 inches under the water surface to keep the pebbles from rolling into the pond. (Mortar is another option, but it will have to be neutralized with vinegar or acid. See Step 6 in Chapter 4, page 71.) The beach will look more natural if you gradually decrease the size of the pebbles as they get nearer the pond. Lay them down thickly enough so that the liner doesn't show through; some coarse sand may help fill the gaps. If your pond is small, keep the beach area small, or the high percentage of shallow water will cause excessive algal buildup.

Gradual Slope

Stone Stop 4"–6" Underwater

Large Stones at Top

A gradual slope with a pebble bottom makes an ideal edging for a wildlife pond. Birds and other animals can easily bathe, drink, and wash food.

BUYING ROCKS FOR YOUR POND

Most stone dealers will sell natural stone for informal ponds as well as stones machine-cut in geometric shapes appropriate for edging a formal pool. If you can afford and handle them, large boulders will look better than small stones. Buy the largest stones you can manage easily, but also look for smaller stones of the same type to fill gaps and create a transition between them and the pond.

A landscape designer, a local nursery, or your water-garden dealer may be able to suggest a local quarry with a good selection and helpful service for do-it-yourselfers. A quarry will offer local stone, which will look more appropriate in your landscape than exotic imports. Ask for local stone if you visit a dealer rather than a quarry. If possible, visit a couple of quarries or dealers to get an idea of what's available. If you call first, you may get a sense of which ones will be most helpful. A visit to a good rock quarry can be a fun experience. You can find rocks with holes for waterfalls, flat rocks perfect for the waterfall lip,

rocks with natural depressions for a Japanese basin, and moss-covered rocks to give your pond an instant weathered look. Rock is usually described as either permeable (allowing water to penetrate) or impermeable. Permeable rock such as sandstone will weather quickly and develop a natural-looking roundness; it provides a good home for moss and comes in a variety of colors. Slate has a handsome sheen when wet. Avoid limestone, as it will turn the pond water too alkaline. Granite is an impermeable stone that, while handsome, is more suited to a formal pool. It is durable but hard to cut.

The dealer will probably deliver the rock to the pond site. It will be up to you to move it into place. A medium to large rock can weigh more than 250 pounds, so it's best to hire a contractor for the job or rent a small backhoe. Even if you're in good condition, enlist friends to help, and allow several days to complete the job to reduce the possibility of muscle strain.

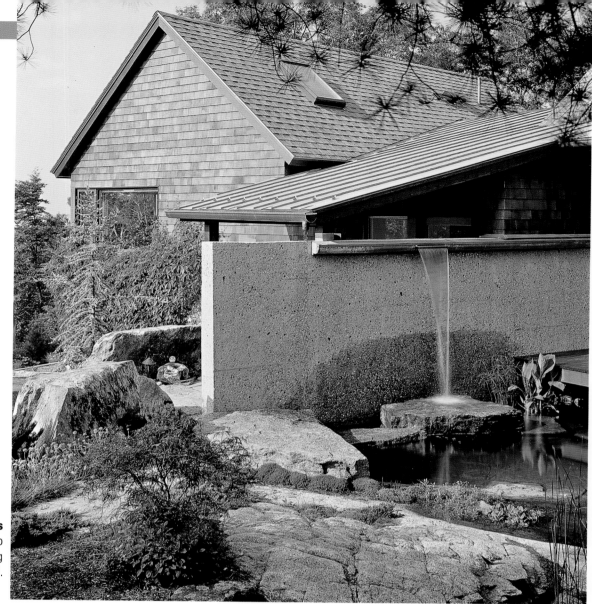

Visit stone yards and quarries to select interesting pieces for your pond.

Designing the Pond Configuration

A formal reflecting pool with no plants or fish only needs to be 12 inches deep. Other ponds with water lilies should be at least 18 to 24 inches deep, which is considered the optimum for those plants. Ponds less than 18 inches deep heat up and cool off more quickly than large, deep ones.

If you plan on having koi, they can survive the cold, but not being frozen. Ice can form to a depth of six inches or more depending on the temperature. The pond should be deep enough to protect the fish from freezing. Deeper ponds can help better insulate koi from the cold.

Shallow and Sloping Areas. Marginal plants need water depths of a foot or less. Separate planting beds or shelves around the pond perimeter can hold these plants. Container plants can be raised on bricks or lightweight plastic milk crates.

Clay ponds should have a shallow bowl shape to make the edges less prone to cracking or crumbling if they dry out. Wildlife ponds often have one side that is a shallow pebble beach so that birds and other creatures have a place to wade.

Don't make your pond's bottom perfectly flat. Slope it slightly toward a sump hole, which will trap dirt and debris and ease cleaning. You can also use this sump area as a drain location or as a place for a submersible pump to improve water circulation. Elevate the pump on a brick (or by other means) to keep it above sediment in the sump bottom. Dig the hole deep enough to accommodate both pump and brick.

A pond's shape can be as simple or elaborate as your resources permit.

The Pond Bottom

Before you begin digging your pond, think about the needs of its future inhabitants. Water lilies require a minimum depth of 18 inches. Koi and other large fish need ponds 3 feet deep. If you want to have marginal plants, such as grass, sedges, arrowhead, and pick- erel weed, you will have to accommodate them in water depths ranging anywhere from an inch or two to a foot, either by building shelves or raising them on bricks or plastic baskets. Sloping the bottom toward the sump hole will make pond cleaning much easier.

Marginal Plant

Small to Medium Water Lilies

Large Water Lilies, Fish

Power Cable

6"–9"
Bog Plants

12"–18" Small/Medium
Water Lilies

24"–36"
Large Lilies,
Fish

Shelf

Bricks Raising Water Lilies to Correct Height

Submersible
Pump

Stone Slab to Raise
Pump above Debris

how|to

Make a Site Plan

If you've selected a site for your pond and you plan to leave the rest of the yard pretty much as it is, a site plan isn't necessary. Otherwise, it's a good idea to develop one. It's relatively easy and even fun to do, and it will help you (and others involved in the project) visualize how the pond fits into the overall scheme. The plan can also be submitted to your local building department for approval if that is required. Local building codes are likely to have requirements relating to setbacks and safety barriers to protect young children. Check before you begin.

Make copies for your records. Once you've finalized the design, make a neat tracing. Attach this final tracing-paper overlay to the base map, and make photocopies. Keep one copy for your files; give another one to building officials; and retain at least two more copies for reference during the project installation. The records will make any further revisions in the pond design easy to note.

Tools and Materials: graph paper (¼-inch grid); tracing paper, several sheets; 50-foot measuring tape; pencil; ruler; site survey map (plat), if available

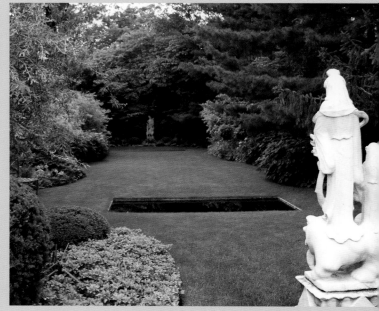

A sculpture and the shallow pool's reflections of sky and trees produce an elegant effect.

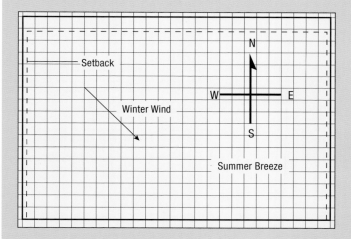

1 **Mark the property lines.** On the graph paper, mark your property lines (a scale of ¼ in. = 1 ft. is standard). If only a portion of the property will be affected (the backyard, for instance), you don't need to include the entire lot. Indicate north, south, east, and west. Also mark the directions of prevailing summer and winter winds. (Ask neighbors or your local Cooperative Extension Service if you're not sure.) Check with the building department to see how far the pond or any added structures must be set back from lot boundaries; mark these setbacks as dotted lines on your plan.

2 **Locate existing structures.** Starting from a front corner of the house, measure the house dimensions, and transfer them to the plan. Again, if only one yard (front, side, or back) will be affected, you need only show the part of the house that faces it. Include the locations of exterior doors and windows on the wall facing the pond site. Measure and mark the locations of your garage, storage shed, and any other detached buildings and permanent structures, including patios, decks, fences, and paved walks. Show any underground or overhead fixtures, such as utility lines and septic systems. Utility companies will mark these for you.

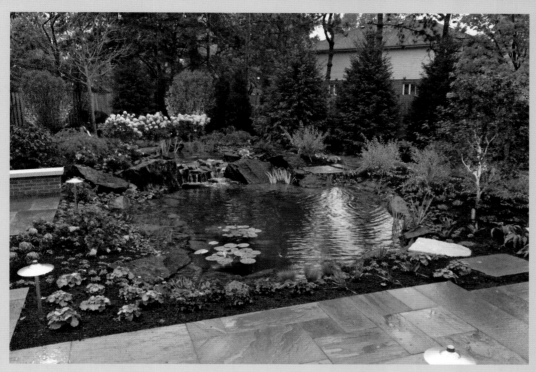

Make a rough drawing and take photos of the site and your property's plat to your local building department to see if permits are required.

3 **Locate plantings.** Mark the locations of existing trees, shrubs, and other major plantings; specify which are to be kept and which need to be removed or relocated. If applicable, make notations on the shade cast by trees, tall shrubs, fences, or other structures near the pond site. Remember to factor in growth of any immature trees and large shrubs.

4 **Locate the pond on overlays.** On a tracing-paper overlay, draw in the exact size and location of the proposed pond. Include edging materials, a waterfall if you plan one, and other proposed pond features, such as walks, planting beds, and fountains. Show the path of new utility lines to the pond. Use as many overlay sheets as you need to design a suitable plan.

PART 2

Installing Your Pond

Once you've chosen a flexible or preformed shell for your pond, installation is next. It marks the end of dreaming and planning and the beginning of years of enjoyment. This section contains instructions to help you through the process.

CHAPTER 4

Start with a Pond Foundation

A flat site is often the easiest place to build a water feature, especially if this is your first one. The most difficult spot is at the bottom of a slope. In nature, ponds tend to be in low-lying areas, but there are several concerns in a garden situation. Low areas collect runoff that may contain pesticides and other toxins, as well as soil and other organic debris. Low areas tend to collect cold air before the rest of the garden.

Depending on where you live, a low spot may be too close to the underground water table. That increases the likelihood that groundwater could bubble up under a liner or heave a pond shell out of the ground.

A good foundation and careful planning will keep your water feature beautiful for years. Consider all of the aspects of the site. A flat location is the easiest for building a pond, although slopes offer dramatic possibilities.

Special Sites

Slopes. As previously noted, a hillside can lend itself to some creative possibilities for waterfalls and streams. On some properties, a slope may be the only choice. If that is the case with you, you'll need to build a retaining wall for the pond. You can do this with soil, using the "cut-and-fill" method. Use subsoil excavated from your pond to build a mound on the downhill side, cover it with topsoil you've removed from the area, and landscape it with plants and rocks.

You can also build a brick or concrete retaining wall on one or both sides of the pond. A wall on the uphill side can be designed so it's almost invisible aboveground. It will help prevent that slope from eroding, and its top edge can keep soil and other matter from washing into the pond. A wall on the downhill side will provide additional support for your liner or shell and the weight of the water it contains, but depending on your slope, it may be visible from below and may obstruct your view of the pond. If you build this wall of stone, you may be able to turn it into an attractive rock garden to complement an informal pond. For a formal pool you can use brick and turn it into a raised bed in which to grow annuals, flowering perennials, or ornamental grasses.

If your property has a high water table, your best solution is to plan on a raised or at least a semiraised pond. You may be able to deal with seasonally poor drainage by installing gravel-filled trenches to divert water around the pond and into a dry well. It will be helpful on the uphill side of a slope to catch runoff before it reaches the level of the pond. A more attractive option is a wetland garden on the uphill side of the pond to catch runoff.

A sloped site offers creative possibilities such as incorporating a naturalistic waterfall.

how to

Install a Flexible Liner

DIFFICULTY LEVEL: MODERATE

Flexible pond liners of PVC plastic or rubber are by far the most popular options for pond foundations. They are both relatively inexpensive (compared to preformed shells) and easy to install, and they provide unlimited creative opportunities in pond size and shape. It's also easy to load a roll of flexible liner into your car's rear seat or trunk. Most flexible liners are black, which gives ponds the illusion of additional depth. You may occasionally see other colors. The liners come in a variety of stock sizes, with larger sizes available as special orders. Some garden suppliers carry large rolls of liner material in standard widths. You simply pull the length you need off the roll. If you don't have a well-stocked supplier within easy driving distance, consider ordering the liner by mail-order or online. Most mail-order suppliers and Web sites have knowledgeable, helpful staff.

ESTIMATING THE SIZE TO BUY

Quality liner material is not inexpensive. Nor will you enjoy calling in your helpers and digging the hole, only to find that you don't have enough liner to fill it. Water-garden expert and supplier Charles Thomas recommends that anyone installing a water garden for the first time should add a foot to the calculations in both directions. Check your math a couple of times, and then have someone recheck your figures.

Tools and Materials: rope and stake (for circular ponds); garden hose (for irregular ponds) or batter boards and string (for rectangular ponds); framing square (for square or rectangular ponds); sharpened stick (for circular ponds); flour, powdered gypsum, or nontoxic spray paint (for marking outlines); measuring tape and calculator

IRREGULAR

SQUARE

1 Outline the Shape. After clearing the site of plantings and other obstructions, outline the pond shape on the ground. For irregularly shaped ponds, use a rope or garden hose to mark the pond perimeter. For squares or rectangles, use batter boards, string, and a framing square to make sure all corners meet exactly at a 90-deg. angle. For circular ponds, make a simple "compass" with a stake, sturdy twine or rope, and a sharpened stick, screwdriver, or other pointed object. Drive the stake in the center of your pond area; attach a rope the length of its radius; and use the sharp stick or screwdriver tied to the other end to mark the pond's outside edge. Go over the marked line with flour, powdered gypsum, or nontoxic spray paint to make it more visible.

CIRCULAR

Plants such as hosta and pontederia (also known as "pickerel weed") create a soft border around this lily pond.

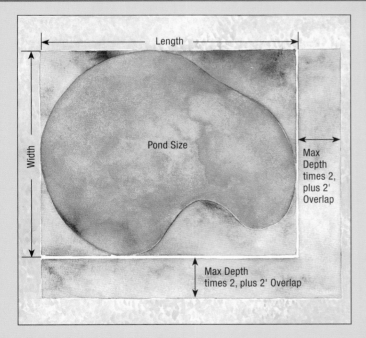

FORMULA FOR LINER SIZE

Liner Width =
Pond Width + 2x Depth + 2-foot overlap

Liner Length =
Pond Length + 2x Depth + 2-foot overlap

Example:
The pond is 24 inches deep and fits inside a 10 x 12-foot rectangle. To figure liner width, add 10 feet (the width), plus 4 feet (the depth, doubled), plus 2 feet (for overlap), for a total of 16 feet. To figure liner length, add 12 feet (the length), plus 4 feet (the depth, doubled), plus 2 feet (for overlap), for a total of 18 feet. You would therefore need a 16 x 18-foot liner for a 10 x 12-foot pond.

2 **Calculate Liner Size.** Measure the overall width and length of the pond; then determine the smallest rectangle that would enclose the pond area. To allow for pond depth, decide on the maximum depth of the pond, double it, and add this figure to the width and length of the rectangle. To allow for overlap around the edges, add an additional 24 in. to the width and length of the liner. This will provide 12 in. of overlap around the pond rim once the liner is installed. It is obviously best to overestimate when calculating the liner size you'll need, particularly if the shape of

the pond is quite irregular. (Refer to the example above, showing how to compute a 16 x 18-ft. liner for a 10 x 12-ft. pond.)

Note that for irregularly shaped ponds, you may need to trim excess liner material to provide an even overlap around the entire pond. If you are creating one or more wetland gardens alongside the pond, you may be able to use the excess for that purpose. Be sure to add extra liner to your calculations if it appears that you will not have enough for a desired wetland.

how to

Construct a Lined Inground Pond

DIFFICULTY LEVEL: MODERATE

Installing a flexible liner in the ground requires four basic steps: digging the hole, laying down the liner, filling the pond with water, and adding stones or other edging around the pond perimeter. Some sites and designs may require a few additional steps.

If you plan to install statuary, read about footings on page 122 before you begin your pond.

Tools and Materials: measuring tape; spirit level; tamper; flexible liner; shovels (flat shovel works best for removing sod; rounded shovel works best for digging); wheelbarrow (for moving excavated soil); straight boards (for checking level); underlayment fabric or old newspapers, carpet, or damp sand; stones for temporary liner weights; heavy-duty scissors or utility knife.

1 Dig the Hole. Use a flat shovel to remove patches of sod within the pond outline and about 6 to 12 in. beyond the perimeter. Digging shallow shelves around the perimeter is optional; they are about 12 to 16 in. wide and 9 to 12 in. below the top edge of the excavation. After excavating the pond area to the depth of the shelf, compact the soil firmly in the shelf area using a tamper. The perimeter should be the depth of the shovel blade. Use a straight board and a spirit level to make sure the shelf is level. Then excavate the rest of the pond. Check the depth frequently by measuring from the bottom of the hole to the top of a long 2x4 or 2x6 placed across the pond. The sides should slope in about 20 deg. from vertical; 45 deg. in loose or sandy soil. Slope the bottom of the excavation about ½ to 1 in. per foot toward the center or one end; at the lowest point, dig a shallow (6 to 8 in. deep) sump hole to facilitate draining the pond for future cleaning.

4 Position the Liner. Work shoeless so as not to damage the liner. To make it more flexible, unroll it and let it warm a few minutes in the sun. Heat will build up underneath it and kill a lawn, so spread it on sun-warmed pavement. Avoid dragging the liner across the ground. With a helper, drape the liner loosely into the excavation, leaving an even overlap on all sides. After it's centered, weight down the edges with concrete blocks, bricks, or stones. Then fill the pond with water.

5 Adjust the Liner. As the pond fills with water, adjust the liner to conform to the sides of the pond and smooth it out. Ease off the stone weights. When the pond is full, trim off excess lining using a scissors or a utility knife. Leave enough around the rim to extend underneath and a few inches behind the first course of stones. To keep the liner in place while you add edging, push large nails or spikes through the liner into the ground every foot or so around the pond rim.

2 Cut a Ledge for the Edging Materials. Using a flat-blade shovel, cut a ledge that is about 12 to 15 in. wide and deep enough to accommodate the combined thickness of the edging and any underlayment. If you will be mortaring the stones, include an extra 2 to 3 in. The top of the edging should be at least 1 in. above the surrounding terrain and overhang the pond edge by a few inches to hide the liner and protect it from the sun. If you'll be installing a statuary fountain that weighs more than 100 lbs, install a 4-in.-thick concrete footing for it before you lay the liner.

3 Make Sure the Pond Edges are Level. Use the same board you used to measure hole depth. Place a level on top of it; then move the board to various points across the length and width of the pond while checking for level. Remove sharp stones or roots from the site. If your liner does not have a built-in underlayment, you need to give it additional protection with pond underlayment from your supplier, 2 to 3 in. of damp sand, old carpet, or a 1-in. layer of newspapers. Pack damp sand or soil into any voids in the sidewalls and bottom. If your soil is mostly sand and your liner is heavy, omit underlayment on the bottom only.

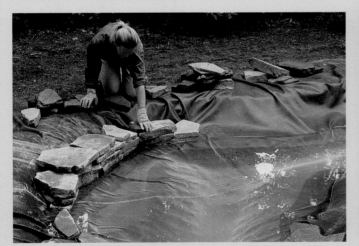

6 Add Edging Materials. A single line of natural stones is the simplest form of edging. Place large stones over an extra layer of liner. Or set stones in 2 to 3 in. of mortar reinforced with metal lath. Treat and allow the mortar to cure for a week. Then scrub the edging with a vinegar solution of 4 parts vinegar to 1 part water to neutralize the lime leaching from the mortar. Drain the pond, rinse the liner, and add fresh water; repeat until the water tests neutral.

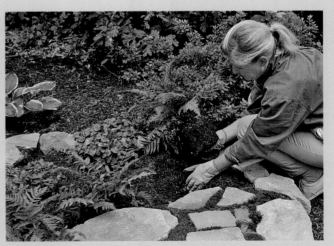

7 Add Plants Around the Perimeter. Tuck plants between rocks—either directly into the soil or in pots sunk into the ground—to soften the edges of the pond. (See the sidebar "A Moss Milkshake" on page 46 for information on how to encourage moss to grow between stones.)

Working with the Terrain

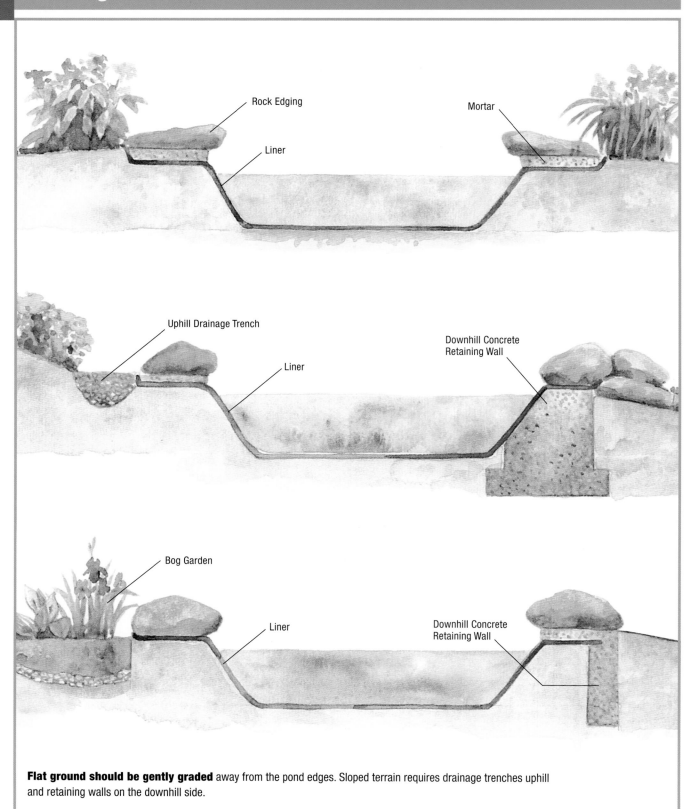

Rock Edging

Mortar

Liner

Uphill Drainage Trench

Liner

Downhill Concrete
Retaining Wall

Bog Garden

Liner

Downhill Concrete
Retaining Wall

Flat ground should be gently graded away from the pond edges. Sloped terrain requires drainage trenches uphill and retaining walls on the downhill side.

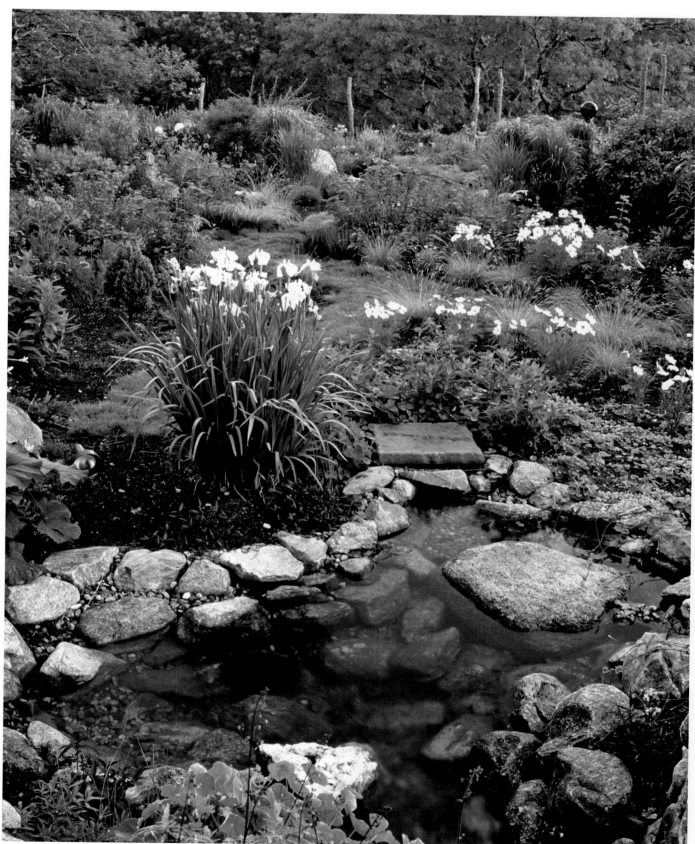

A small shallow pond and various plantings add interest and color to this hilly landscape.

A small deck and chairs overlooking a pond and surrounded by greenery is a perfect at-home getaway for relaxing and reflection.

Planting-Shelf Options

Although some pond designs have shelves all the way around the perimeter for containerized plants, these are optional. On a practical level, you will often discover that containers are too big or the wrong shape for such shelves. Many water gardeners find that raising their containerized plants on bricks or plastic milk crates allows them to be more flexible about the placement of their marginal (shallow-water) plants. Another option is to create permanent planting areas that allow you to grow your plants without containers but still keep them from spreading. To create planting areas for marginals, excavate a ledge wide enough to allow you to lay a stone or brick retaining wall along the outside edge on top of the liner. Mortar the stones or bricks only enough to keep them in place because it's no problem to have water seeping between them. Fill the area with good garden soil. After planting, top the soil with gravel to keep it from being dislodged. The shelf shouldn't be wider than about a foot, so you can easily reach plants for deadheading, dividing, and other chores.

Planting Beds. In formal pools, some people use bricks to create permanent planters for water lilies in the middle of the pond. In a deep koi pond, permanent planting beds with edges 12 inches below the surface and 24 inches across will hold the largest water lilies and protect them from the fish. (Koi are less likely to bother plants this close to the surface.) For marginal plants, build the planter walls so that the edges are 6 inches below the surface to accommodate a wide range of species. You can create deeper areas within the planter for species that need to grow 8 to 12 inches below the surface. Different plants grouped together look more natural in such beds, but obviously you can't rearrange them as easily as with containers. Such large planter beds are heavy; installing a concrete footing under your liner will help protect it.

You can build permanent shelves into the side of your pond. But many water gardeners find that raising container plants on bricks, plastic crates, or other platforms gives them more flexibility in plant placement.

Planting Pockets

Spaces between pondside stones allow for container plants or inground plantings. Give the latter good garden loam topped with gravel.

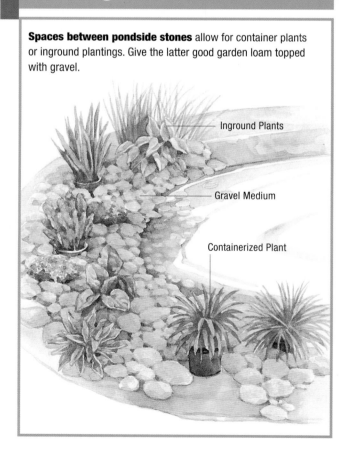

Inground Plants

Gravel Medium

Containerized Plant

Planting Options

Wide Shelf

Koi-proof Planting Area

Central Planting Bed

Deep Shelf

Container Platform

Although you wouldn't want to include all of these in one pond, this drawing illustrates the many possibilities for creating permanent planting areas within a water feature. Large central planting beds require a concrete footing if you're using a flexible liner.

Plant Island

Shape a flat-topped mound of earth lower than the water level, and cover it with the liner. Build a retaining wall of upside-down sod pieces around the perimeter, and fill the center with heavy garden soil. For a dry island, build a flat-topped mound 6 to 12 inches higher than the water level, and drape the liner over it. Cut a hole in the center of the liner. Dig organic matter into the soil before planting it with perennials or small shrubs. Upside-down sod can hide the liner around the edges.

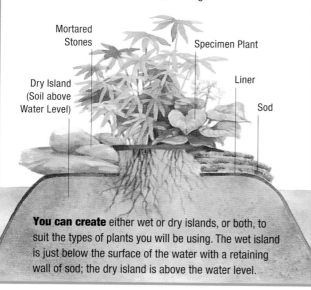

Mortared Stones

Specimen Plant

Dry Island
(Soil above
Water Level)

Liner

Sod

You can create either wet or dry islands, or both, to suit the types of plants you will be using. The wet island is just below the surface of the water with a retaining wall of sod; the dry island is above the water level.

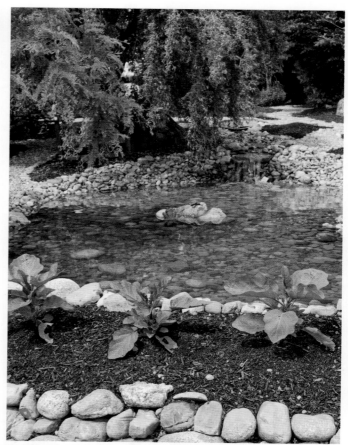

Gravel and mulch add a natural look around the pond, and they provide a surface that you can walk on to deadhead or divide plantings.

Extra Support for Pond Foundations

A pond constructed in soil that is sandy or soft or where you'll use large boulders will need extra support for the pond edges. A simple way to achieve this is placing a line of concrete blocks along the edge where the soil will be excavated. The blocks need not touch, so they can be placed in an informal, curving line. The blocks can also provide support for preformed pond shells, as they'll help contain the outward pressure when the pond is filed. It's also easier to lay stone edging without using mortar on the resulting flat surface. A carpenter's level will verify that the blocks are even when installed.

Bring the liner's edge up and over the concrete blocks (or poured concrete if that is what you use). Underlayment (special pads) under the pond liner will help prevent punctures from any sharp edges on the blocks. Extend the liner a foot or more beyond the cement blocks so they are hidden. If you prefer using poured concrete rather than individual blocks, bring in professional expertise. Many landscaper contractors specialize in pond installation. For large projects, that may be the way to go if your resources permit.

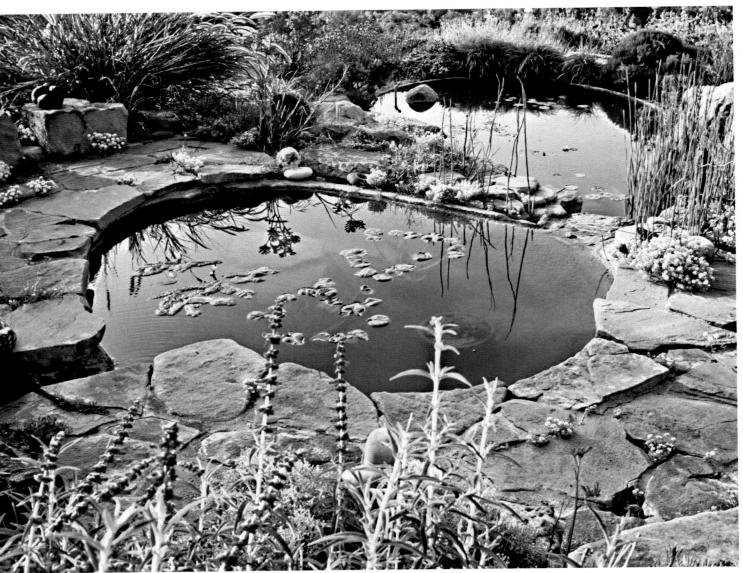

Buried concrete blocks along the edge provide extra support for this pond's preformed liner.

Pond netting, which protects koi against heron attacks, should be supported above the water.

Optional Cement Overliner

A thin layer of cement-like material spread over the liner will protect it from the damaging effects of ultraviolet rays as well as from punctures caused by waders in the pond. Plastic cement is the material of choice for a liner mixture because it contains latex additives that make the mixture highly resistant to cracking. Most lumberyards and masonry suppliers carry this product; mix 1 part plastic cement to 4 parts sand to make a good liner mixture. If you like, you can add coloring agents to the cement and/or produce various surface textures by brooming or troweling before it dries.

After installing the flexible liner, cover it with a layer of chicken wire to provide reinforcement. Hand-pack a 1-inch layer of plastic cement into the chicken wire over the entire surface of the pond; wear heavy gloves for this procedure. Start packing cement at the base of each side-

Pond Supports

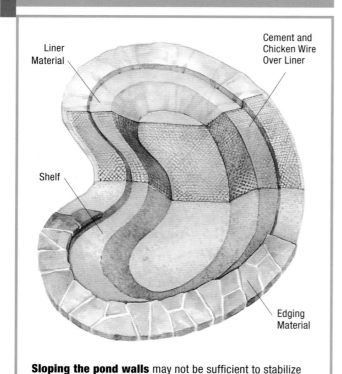

Sloping the pond walls may not be sufficient to stabilize them if the soil is very sandy or crumbly. Mortar may be needed to significantly strengthen the sides; a cement overliner with chicken wire adds stability to the entire pond area. It is applied to the pond sides and entire bottom.

Nonsupport versus Support

Lack of edge support can cause granular soil pond sides to shift.

With edge support, pond sides are secure.

(Loose Granular Soil)

(Loose Granular Soil)

wall, building up to the top in 6-foot-long sections. After the sidewalls are covered, do the pond bottom. Brush or trowel the surface smooth; then allow the plastic cement to harden (about 10 to 12 hours, or overnight).

Once the cement has hardened, fill the pond with water. Add 1 gallon of distilled white vinegar per 100 gallons of water; allow this mixture to stand one week. (The vinegar serves to neutralize the lime leaching from the cement.) Drain the pond. (See page 194 for information on draining a pond.) Rinse the overliner thoroughly before refilling the pond with fresh water. Test the pH of the water before adding fish or plants. (For more on pH, see "What's In Your Water" on page 181.) If the water tests too alkaline, repeat the vinegar treatment and test again.

Installing a Preformed Shell

Rigid, preformed pond shells of molded plastic or fiberglass are quick to install and resist punctures better than flexible liners. You don't have to fret about creating the design, and if you move, you could conceivably take the pond with you.

PREPARING THE GROUND

Although the conditions for a rigid shell aren't as exacting as for a liner, the ground where you install a preformed pond must be free of rocks, projecting roots, and other sharp objects and—above all—must be stable. The shell, which can weigh several tons when full of water, will need to be fully supported by firm, well-packed earth. Any air pockets or bumps can cause it to crack or buckle.

Groundwater (from a high water table) can erode loose or sandy soil around the shell. In cold climates, frost heaving can deform or buckle it. If you anticipate either of these conditions, make the excavation about 6 to 8 inches deeper and wider than the shell. Then backfill the hole with 3 to 4 inches of smooth pea gravel, top with 2 inches of sand or finely sifted soil, and tamp firmly. (If you plan to install a statuary fountain, stepping-stone boulders, or other heavy objects in the pond, read about footings in "In-Pond Statuary" on page 122 before you begin construction.)

These durable plastic or fiberglass foundations, above, come in many shapes and sizes, but minus the unlimited design options of flexible liners.

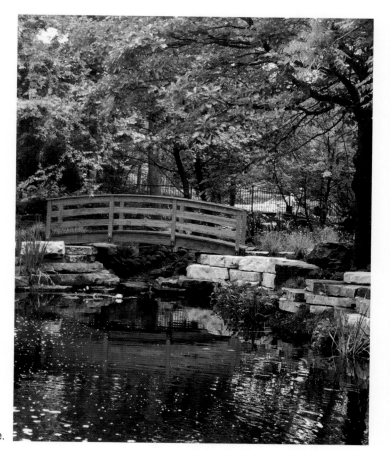

Large, natural stones are used to support a hefty bridge.

how to

Construct a Preformed Inground Pond

Once you dig the hole, you'll have to remove any rocks or other sharp objects. For added protection to the liner, cover the bottom of the hole with 2 to 3 inches of damp sand or finely sifted soil. (For thinner shells, you may also want to use an underlayment fabric; see "Flexible Pond Liners" on page 48.) Tamp all surfaces. Then use a spirit level to make sure the bottom of the excavation is perfectly level in all directions.

Tools and Materials: preformed shell; plumb bob or spirit level and stakes; rope, garden hose, or nontoxic spray paint (for marking outlines); shovel and tamper; damp sand or finely sifted soil; measuring tape; long, straight 2x4; spirit level; edging material; mortar and mixing equipment; vinegar or commercial concrete-curing agent (optional)

1 Mark the Shell Outline. Except for very small ponds, you will need help with installation because you will be lifting and moving the shell several times. Place the preformed shell upright in the desired location. Use a plumb bob or a spirit level and stakes to transfer the shape of the pond rim to the ground, and mark the outline with a rope, garden hose, or nontoxic spray paint. Use stakes (spaced about 12 in. apart) to keep the rope or hose in place.

The outline of the preformed pond liner is mostly visible, above, but it does not detract from the appeal of the water feature. Small, not-too-heavy rocks can be arranged on top of the liner's edge if you wish to make the pond blend seamlessly into the landscape.

2 **Dig and Prepare the Hole.** Excavate the hole, allowing an extra 2 in. around the perimeter and 2 in. in the bottom of the hole to be backfilled with sand. If the shell has shallow-water shelves, dig the hole only to the depth of these shelves; then tamp the outside edges of the bottom firmly. Put the shell in the hole, and mark the outline of the bottom of the pond. Remove the shell, and dig out this lower portion to the distance between the bottom of the shelves and the bottom of the pond (plus 2 extra in.). Flatten the bottom with the edge of a board, and firmly tamp the soil. (Thinner shells must have firm support under the shelves as well as on the sides and bottom.)

3 **Set the Shell.** Place the pond shell into the excavation, and check the height of the rim. The rim should be about 1 in. above the surrounding ground to prevent runoff from entering the pond. Add or remove sand from the bottom of the hole (and soil from the shelf support) until you achieve the desired height.

4 **Level the Shell.** Place a long, straight 2x4 across the shell rim in several places, and check with a spirit level. If the shell isn't level, pull it out of the hole and relevel the excavation. The pond must be perfectly level before you add any water. Even a few inches of water in the pond bottom will make the shell virtually impossible to move.

Once the shell is level, start filling it with water slowly. As the water level rises, backfill the hole around the shell with sifted dirt or damp sand, tamping it gently with a shovel handle or the end of a 2x4. Make sure you fill any gaps or holes, especially around any shallow-water shelves. Check the rim for level frequently. Don't allow the water level inside the pond to rise above the backfilled earth outside the rim, or else the shell may bulge outward.

5 **Add Edging.** When the shell is filled with water, you can conceal the exposed rim with rocks, masonry materials, or overhanging plants. If you use flagstones or flat pavers, allow them to overhang the pond edges by 1 to 2 in. Don't allow the full weight of large rocks to rest on the pond rim, because the weight may deform or damage the pond walls. Instead, embed the rocks in a 3- to 4-in.-thick bed of mortar, raised slightly above the lip of the shell, or bury a line of concrete blocks along the rim of the shell. If you use mortar, neutralize the lime in it with distilled vinegar after the mortar has cured for about a week, as described under "Constructing a Lined Inground Pond," step 6 on page 71.

BUILDING A SEMIRAISED POND WITH A PREFORMED SHELL

It's possible to install some of the thickest preformed pond shells completely aboveground using a skirt of wood, brick, or masonry block to hide the sides and to hold up the rim. But it's difficult to give even the sturdiest shells enough support to keep them from buckling and shifting.

Do-it-yourselfers will have better luck with a partially raised pond, which involves sinking the lower part of the shell up to the shelf level and building a low wall to mask the raised portion. As with an inground pond, make the excavation 2 inches deeper and wider than the shell, line the bottom of the hole with 2 inches of sand, and set the shell in place. Then build a wall from the ground to the lip of the pond, backfilling behind the wall with soil (or concrete) as you go. If your wall is stone or other masonry, you'll need to have a concrete footing (foundation) installed to support the wall before you start constructing it. The footing should be at least twice the width of the wall and a minimum of 4 inches deep (even deeper in colder climates, with a layer of gravel underneath; check local codes). Use reinforcing bar (rebar) for stability. Place cap stones over the lip of the shell to hide it; secure the cap stones with mortar.

There are a variety of design treatments that can be attempted with a semiraised pond. Your local water-garden dealer is the place to start looking for ideas. He or she may be able to show you excellent examples of a semiraised pond or suggest a design.

Geometric Semiraised Ponds. These are the easiest shapes with which to work. You can support any straight-sided geometric shape (rectangle, square, L-shaped) with a fairly basic design of concrete block, which is fast, economical, and durable. Then you have an extensive choice of materials to decorate your wall, including easy-to-apply veneers that look like old brick or various types of natural stone. More-skilled do-it-yourselfers may choose to build the support of concrete, in which case they will first need to build supports of plywood and 2x4 stakes. Remember to make any provisions for wiring and electrical hookups for pumps and lighting before you begin erecting your support wall.

Semiraised Pond

This style can be a handy compromise when working with preformed shells. It is sturdier than a fully raised preformed shell, yet the inital excavation will be easier than that of a sunken pond.

Free-Form Semiraised Ponds. A preformed pond shell with an irregular outline will be more challenging to enclose with a support wall than a shape with regular edges. Standard 16-inch concrete block may be too large to adapt to the curvature of your shell; brick may be a better choice for following a free-form path.

Using concrete would allow you to follow the pond edge more precisely, but you will need to find flexible materials with which to make your form. These might include flexible plywood or plastic sheet laminates.

This pond, above, is built from a preformed shell raised partway out of the ground. But a woodland setting creates a more informal impression than that of more geometric forms. Creating the same free-form design, right, as might appear in nature, would not be possible with a rigid shell.

Mortared brick, stone, or concrete are all excellent choices for supporting the walls of a raised pond, such as this one, left.

Moving Water Features

Moving water adds sound and activity, invites birds, and creates soothing background "music." It may be a waterfall, a stream, a fountain, or a formal pool with water gently spraying from scuppers. There's a practical benefit, too. Moving water provides aeration, increasing oxygen for fish and other pond life.

Design Pointers

The type of moving water you choose depends on the style (formal vs. informal) as well as your terrain. For an informal pond, even the smallest stream should look natural, edged with a variety of boulders and rocks. A tall waterfall works on a steep slope, but if the terrain is flat, it will look artificial. For a formal pool, you may want a straight-sided canal or steps of flowing water. Masonry blocks, bricks, stone, and ceramic tiles are all materials that work with formal water features.

SHAPING A WATERFALL

Keep a waterfall in scale with the pond. A small trickle in a large pond won't be very dramatic, nor will it be very effective at recirculating and oxygenating the water. And a large cascade gushing into a small pond will stir too much of the water surface, churning up sediment and making it nearly impossible to raise fish, water lilies, and other aquatic plants that prefer still water. If you want both a large, splashing fall and aquatic plants, you'll need to design the pond so plants can be placed well away from the wave action.

Resist the temptation to be too flamboyant. To maintain the main pond's water level, the surface of the fall or stream should be smaller than that of the pond. And a big, splashy water show can speed the loss of pond volume through evaporation. You can hold evaporation to a minimum by keeping the falls low and the watercourse relatively short. For the same reason, small, deep basins are preferable to larger, shallow ones. As you proceed, you must also minimize any possibility of leaks between rocks along the bank and behind the falls.

Creating a watercourse such as this, left, gives you an opportunity to combine artistic flair with engineering skill. But if this is your first such project, you may want to consult an expert.

Streams associated with formal ponds are similar to canals; they usually have straight sides and uniform edging.

The sound of moving water, even from a small stream such as this, is a delightful feature next to a patio.

Creating a realistic stream design requires deft placement of rocks and plants.

Waterfalls. These look best and are less prone to water loss when large, overhanging rocks are used for the lip of the falls. Use smooth, flat flagstones to produce a wide, thin curtain of water, or direct the water through a narrow gap between large boulders to produce a gushing effect. Creating a hollow space behind the falls will amplify and echo the sound of falling water. While the lips of informal falls are formed from naturalistic materials with irregular shapes, those of formal waterfalls can be brick, tile, flagstone, or landscaping ties. Some formal designs incorporate a sheet of clear acrylic plastic to create a wide, nearly transparent curtain of water. The plastic itself is all but invisible when the falls are in operation.

SHAPING A STREAM

For some people, a trickling rivulet is more picturesque than ocean waves. A winding stream is a particularly apt addition to a woodland or a rocky hillside; it's also at home on a prairie, where a waterfall would look contrived. Although you'll need a pond to feed your stream (unless you bury a water tank to take its place), you can make the stream the predominant feature by virtue of its length, placement, or elaborate planting and rock surrounds.

Stream Design. Nature usually arranges streams into a series of short, fairly flat sections separated by low falls or cascades. In a home water garden, streams need to be as level as possible so that they will retain some water when the pump is turned off. Alternating between wet and dry conditions can shorten the life of plastic or fiberglass foundation materials and crack mortar or concrete. And a stream that holds some water at all times also looks more realistic. A drop of 1 to 2 inches per 10 feet is all that's needed to make the stream flow downhill. At that point, changes in width can change stream speed.

Stream Speed. To increase the speed of a stream's current, bring its banks closer together; for a more leisurely current, move the banks farther apart. If you want to grow shallow-water plants along the edges, a deep, wide, slow-moving stream will be preferable to a fast, narrow one. But avoid large areas of slow-moving shallow water, which can quickly become clogged with thick mats of algae.

In either case, twists and turns in the course will make it look more realistic than will a straight channel. Vary the size of the rocks along the banks and the distance between the banks. Placing large rocks inside the watercourse will create rapids; placing smaller stones and pebbles will produce a rippling effect. Either approach will also make the stream look and sound more natural. Straight or parallel channels are appropriate only for formal designs.

Choosing and Buying a Liner

To prevent water loss between rocks or other edging, artificial waterfalls and streams are lined with the same types of materials that are used to line a pond. Most of the same purchasing, design, and installation considerations also apply. In addition to the liner, remember to purchase sufficient underlayment material to cover the entire watercourse. (See the discussion of underlayment under "Flexible Pond Liners" on pages 48-49.)

The stream should be in proportion with the pond.

FLEXIBLE LINERS

The easiest and most versatile material to use is a flexible liner, which will adapt to both formal and informal waterfall designs. Ideally, you should use one large piece of liner for constructing both the main pond and the waterfall or stream to provide a continuous, seamless barrier. In practice, though, it's not always easy to align one large square or rectangular sheet of liner with the selected watercourse site without creating large amounts of waste material.

If the watercourse will be approximately the same width along its entire length, you can use one long strip of liner. However, if the watercourse consists of pools and cascades of different lengths and widths, or if you have designed several bends in a meandering stream, you may need two or more separate pieces of liner. You still may be able to save money by ordering one large sheet of it and then cutting one or more strips from it to line the watercourse. This may cost less than if you were to order separate sheets for the watercourse and pond. Tape or glue the sheets together where they overlap, using seam tape or adhesive available from the liner dealer.

Flexible Liner Watercourse

To determine the amount of liner you'll need for your watercourse, measure the width and length of the course, and then add twice the depth of the fall or stream plus 2 feet to allow a foot of overlap on each side. (See the sample calculations on page 69.) If you plan to create wetland areas on either side of your fall or stream, add in this additional width. If you'll be piecing the liner along its length, add at least 12 inches (for each junction) to allow sufficient overlap to prevent leakage at joints. When planning the main pond, make sure the liner for the main pond is large enough to extend upward into the first catch basin.

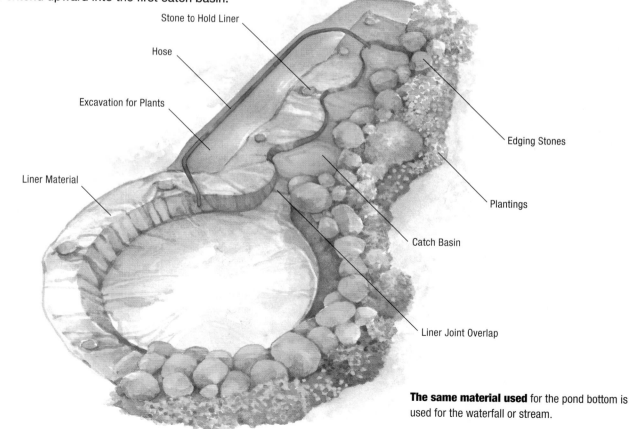

The same material used for the pond bottom is used for the waterfall or stream.

Moving Water

The water for your fall, stream, or fountain is recirculated from your pond by a small electric pump. Buy one that's big enough to operate your waterfall and any other water feature in your pond.

In general, a pump that recirculates one-half of the pond's total water volume per hour will provide the minimum flow for a pleasing proportion of moving water for the size of the pond. For example, if the pond holds 1,000 gallons of water, buy a pump that will deliver at least 500 gallons per hour at the top of the falls. For a larger, bolder cascade, select a pump that will turn over the full 1,000 gallons in one hour. It's better to err on the side of a too-large pump than have one that's too small.

You can also calculate the amount of water required for cascades of various sizes. First measure the width of the spillway over which the water will flow. Then decide how deep you want the water where it flows over the lip. For a light sheet of water (¼ inch deep), you'll need a pump that produces 50 gallons per hour for each inch of lip width. For a heavy flow (1 inch deep), look for a pump that produces 150 gallons per hour for each inch of lip width. For example, if the falls will be 6 inches wide, you'll need a pump that can deliver 300 gallons per hour for a ¼-inch-deep flow or one that delivers 900 gallons per hour for a 1-inch-deep flow.

The right size pump, which will recirculate the pond's water efficiently, will provide a suitably streaming cascade.

PREFORMED WATERFALLS

Most companies that make preformed fiberglass or plastic ponds also offer preformed waterfall runs or courses of the same material. These are installed much like a preformed rigid pond shell. (See "Installing a Preformed Shell" on page 81.) The units consist of one or more small basins with built-in cascades and a lower lip that empties into the pond. You can combine two or more short watercourses to produce a longer watercourse, with each unit emptying into the one below it.

Styles. Informal preformed watercourses are shaped (and sometimes colored) to simulate natural rock, although most look fake unless the edges are disguised with overhanging stones or other materials. Formal preformed waterfalls are usually smaller versions of square or rectangular preformed ponds, with the addition of a built-in lip or spillway.

Materials. Fiberglass and plastic watercourses are lightweight and inexpensive. But as with preformed ponds, the sizes and designs are limited. In fact, preformed watercourses are often designed for use with a specific pump size. On the other hand, you may find it an advantage that your design has been worked out in advance because you can skip some planning and measuring. Preformed watercourses made of cement or reconstituted stone are also available. Although these are more substantial and natural-looking than plastic or fiberglass units, they are much heavier. As a result, the practical size of these units is limited to only a few square feet.

A smooth, flat overhanging stone provides a perfect lip for a wide, thin curtain of water. Hollow space behind the waterfall creates a pleasing echo of falling water.

Determining Pond Capacity

In order to buy the right size pump, you need to figure your pond's capacity in gallons of water. (You'll also need this information for choosing a filter and determining correct dosages of plant fertilizers, fish medications, algaecides, and other chemical treatments.) The most accurate way to determine pond capacity is to attach a flow meter to your faucet or water-supply line and record the number of gallons used when you fill the pond.

Here's a less accurate but easier and less expensive method: turn on the garden hose at a steady flow rate, and time how long it takes to fill a 5-gallon bucket (say, 10 seconds). Then time how many minutes it takes to fill the pond at the same flow rate (say, 20 minutes).

Now figure out the flow rate of the hose in gallons per minute (5 gallons in 10 seconds x 6 = 30 gallons per minute). Next, multiply the gallons per minute by the number of minutes it took to fill the pond (30 gallons x 20 minutes = 600 gallons).

If it isn't practical to fill (or refill) the pond with water, calculate capacity in gallons using one of the following formulas. Each assumes that the pond sides are straight (or steeply sloped) and that the bottom is flat.

■ **Rectilinear ponds:** If the pond is roughly square or rectangular, measure its average depth, width, and length. Then multiply the three figures to determine cubic feet. Multiply the cubic feet by 7.5 to get capacity in gallons.

■ **Circular ponds:** Multiply the diameter by the diameter (diameter squared) times the depth times 5.9.

■ **Oval ponds:** Multiply the depth by the width by the length by 6.7.

■ **Free-form ponds:** It's tough to calculate the volume of an irregularly shaped pond accurately. For the closest estimate, determine the average depth, width, and length, and then use the equation for oval ponds.

Other Considerations. Placing the recirculating pump or pump inlet close to the falls increases the pump's efficiency because the pump then needs to push the water a shorter distance. (You'll also need less tubing or pipe between the pump and the head of the falls.) As a rule, every 10 feet of horizontal pipe or tubing is equal to 1 foot of vertical rise in reducing the performance of the pump. Thus, theoretically, you could power a 30-foot stream with the same pump you would need for a 3-foot waterfall. (That's only theoretical because the stream will have a modest incline, and the fall will have at least a short horizontal run.)

Buy a pump that is slightly more powerful than you think you'll need. You can always restrict the flow if necessary. Some pumps have valves that let you adjust the flow. If yours doesn't, you can restrict the flow by installing a separate valve on the outlet, or discharge, side of the pump or by using a special restriction clamp that attaches to the outlet tubing. (Never restrict the flow on the outlet side by more than 25 percent, however, or you'll burn out the motor.) Before buying the pump, find out if the dealer will allow you to exchange it for a larger size if it turns out to be too small to operate the waterfall to your satisfaction.

Pump Performance

Pump Head (Lift). When shopping for a pump, check the performance charts that come with the product. Most pumps are rated in gallons per hour at various heights above the water surface. This height is referred to as *head* or *lift*. The higher you place the discharge for the waterfall above the pond, the lower the pump output (because the higher your waterfall, the harder the pump has to push to deliver water to the top). For example, a pump that delivers 300 gallons at a 1-foot head may deliver only 120 gallons at a 4-foot head.

In pump-performance charts, manufacturers also provide a maximum head figure, which is the theoretical maximum height to which the pump can lift water. For best pump performance, purchase a pump whose maximum head height is well above the total height of the falls. You can buy moderately priced pumps offering a maximum head height of more than 20 feet.

If you intend to incorporate a fountain in addition to your waterfall, you need to add to your overall figure the gallons per hour required to operate the fountain. If you're adding fish, you'll need a separate mechanical or biological filter, which will further restrict flow and thus necessitate a bigger pump. (Your choice of filters will be limited with certain types of pumps; other pumps are more versatile. See "Filtration" on page 182 for more on filters.) Your pump supplier can help you work out details for these more complicated setups.

Pumps are rated by the amount of water they can deliver at various heights (the head).

Large overhanging rocks, such as flat flagstones, can be used to form an informal, natural-looking waterfall.

SUBMERSIBLE OR EXTERNAL PUMP?

Submersible pumps, as the name implies, are submerged in the water and are removed only periodically to allow cleaning of the built-in filter or strainer that keeps them from getting clogged with leaves and other debris. Submersible pumps are used in most garden ponds for a number of good reasons. They run cooler and more quietly than external pumps and are generally less expensive. In most cases, they're more economical to install and to operate because they require less plumbing. Reasonably priced models range in capacity from 180 to 1,200 gallons per hour; high-capacity models will handle up to 3,400 gallons per hour.

If a submersible pump doesn't work with your pond design, you can buy a pump designed to operate either in open air or submerged. Compact in size, these devices are a good compromise in situations where a submersible pump would pose safety hazards or be prone to damage and where a typical external pump would be too big for the pond. Their capacities are similar to those of submersible pumps. For external operation, these pumps usually need to be placed in a dry sump below the water level of the pond. Dig a hole deep enough to accommodate the pump but above the water table; provide a cover for the hole that's easy to camouflage and to remove for inspection or maintenance.

External pumps are those that sit outside the water, like those used for swimming pools. They're usually appropriate only for very large waterfalls and fountains or in situations where a submersible pump would be dangerous or impractical—such as in a pond that doubles as a wading pool. With capacities ranging from 2,400 to more than 8,000 gallons per hour and a maximum head of up to 80 feet, external pumps are overkill for most backyard ponds, and the noise they make can distract from the pleasant sounds of your water feature. They also require their own housing to protect them (which is difficult to camouflage). If you're installing a

swimming pool, though, you might consider plumbing the pump and filtration system to operate a pond and waterfall also.

1,200-gph Submersible Pump with Prefilter

Adjustable Flow Submersible Pump

500-gph Submersible Pump

Pump Kit with Fountainhead

DETERMINING QUALITY

When selecting a pump, buy the best you can afford—even if it's a small one. The least expensive (and least durable) pumps have a shorter life span. Suitable only for relatively small water features, they also tend to clog more easily.

Moderate-Quality Pumps. Most moderately priced pumps have aluminum or cast-iron housings with a corrosion-resistant epoxy finish. They tend to be tougher and more impact-resistant than plastic pumps and come in a wide range of capacities. Aluminum-housed pumps are the less expensive of these two types and will corrode more quickly in salt water, chlorinated water, or water frequently treated with pond chemicals.

High-Quality Pumps. The most long-lasting (and most expensive) pumps are a combination of brass, bronze, and stainless-steel components and housings. These pumps will withstand a variety of water conditions—including salty and chlorinated water—and can handle continuous operation. As a rule, they come only in

larger sizes (capacities of 800 gallons per hour or higher). If you expect the pond to be a permanent feature in your yard, these pumps are well worth the extra initial cost.

Efficiency. Compare the pump's amp rating (or wattage, if it's given) to its output in gallons per hour. If two pumps have the same output, the one with the lower amp rating is more energy efficient. Many pumps come with a 6-foot cord, which won't work if local codes require the electrical outlet to be 6 or more feet away from the pond edge. You can usually order longer cords from the pump manufacturer as an option. Use only cords and plugs designed for use with the pump. Don't use extension cords unless they have a built-in ground-fault circuit interrupter (GFCI).

It's a good idea to order all the required fittings, valves, and pipes needed to operate your waterfall at the same time you order your pump, as well as other features such as a separate filter or fountain.

ELECTRICAL REQUIREMENTS

Your pond will require an underground electrical cable from your home's power source, not only for a pump but also for any underwater or perimeter lighting. In many municipalities, a licensed electrician must do the wiring. In all cases, check local codes for outdoor electrical requirements before you start.

For Outdoor Components. Make sure all outlets, wiring, and connections are designed for outdoor use. The National Electrical Code (NEC) does not, but local codes may, require that you put the cable in conduit. When a circuit is protected by GFCI as that for any pond must be, the NEC requires only that the cable be 12 inches deep. But consider burying the cable at least 18 inches deep to prevent it from being disturbed by spades, rototillers, or other gardening equipment.

For Pumps. Most small submersible pumps come with a waterproof cord that you simply plug into a three-prong electrical outlet near the pond site. You must protect this receptacle with GFCI in a weatherproof outlet box with a watertight-while-in-use lid. With some larger pumps (both submersible and external), you hard-wire the cord directly into a circuit, en-

closing the connection in a weatherproof junction box near the pond. The latter requires a GFCI breaker wired into the circuit, either in the main electrical panel or in a subpanel. In either case, you should wire a switch into the circuit so that you can control the pump and lights from inside the house. If possible, locate the outlet or junction box in an inconspicuous and protected area, such as under a deck or against the side of a building. It's best to put the pump and pond lights on a separate circuit, with their own breaker at the main service panel. If you tap into an existing branch circuit, make sure it can handle the additional load of the pump and any outdoor lighting.

Every electrical component must be rated for either underground or outdoor (exterior) use.

Plumbing Your Moving-Water Feature

Plumbing for most pumps is relatively simple. Complexity will vary depending on the pump model, the length of the pipe between pump and outlet, and the number of water features the pump will operate.

Locate the pump as close as possible to your moving water feature. For submersible types, this usually means placing it at the base of the falls (or statue). Remember to raise submersible pumps a few inches off the pond bottom with a brick or a stone to prevent silt and other sediment from clogging the pump intake. For nonsubmersible types, you'll have to use your creativity to find a spot that's relatively close to the pond yet as unobtrusive as possible.

Tubing. Some pumps are sold with a length of inexpensive clear plastic tubing, which is a larger-diameter version of the type used for aquarium pumps. Although such tubing is adequate for short runs, it has several drawbacks. First, the thin walls of the tubing are easily crushed or kinked, so you can't bury it underground or make it conform to sharp bends. Conversely, if the tubing is exposed to sunlight, algae will build up on the inner walls, restricting flow. Because exposure to sunlight will eventually make the tubing brittle, it must be replaced periodically.

One solution is to run a short piece of flexible tubing from the pump to the edge of the pond, connecting it to a rigid PVC pipe that runs from there to the top catch basin at the head of the falls. Alternatively, you can use a higher-grade flexible tubing for the entire run, either a reinforced type or a special black-vinyl tubing sold by pump suppliers. Make sure the diameter of the tubing meets or exceeds the size recommended for your pump model because a smaller diameter will restrict water flow.

Plumbing Waterfalls. When plumbing the waterfall, keep sharp bends and right-angle pipe junctions to a minimum, as these tend to restrict flow. Lay the outlet tube along the ground as close as possible to the edge of the watercourse. Camouflage the outlet tube where it runs between the pond and the top of the watercourse with rocks, plants, or mulch. It's best not to mortar it permanently behind your landscape rocks because you'll need easy access to deal with any future maintenance problems.

Water Pressure. When you run the end of the outlet hose or pipe into the top of the watercourse, you may find that the water pressure produces a strong jet, causing water to splash outside the catch basin. If this happens, either run the hose under a small pile of rocks in the catch basin, or fit a short section of larger perforated pipe or hose over the end of the outlet to break the force.

You can camouflage plumbing and electrical outlets with small rocks around your pond.

Fittings

Pump suppliers offer a wide range of fittings and adapters to connect pumps to various water features. Use nontoxic plastic valves and fittings wherever possible; brass and other metal fittings can corrode with time and may be toxic to fish. Most fittings for flexible plastic tubing are a barbed, push-fit type; when using these fittings, install hose clamps at all connections to prevent leaks. Fittings and connections for rigid PVC pipe are either screwed on or welded on using PVC cement. Some pumps require brass fittings on the pump discharge, which may or may not include a flow-control valve. Depending on the pump design, you may need to install an adapter fitting so that you can attach flexible tubing or rigid PVC pipe.

If you add a T-fitting with a diverter valve to your pump discharge, as shown in the drawing below, you will be able to operate two water features, such as a fountain and a waterfall, at the same time. However, you can accomplish the same result by installing a plain T-fitting plus an in-line flow-control valve in the shorter of the two pipe runs. Both types of fittings will allow you to regulate the amount of water that is supplied to each feature.

If you don't install a diverter or flow-control valve, the pumped water will take the path of least resistance (i.e., the shorter pipe run). The result will be either too little flow to operate one feature or too much flow to the other, or both. The pump should have enough capacity to operate all attached features.

The right fittings and valves, in this case a T-fitting and a diverter valve, let you run several water features simultaneously.

Purchase a pump for your waterfall that is a bit more powerful than you think you'll need. You can always restrict the flow.

Good Planning. As with all aspects of your pond design, careful planning is paramount. If you buy a pump with the intent of operating only one water feature and decide later that you would like to add more, you will face the choice of either buying a new, larger-capacity pump to run all the features simultaneously, or buying a second pump. The latter choice would allow you to power them independently (so that you can run your waterfall but not your fountain and vice versa), but may require additional electrical work or the use of an outlet that was originally planned for lighting. Water garden suppliers report that return customers inevitably want larger ponds with additional features. Thus your best bet may be to think big in the beginning and plan for all future contingencies.

Maintain Pond Levels Automatically with a Float Valve

Because ponds and fountains recirculate water, you don't need to run a water line directly into the pond or fountain. Just make sure there's an outdoor faucet nearby so you can add water to the pond from a garden hose. Small ponds in particular may require topping off every week or so during the hottest months of the year.

To eliminate this chore, install a float valve. This device floats on the water. When the water level drops, the float lowers, opening a valve that allows more water to be fed into the pond through a pipe or tubing connected to a nearby faucet. These inexpensive setups are available through water-gardening catalog suppliers and nurseries that carry water-garden accessories. Simple ball-cock valves, such as those used in toilet tanks, will also work. These are larger than float valves, however, and therefore harder to disguise.

An inexpensive float valve can be clamped to a short steel rod mortared between stones just below the waterline. The valve is connected to the main water supply with a ¼-inch-diameter copper or plastic tube. When installing such a system, make sure there's no chance of pond water siphoning back into the water supply and contaminating your drinking water with fish waste and other toxic substances. Most building codes require some form of backflow preventer (also called anti-siphon device).

Inexpensive types screw onto a faucet (just be careful to install it facing the right direction). For added protection, install a check valve (almost as inexpensive) on the faucet before you install the backflow preventer.

¼" Copper or Plastic Tubing
(To Water Supply)

Shutoff Valve

Float

Desired Waterline

Pond Liner or Shell

Steel Rod

Clamp

Installing a diverter valve will allow you to create separate effects such as the small waterfalls shown here.

Installing a Submersible Pump

Submersible pumps add movement and sound to a water garden. They're very easy to install and relatively uncomplicated to maintain. If the pump will be used only for filtration, place the submersible pump/filter in your sump or in the deepest part of the pond. Run the outlet tube to the far end of the pond for better circulation. If the pump will be feeding water to a falls or fountain, locate the pump as close as possible to the foot of the falls or the fountain. Plumbing connections at the outlet hose (or pipe) must be high quality and the necessary electrical connections must meet required electrical codes. Raise the pump several inches off the pond bottom to prevent frequent filter clogging.

Tools and Materials: submersible pump/filter kit; outlet hose & fittings (sufficient length from pump to top pool of falls); electrical outlet accessibility; platform material (to raise pump off pond floor); material (stone, gravel) to hide lines and cables

Basic Installation Tips
- Place pump on a brick at the bottom of the pond.
- Keep bends and right angles in tubing to a minimum to maintain a steady, even flow.
- Disguise all hoses and electrical lines under mulch or rocks.

Switch
Junction Box
6' Min.
Waterproof Cord
Pump
Plug
18" Min.
Conduit

Adapter
Flexible Tubing
Flexible Tubing
Pump
Adapter
Rigid PVC Pipe (Buried)

A narrow stream splashes over a stone ornament, creating a spray as it empties into this pond.

Install a Lined Watercourse

DIFFICULTY LEVEL: CHALLENGING

If you're using a flexible plastic or rubber liner for your pond, it's easiest to excavate for the watercourse and install its liner at the same time. You can, however, also add a lined watercourse to an existing pond with any material at a later time.

Tools and Materials: Flour, nontoxic spray paint, or stakes and string (for marking outlines); shovel; tamper for compacting soil (or a scrap of 2x6 nailed to the end of a long 2x4); spirit level; long, straight 2x4 (for checking level of large areas); concrete blocks (optional, to pro-vide increased support for outer edges and/or waterfall lip); pump, tubing, and connecting fixtures; adhesive or tape for liner joints (optional); heavy-duty scissors or utility knife for cutting liner and underlayment; underlayment; liner; 3-inch or longer nails (to hold liner in position); edging material such as rocks; mortar (optional, for securing stones along edges); landscaping materials (rocks, plants); watering can or hose

1 Grade the Site. If you're working on flat ground, you may want to rough out the shape, left, of your watercourse before you begin changing the grade. Then build up a berm of compacted soil next to the pond at your waterfall location (this is a good way to make use of the soil excavated from the pond). Make the berm wide enough to accommodate the watercourse, with sufficient space around the perimeter for rocks, plants, and other landscaping materials. Tamp the soil firmly to compact it. Slope the sides gently away from the proposed excavation to prevent rain from washing dirt into the watercourse. Avoid steeply sloped mounds, which not only look unnatural but will be more prone to soil erosion. If you are work-ing on a naturally sloping site, especially one that is very rocky, it will dictate the shape of your watercourse to a great extent. Now working on your slope—natural or otherwise—cut a series of level terraces to create what looks like a staircase. Each terrace will serve as a catch basin for your waterfall or stream. For a stream, you will have long steps with short risers; for a steep waterfall, you will have shorter steps with taller risers. Make each step large enough to accommodate rocks or other edging material or concrete supporting blocks if you are using them, right.

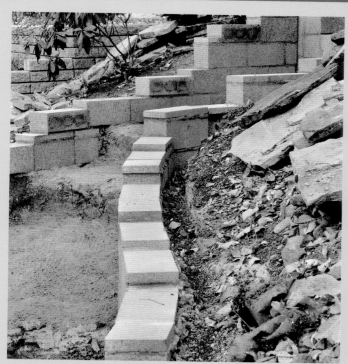

2 Creating Catch Basins. You want each one of your stair steps to hold water even when the pump is turned off. Things will always look natural as a result. There are several ways you can accomplish this. If you are using concrete block supports, which is essential when you are working with either sandy or flinty soil, they will form the sides of your catch basin. (They will look straight and artificial, but you will make them look natural later by artful placement of rocks on top of and around them). Dig your terrace and shape it so that it slopes backward slightly, away from the pond.

If you are working with clay soil that packs solidly you may not need concrete blocks. Instead, you can excavate a catch basin in the middle of each stair, leaving a ledge of earth on which to place your edging stones. (Even if you have clay soil, however, the concrete blocks are a good idea if you are edging your stream with large, heavy boulders.) If the basin is large enough, you may want to cut another ledge around the perimeter in which to set partially submerged boulders. But remember that the finished watercourse will look smaller than the excavated holes once the rocks or other edging materials are in place along the sides.

The catch basins are mini versions of the main pond, so follow the procedures outlined in steps 1 through 7 on pages 70–71 to dig and level the basins. As with your pond, your stream should be level across its width. To make sure that it is, use a spirit level placed on top of a 2x4.

Now on the leading edge (the edge that is the closest to the pond) of your terrace or catch basin, you need to provide a stable base for the waterfall lip. Do this by creating a berm that is at least 12 in. wide. You can use well-compacted soil, but again, when you are dealing with loose or sandy soil, use concrete blocks or poured concrete for a firmer base.

3 Install the Tubing and Pump. Position your pump at the foot of the lowest falls. (Elevate it on a brick or a flat stone; raising it a few inches off the bottom will keep sediment from clogging the pump intake.) If your pump isn't a submersible type, put it close to the base of the falls. Run the pipe or tubing, left, from the pump alongside the watercourse from the point where it exits the pond to the top catch basin or head of the falls. (For more information about choosing and installing pumps, see pages 90–102.) All fittings must go together securely so that no leaks occur, right.

Continued on next page.

howto

Install a Lined Watercourse (cont'd)

4 **Position the Liners.** If you're using underlayment, position it first, right. If you're using a single liner for the pond and watercourse, drape the liner over the entire excavation and over the supporting concrete blocks if you have used them, opposite top. Then slowly fill the pond with water to hold the liner in place, allowing the liner to settle before filling the watercourse.

If you're using separate pieces of liner, start by fitting the liner for the main pond, allowing enough overlap at the waterfall end to extend up and over the first waterfall lip. Cut and fit the next piece of liner in the lowest catch basin, providing at least 12 in. of overlap with the main-pond liner. Overlap the liners for additional catch basins in the same manner.

For additional protection against leaks, you

5 **Position the Edging Stones.** Position the overhanging rocks or other edging materials, left, across the waterfall lip, inset, and on either side of it. For a more natural effect, place stones behind the waterfall beneath the lip to hide the liner. The top surface of the lip stones should be just slightly below the water level of the stream or basin, above left, so that water will flow from one basin to the next without overflowing the banks. The last major stone to be laid is the one on the exit spillway, above right. The type of stone and its positioning will determine the pattern of the waterfall entering the pond.

can join adjacent liner sections with a special liner adhesive or tape available from your supplier, although with sufficient overlap this is not necessary.

Next, it's important to check for level. Use a hose to fill the catch basin(s) with water to settle the liner in place, as you did for the pond.

Check for leaks, and note the water level around the rim of each basin. If you see any high or low spots, remove or add soil beneath the liner to level the basin.

Then, to keep the liner in place while you add edging material around the water feature, push large nails through the liner into the ground every foot or so around the overlapping edges. (Note: you do not have to remove the nails later.)

Alternately, you can use several large stones to keep the liner positioned until you have installed all your edging.

6 **Fine-tune the Waterfall.** Now install your pump. (See "Installing a Submersible Pump" on page 102.) Turn on the pump and notice how water flows over the lip; adjust the height and angle of the stones, if necessary, to provide a pleasing cascade. When you're satisfied with the results, place your remaining stones along the edge of each basin, on top of your concrete blocks or along the ledge you've shaped around the perimeter of each basin or along the stream banks. Hide the liner edges with the edging rocks, or bury it with soil. Mortaring the rocks in place prevents them from slipping into the watercourse. You can place more stones in the watercourse to alter the flow pattern, but avoid using gravel in the streambed because it will become clogged with algae and silt.

Last, add landscaping. If you're building a natural-looking watercourse, arrange additional rocks on and around the mound for the waterfall and near the stream. Use boulders, medium-size rocks, and small pebbles to avoid making the waterfall area look like a pile of rocks. Make planting pockets between stones for installing low shrubs, grasses, ground covers, and other plants.

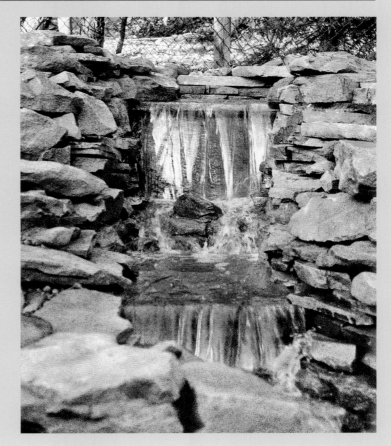

how to

Install a Preformed Watercourse

DIFFICULTY LEVEL: MODERATE

Just as with a lined watercourse, you can install a preformed watercourse at the same time as your pond or you can add it later. If you're planning to install more than one unit, see the instructions in step 5 before beginning your project.

Tools & Materials:
preformed watercourse; pump, tubing, and connecting fixtures; flour, nontoxic spray paint, or stakes; landscaping materials (rocks, plants); concrete blocks (optional), mortar (optional); shovel, fine sand, ruler (to measure sand depth); tamper for compacting soil; cement and mixing equipment (only for precast stone and cement units); spirit level and long, straight 2x4

Plantings will blend the watercourse into the landscape.

Excavated Pocket

1 Grade the Site. If you're working with a natural slope above the pond, excavate a pocket in which to place the watercourse. On flat ground, build up a berm of firm soil to support the shell at the appropriate height above the pond. The sides of the berm should slope gently away from the watercourse and be wide enough to accommodate rocks or other materials used to disguise the edges. Firmly tamp the built-up soil. Test soil firmness to see that the watercourse won't sink unevenly into it. Next, set the preformed watercourse in position on top of the mound and mark its outline on the ground with flour, nontoxic spray paint, or a series of short stakes.

Water Level

4 Test the Watercourse. Fill the unit with water and check the water level around the rim to make sure the unit remained level during the backfilling. If you haven't already done so, install the pump; attach the outlet tubing to it; and fill the main pond. Then pump water down the course. The water should flow evenly over the lip and any built-in cascades at a level of about 1 in. below the rim. Adjust the pump flow rate if necessary.

Tubing Alongside Excavation

2 **Dig the Hole.** Dig a hole to match the size and shape of your preformed watercourse unit. Tamp the soil firmly to keep the sides and bottom from bending and warping when filled with water. If your soil is loose or sandy, create extra support with an encircling collar of concrete blocks. (See "Extra Support for Pond Foundations" on page 78.) Lay the unit in place to see if it fits. If not, lift it out and either add or remove soil as necessary.

3 **Place the Watercourse.** Position the lip over the pond edge. Use a spirit level to make sure basins are level in all directions. Backfill around the edges (and between concrete blocks if you used them) with fine sand to a height of 1 to 2 in. below the outside edge of the shell, or as recommended by the manufacturer. Run the pipe-outlet tubing into the top basin. Secure it at the top with rocks, or as specified by the manufacturer.

5 **Place any Additional Units.** If you'll be installing additional sections of watercourse, follow steps 1 through 3. Then, after installing and leveling each one, you'll need to test them by filling all of them with water and allowing the water to run down the rest of the course (step 4). Make any needed adjustments at this time to the height and position of the unit. Make sure each unit is firmly positioned before installing the one above it.

6 **Add Landscaping.** Install edging material above ground level. If water runoff is heavy, mortar stones for a better seal. Dense planting will help prevent erosion and deter water pollution. Turn on the pump. Position the pump outlet pipe or tubing at the top of the watercourse and disguise it with rocks or plants. Run the watercourse continuously for 48 hours; then recheck it for settling and readjust the flow or the position of the hose if necessary.

CHAPTER 6

Fountains and Light

The soothing sound and delightful sight of moving water are great reasons for adding a fountain to your garden. A fountain can be placed near a front entry or off a deck or patio. With lighting, it can create a dramatic focal point in the evening.

Style and Placement

There's a fountain for just about every style garden—formal or informal. Materials may be concrete, resin, marble, fiberglass, cast stone, bronze, or granite. Cast stone fountains are molded into virtually any design. They look like they were carved from real stone, but they are lighter weight.

Consider not only sound, style, and size, but also the relationship to other landscape elements. If the fountain will be placed in a pond, keep in mind its effect on your plants and fish. Sound is one of the greatest benefits of a fountain, adding music to your landscape and masking traffic and other noises. The effect can range from the creek-like burble of a low geyser to the high, musical tinkle of a fine spray to the deeper, rainy-day resonance of a tall water column. Think about which type of sound will bring you the most enjoyment. Even on the smallest patio or in the tiniest yard, you can enjoy the soothing sounds of a fountain by installing a self-contained unit, a wall fountain that spills into a small basin, or a cobblestone reservoir.

SPRAY OR STATUARY FOUNTAINS

Fountains of all styles come in two basic types: spray fountains (essentially just water nozzles, or jets, that spray water in different patterns) and statuary fountains, which spray water from a sculpture or figure. Fountains with elaborate spray patterns and classical statuary are suitable for a formal design. In a pond that's informal but not meant to mimic nature, a simple spout will suffice. As a rule, fountains look out of place in a wildlife pond, unless you choose a simple model that bubbles up from the surface like a natural spring.

A fountain should suit the style of your garden and your house. This one with its classical motifs, such as the acanthus leaves, blends well with the formal style of the home's architecture.

A sugar kettle fitted as a fountain offers soft bubbling tones.

Almost any spray-type fountain works with a modern-style home and pond; for statuary, look for a contemporary sculpture. For a bungalow or a farmhouse, an old water pump is the perfect accessory for a small pond or basin.

ENVIRONMENTAL CONSIDERATIONS

Also consider the overall shape of your pond. With a square or circular pond, fountains typically look best in the middle. If your pool is rectangular, you may want to install a line of pipes down the center spraying to the sides.

Look around and notice the shape of existing landscape elements, or envision shrubs or other large features you plan to add. You can complement the shape of nearby plants or garden furniture by choosing fountains that have vertical or rounded spray shapes, for example.

Water trickles from a stone fish in a formal pool.

Wind Strength. Wind is also a factor that will affect the style of fountain that will work best in your garden. If you have a windy site, fountains that create a fine spray of droplets, or those that produce a thin film of water, such as a bell fountain, are unsuitable, as their pattern or symmetry will often be disturbed. If this is your situation, look for a geyser style that shoots up a heavy column of water.

Water Disturbance. If you want to grow floating or marginal plants, keep in mind how much the fountain will disturb the water surface of your pond. Water lilies and many other pond flora can't tolerate splashing or moving water; they'll need to be kept to the edge of the pond if you choose a tall, exuberant style of fountain. A low water column or the semispherical bell pattern will disturb the surface less than other designs would. If fish are more important to you than plants, however, choose a splashier fountain for more aeration.

Pond Size. The size of your pond will limit the size of your fountain. In a totally sheltered, windless garden, a fountain jet could be as high as the pond is wide, but this is a rare condition. The more usual guideline is to make the height of your fountain no more than half the width or diameter of your pond to avoid drenching pondside benches, light fixtures, decks or patios, or you and your guests. Also, if the spray is too large for the size of the pond, the resulting water evaporation will lower the pond's water level.

Spray-Fountain Patterns

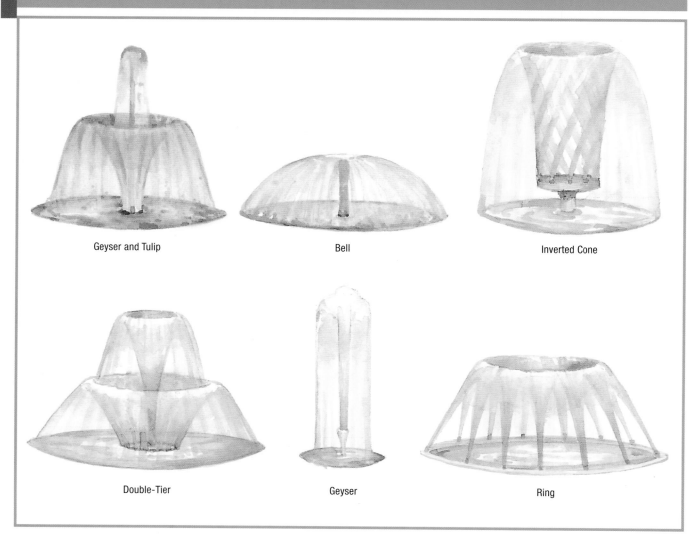

Geyser and Tulip

Bell

Inverted Cone

Double-Tier

Geyser

Ring

In this large naturalistic pond, two spray fountains look like natural geysers between the rocks.

Spray Fountains

A spray fountain consists of a nozzle or ring attached to the outlet pipe of a pump at or above the pond's water level. The simplest style is a length of vertical pipe, run to a level just under the water surface, which provides a natural-looking geyser effect. Adding a narrow nozzle to the pipe will give you a taller, more dramatic geyser. Because geysers introduce air bubbles into the spray, they are especially good for aerating the water. (But size and place them carefully to avoid stirring up silt and sediment in the pond, producing cloudy water.) To be visually effective, high, showy geysers require powerful, large-capacity pumps.

Most spray fountains come as complete kits. Such kits include a molded plastic nozzle, the right-size pump, various fittings for installation, and a flow-control valve which allows you to adjust spray height. Some kits contain several spray heads to change patterns. Others come with a tee fitting and diverter, which you'll need to attach a second feature, such as a waterfall or filter. Before you assemble any of the kit components or other features, be sure that your pump has the power for these add-ons.

You can also purchase a floating fountain that is very suitable for short-term or periodic use. These relatively

FAR EAST FOUNTAINS

In a Japanese-style garden, you can create a simple bamboo spill fountain or the more complicated *shishi odoshi* (stag scarer). The simple bamboo fountain can be displayed in concert with a *tsukubai*, a basinlike stone used for washing one's hands and face in preparation for the Japanese tea ceremony. Set the stone basin on rocks so that water spills into it from the pipe and then spills over the edge onto the rocks before being recirculated. Instead of drawing its water from a reservoir, a *shishi odoshi* could substitute for a waterfall in a small stream; this device was originally used as a noisemaker to keep deer and other animals out of the garden. You can buy these deer chaser features ready-made.

Instead of hooking your pump to a pipe and nozzle, attach the pump outlet to rubber tubing, and run the tubing through a bamboo pole. Be sure to hollow out all the bamboo "joints" so that the tubing will pass through. (You may have to split the cane and glue it back together.) To join this vertical bamboo pipe and your spout at a slightly downward-facing angle, make an elbow joint with a block of wood or a short section of bamboo. Working from both sides, use a drill to create the angle.

To make the rocking stag-scarer fountain, hollow out a second length of bamboo. Cut one end at an angle, and plug the other end solidly so that the bamboo will hold water. Mount this on a horizontal arm below the first water outlet, either through a hole in your first vertical delivery pipe or on its own support in front of the upper pipe. Your goal is for the upper pipe to slowly

feed into the lip of the lower pipe. When the upper half of the moving pipe fills, it will tip down, spilling out the water; once empty, it will bounce back to its original position. Adjust the water flow so that the rocking pipe fills and empties rhythmically. To get the noise-making effect, position a stone under the closed end of the bamboo; the pipe will strike it when it returns to its original position.

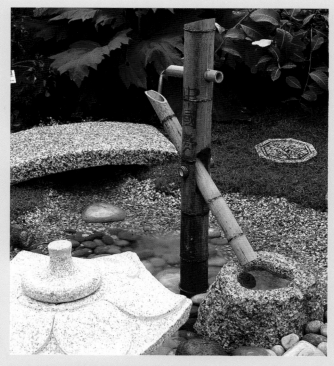

This stag scarer fountain sends water through two bamboo pipes from an underground reservoir.

inexpensive spray fountains are designed with a built-in nozzle that attaches to an existing pump without plumbing (if your pump has an unused discharge valve).

Higher-quality nozzles can be disassembled to make cleaning the jet holes easier; lesser-quality nozzles are more difficult to clean. Brass nozzles are generally used for larger water displays, but they're more expensive than plastic. Keep in mind that nozzles with small holes clog easily and will require frequent cleaning. (Cleaning isn't a big production—just disassemble the nozzle, and hose it off or brush it with an old toothbrush.) Your nozzle will be less likely to clog if your pond also has a mechanical filter.

Connecting a Spray Fountain

DIFFICULTY LEVEL: EASY

Installation is relatively simple but varies depending on the type of fountain, pump, and fittings. The easiest route to a spray fountain is to buy a complete kit and follow the instructions given for its components. The fittings either push or screw together, so the fountain can be easily assembled in just a few minutes.

Tools and Materials: Saw (to cut PVC pipe); adjustable wrench; necessary adapters; PVC pipe (cut to length); elbow fitting (for side discharge pumps); prefilter or filter screen (if necessary); bricks or prop material.

Installation. On most submersible pumps designed for fountains, the water outlet is on top. This conveniently allows you to attach the rigid vertical PVC discharge pipe directly to the outlet. (You may need an adapter fitting on some units.) Cut the pipe to extend the required distance above the water level (typically 4 to 6 inches), and then simply attach the spray nozzle. For pumps with a side discharge, you'll need to install an elbow fitting.

To prevent the nozzle from clogging, buy a special prefilter or filter screen that attaches to the pump inlet. Some units combine the pump and filter in a single housing. The filter should be easily accessible for routine cleaning.

Once you've attached the fittings and spray nozzle according to the manufacturer's instructions, place the pump in the pond on a flat, level surface such as a short stack of bricks. (Raising the pump off the bottom lessens the chances that it will get clogged with debris.) Both pump and discharge pipe must be firmly supported, so the pipe remains perfectly vertical.

If the unit has a tendency to tip or to move out of position once it's running, place a few bricks along the sides of the pump to hold it in place. (If it still tips, try a brick on top for more weight.) Follow the guidelines given in "Electrical Requirements" on page 95 to provide the appropriate electrical connection for the pump.

Spray Nozzle

Diverter to Second Feature

Flow Control Valve

Filtered Inlet

Submersible Pump

Electric Cable

Many are sold as kits. When buying a pump separately, be sure it's powerful enough for the job.

Water cascades over the sides of this ceramic pot and into a small pond filled with cobblestones and grass.

How to Build a Cobblestone Reservoir

DIFFICULTY LEVEL: EASY

Here is a natural water feature that installs easily and requires no pond. It can be placed almost anywhere.

Tools and Materials: Shovel; scissors; spirit level; large plastic bucket, tub, or garbage pail reservoir; galvanized wire mesh (at least 5 inches larger than the diameter of the reservoir); submersible pump; foaming gusher or bubbler spray-fountain kit; flexible pond liner (polyethylene is sturdy enough); small, smooth pebbles or river rock (approx. 2 to 4 inches in diameter, or larger than the wire mesh)

Installation. This simple water feature gives the illusion of a natural spring or geyser welling up from the earth and returning to it. It's a good stand-alone fountain if you don't want the hassle of maintaining a large pond. Even better, it makes a safe water feature for families with toddlers and small children.

The reservoir can go in a lawn or a flower bed or be sunk in a flagstone terrace. It can be as small as a dinner plate or a garden centerpiece 4 feet or more across; the vertical gusher fountains or bubblers usually used with these features can be adjusted to shoot water from 3 to 24 inches or higher, depending on the size pump you attach to them. Seek the advice of your water-garden supplier if you have any questions about buying the pump and fountain to match the desired size of your reservoir. As with any fountain, you need to have easy access to electrical power with a ground-fault circuit interrupter, or GFCI. (See page 95.)

Begin the installation by digging a hole in which to place the fountain assembly. You'll need a hole slightly larger than your plastic bucket or tub. Lower the bucket into the hole, and use a carpenter's level to make sure it is straight. Backfill the hole with soil, and create a bowl shape around it, sloping up.

Next, place the liner over the reservoir, and push the material down slightly into the bucket. Using scissors, cut a hole that's big enough to allow you to lower the pump to the bottom of the reservoir. Make sure the edges of the liner slope down toward the bucket; the liner needs to collect water from your fountain and return it to the bucket. Center the wire mesh over the lined reservoir, cutting a hole in the mesh large enough for the vertical pipe that connects to your fountain. Trim the pipe if needed so that it will be hidden by your stones.

To test the assembly, fill the bucket with water. Arrange stones around the fountain. A fountain kit with a flow adjuster will allow you to experiment with higher and lower geyser settings. When you are satisfied with the effect, arrange stones out to the edge of your liner, trimming off its corners.

This cobblestone reservoir is easy to assemble. It requires no pond and can be placed practically anywhere. Select smooth, matched stones bigger than the holes in the wire mesh.

A pair of "lotus" fountains offers a low burble of water that bubbles up from the center of each "flower" in this pond.

Statuary Fountains

There are fountains and statuary for every taste and function. You can choose a classical Greek figure or a wall-mounted gargoyle or sleek stones that bubble water from the top. Whimsical fish, frogs, and birds spout water, as do as contemporary scuppers attached to a wall. Many can be found at garden centers, big box stores and online, but landscape contractors also have access to higher-end products. Fountains and statuary are made from many different materials, including precast concrete and resin, stone, marble, bronze, and other metals. Modern sculpture fountains can be found in copper, brass, or bronze. If you are scouting resale shops, flea markets, or antique stores, be aware that some older statuary was often made from lead, which can be toxic to fish and other aquatic creatures.

Statuary fountains are sometimes sold as separate units or kits, designed to be installed in or next to a formal pool or pond. A pump must be installed to move the water. Other statuary fountains are sold as complete, self-contained kits with precast reservoir bows and integrated pre-plumbed pump-and-filter systems. They are designed as stand-alone water features.

INSTALLING A STATUARY FOUNTAIN

Most statuary fountains come with installation instructions. Use them in combination with the guidelines that follow to install the unit you've chosen. As with any moving water feature, you'll appreciate being able to turn the fountain on and off from indoors, using an outdoor outlet controlled by an indoor switch. If you do not have electrical expertise, hire an electrician.

Self-Contained Fountains. This type of fountain includes a pump, a power cord, and all fittings. Typically, a small submersible pump sits in the statue pedestal, which sits in a reservoir bowl. Water spills from the fountain into the reservoir bowl, where it gets pumped back to the top. Units such as these can be placed anywhere within reach of a power supply. The pump cord runs from an overflow area inside the pedestal, down through a tube in the hollow base. Make sure the design of the unit you buy provides some way to gain access to the pump for cleaning and maintenance.

To install the fountain, set it on a sturdy, level base, fill it with water, and plug it in. Check the water level frequently and refill the reservoir when needed; water can evaporate quickly from these shallow reservoirs. Follow the manufacturer's recommendations for safety pointers and maintenance.

Water cascades from this mystical water creature into a seashell below.

Wall Fountains

A wall fountain usually spills water through statuary—such as a mask or a decorative plaque—into a basin that hides a small pump. The statuary can be terra-cotta, plastic, fiberglass, cast concrete (often designed to mimic terra-cotta or stone), or metal. A stone water feature will be more expensive than one made of these other materials. Stone and cast-concrete wall fountains require a wall strong enough to support their weight, as well as sturdy, well-secured mounting hardware.

Wall fountains look best if the return pipe doesn't show. Thus the best place for these fountains is a free-standing wall that allows you to run the plumbing behind it. However, this is rarely practical for many of the situations where these small features work best, such as on a townhouse patio. Alternatives include hiding the tubing with vines or chiseling a vertical niche down the wall in which to run the tubing and then mortaring over it.

A more satisfactory option is to build out the wall using similar material—a new line of bricks, for instance, or an enclosure covered with clapboards to match your home's siding. Mount the fountain on the new surface, and run the pipe behind it.

If the fountain doesn't come with its own basin, homemade options range from building an elaborate brick or concrete reservoir to recycling a half barrel or an old sink or trough. Don't make the catch basin too small or rapid evaporation will necessitate frequent topping off. To keep splashing to a minimum, mount the fountain no higher above the catch basin than the diameter of the basin.

Informal water features call for something casual, such as this whimsical spouting toucan.

High-Strength Attachment Wall

Poured Concrete Foundation

Power Cord

Return Pipe

Submersible Pump

Mount the fountain no higher above the catch basin than the diameter of the basin.

In-Pond Statuary

The mechanics of installing fountain statuary in the pond are relatively straightforward. The hardest task is dealing with the weight of the statue. If it and its pedestal weigh more than 100 pounds, a concrete footing is needed to support them before installing a flexible liner or preformed pond. On top of the liner or shell, mount the statue on a hollow in-pond pedestal. Or build your own pedestal with mortared bricks, stones, or other masonry. Then use flexible tubing to connect the pump to a supply pipe that projects from the statue's base.

The footing under the pond shell or liner should be a 4-inch-thick concrete subbase, a few inches wider and longer than the statue base or pedestal. If you forego a footing, the statue's weight may crack the rigid pond shell or tear the flexible pond liner. The footing must be smooth and level to give stable support; unless you have experience pouring concrete, hire a good contractor. For lighter statues, all you need to

do is compact the soil firmly under the statue location with a tamper before installing the shell or liner. If you are unsure how firmly compacted the soil is, rent a powered compactor or a roller for this purpose. Once the shell or liner is installed, you're ready for the next step. (See pages 64-85 for installing shells and liners.)

Protect flexible liners with a small piece of liner underlayment under your pedestal. If you've purchased a pedestal, place it in the pond. If you haven't, build a pedestal by mortaring bricks or stones. Leave an opening near the bottom of the pedestal through which to run tubing from the pump to the statue. Use a spirit level to check your work as you build up the height of the pedestal, as the top needs to be absolutely level.

(If you doubt your handiwork or are installing a valuable statue, hire an experienced contractor.) To facilitate cleaning and other maintenance chores, leave the pump outside the pedestal. Situate it as close to the pedestal as possible, and then run flexible tubing from the pump up through the pedestal into the statue. Be sure that you allow enough tubing at the top to connect easily to the statue.

With a helper, move the statue into position on the pedestal. While your helper tilts the statue slightly, reach underneath to make the connection between the pump outlet tubing and the pipe projecting from the statue's base. (You may need an adapter fitting. Check before you have the statue in place.) Secure the connection with a hose clamp, and then rest the statue in its final position. Don't mortar or otherwise attach the statue to the pedestal—you may need to replace the outlet tubing later.

Fountain Statuary

Spray Nozzle

Hollow Pedestal

4" Concrete Footing

Flexible Supply Line Tubing

Submersible Pump

Pond Liner

Heavy statuary fountains require a 4-in. concrete footing under the pond liner or shell.

Heavy statues and pedestals—those 100 pounds and over—require a concrete footing for support.

Lighting

Lighting adds a magical touch to your landscape. Bistro lighting over a patio creates a relaxing vacation feel. Accent or sculptural lighting produces a sense of depth and punctuates plants and architectural elements. Path lights offer safe passage through the garden, illuminating steps and landings. Ornamental "downlighting" fixtures placed knee-high at intervals along the borders of a walk or attached to step railings provide subtle light for you and your guests to navigate the garden and around water features. Moon lighting (or uplighting) supplies dramatic views of tree trunks and branches—distinct from daytime views.

Lighting fountains, ponds, waterfalls, or streams increases the enjoyment of your water features. When well placed in clear water, underwater lights can highlight water lilies, waterfalls, and other features. But poorly placed underwater lights create glare. They also eliminate pond reflections of the moon or of garden features you highlight with aboveground lights.

A few lights well positioned in the landscape around a water feature are generally more effective than underwater lights. You can create dramatic nighttime reflections by directing hidden, ground-level spotlights up toward surrounding trees or tall shrubs. Waterfalls or fountains will sparkle when you direct lights toward them from the pond edges. Keep it simple: a few well-placed spotlights or accent lights will produce a more desirable effect than

Effective lighting highlights trees and water features to add to the nighttime ambiance.

Thoughtfully placed lighting highlights both the water and special architectural elements.

Fixture Kit

Clear or Colored Lens Choices

Position Fixture to Highlight a Specific Pond Feature

Specially Sealed Underwater Fixture

A number of lighting suppliers now offer fixture kits. If you select a low-voltage (12-volt) system, you will have a lighting arrangement that is less expensive to buy and easier to install than a standard 120-volt system.

strong floodlights that light up the entire yard. Move the light fixtures from one location to another to get a satisfactory glow.

FIXTURE TYPES

You can choose from two basic systems for your lighting fixtures: standard 120-volt systems and low-voltage (12-volt) systems. Standard-voltage systems run directly on household current; 12-volt systems require a transformer (to reduce the voltage), which is connected to a 120-volt power source. As a rule, 12-volt systems are much safer and easier to install than standard systems. The 12-volt fixtures and bulbs are also much less expensive; most use standard automotive-type bulbs. You can even buy these fixtures as do-it-yourself kits, although these offer a limited number of lights and effects. Because low-voltage lamps don't produce as much light as standard systems do, they're best for lighting pathways or providing subtle lighting around ponds. They aren't as effective in illuminating large areas as 120-volt floodlights are. No matter which system you choose, make sure the fixtures, bulbs, connectors, and junction boxes are designed for outdoor use. Because outdoor lighting will be exposed to the weather, the circuit should be protected by a GFCI. Check local codes for additional requirements.

Bulbs for outdoor lighting vary in both intensity and color. For standard and low-voltage systems, ordinary tungsten bulbs are the cheapest and most readily available. They come in a variety of wattages, giving you a choice of intensity. The type most commonly used has thickened

lenses and built-in reflectors. They come in the form of spotlights, narrow floodlights, and broad floodlights in both high and low voltages. More-expensive high-intensity halogen bulbs are becoming popular for outdoor lighting because they produce more light per watt than tungsten bulbs and have a longer life span. They produce incandescent light that's a bright, clear white yet still natural-looking.

Other high-intensity bulbs include mercury vapor (bluish white), sodium (amber yellow), and metal halide (intense, harsh white). In general, the light they produce is too bright and artificial to be appealing around a pond; they're best for lighting up streets and large parking lots.

For underwater lighting, you need special bulbs and watertight housings. You can buy colored lenses for underwater and general lighting. If you plan to highlight plants and trees, choose colored lenses carefully to avoid giving foliage an unnatural appearance.

FIXTURE PLACEMENT

To highlight fish or submerged plants, position lights around the edge of your pond. Point one up toward a waterfall or tuck one in behind it and aim the light up toward the fall. Angle two at the foot of a fountain to allow its spray to sparkle.

Avoid situating aboveground fixtures where they will create glare off the water surface or shine in the eyes of viewers. To get a sense for placement, it may help to experiment first with one or more bright flashlights.

Hide Lights from View. Fixtures with a black or dark green finish will be the least obtrusive. Hide fixtures among plantings, beneath a deck overhang, behind a tree, or within its canopy. Or recess fixtures below ground in light wells. Prefabricated units consist of a bulb and reflector encased in a watertight housing with a metal grille or clear plastic cover. If you're installing other types of fixtures belowground, be sure they are waterproof.

Wires and conduit can be buried underground. Conceal low-voltage systems under a layer of mulch. Install junction boxes and transformers for low-voltage systems aboveground. You can make them less visible with judicious placement of plant containers, small shrubs, or ornamental grasses.

Underwater Lighting

Fountain Kit with Integral Underwater Lights

Lights Swivel for Effects with Fountain

This can be dramatic and eye-catching, but easily overdone. So go slowly and start simply. Low-voltage systems are the safest and easiest to install.

CHAPTER 7

Bridges and Stonework

Bridges and stepping-stones offer a fun way to cross your pond. They also offer another viewpoint from which to enjoy fish and plants. Include them in your plans while you are designing the pond rather than trying to add them later. You may need a permit to install a bridge, so check with your local building inspector about codes before you begin.

Wooden Bridges

A bridge can be as simple as a weathered plank across a narrow stream or as ornate as a red-lacquered Japanese "camelback." The latter adds architectural interest and allows you to pause and reflect, just like the French artist Monet did at his garden in Giverny. Some thoughtful planning and placement will add to the charm of your pond. Give visitors a reason to get to the other side, such as a bench, a garden ornament, or interesting plants.

Size Matters. The bridge should be in proportion with the pond or stream in length, width, and height. Make it wide enough to cross easily and safely, and so that it won't collapse under the weight of a few people. A bridge should be at least two feet wide. For a very narrow stream or a small natural pond, a couple of wide, sturdy planks laid from one bank to the other may suffice. Bridges more than 12 to 18 inches above the water's surface will need handrails, both for safety and for aesthetics.

A sturdy foundation for the support posts is essential no matter what the size of the bridge. If the bridge spans more than 8 feet long, consider consulting a building contractor, because bridges of this size require larger beams, additional supports, or both.

In a true Zen garden, above, a red bridge represents a transformation from worldliness to wisdom.

Building a bridge such as this one, opposite, requires using treated lumber that is rated for marine or seawall use.

Whether you build it yourself or work with a contractor, specify the use of rot-resistant lumber as well as rust-resistant hardware and fasteners. Lumber used at or near the ground should be rated for use in the ground or in contact with soil. Treated lumber rated for marine or seawall use is sometimes used for small bridges. Be aware that treated lumber may contain chemicals that are toxic to fish and plants. Leftover treated lumber should not be burned because the chemicals become airborne. (Check with your lumber supplier or county sanitation department for disposal instructions.)

Not sure how to design a bridge? Building plans follow for the one described in the next pages. You can build a simple footbridge across your pond with doubled 2x8s for support beams, 2x6s for decking and handrails, and 4x4s for the posts. Use pressure-treated lumber and galvanized carriage bolts and nails. The following instructions are for a 5-foot-wide bridge that can span a pond or stream up to 6 feet across.

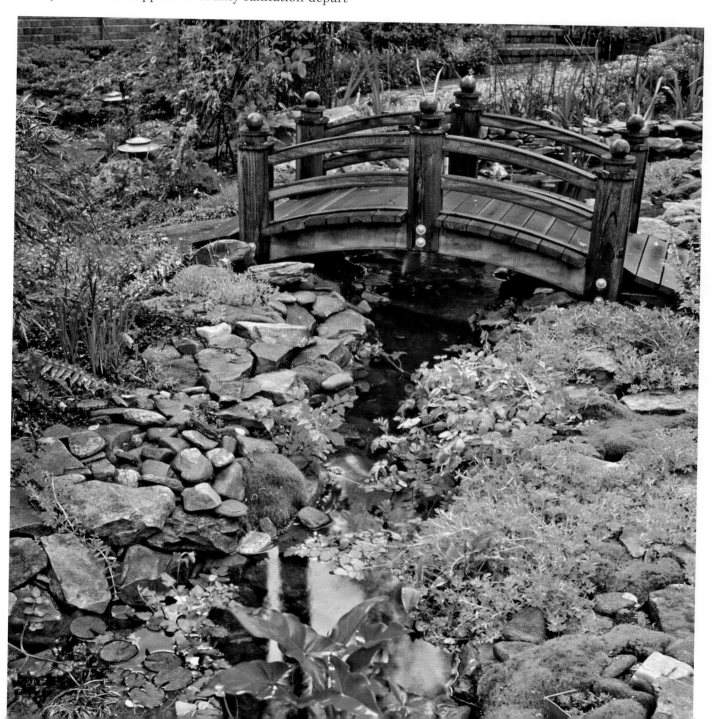

how to

Add a Footbridge

DIFFICULTY LEVEL: CHALLENGING

Tools and Materials: Measuring tape; circular saw; hammer; mortar hoe; wheelbarrow or mortar pan; spirit level; drill, ⅝-in. spade bit, ½-in. spade bit (for optional handrail); wrench; portable saber saw; power sander; six 8-ft. 2x8s; six 4x4s (length depends on depth of postholes and handrail); nine 10-ft. 2x6s; two 8-ft. 2x6s (for optional handrail); 1 cu. ft. gravel; concrete (amount depends on depth of postholes); six 20d common nails; 3 lbs. 10d galvanized common nails; 1 lb. 8d galvanized common nails; twelve ½ x 7½-in. carriage bolts, nuts, washers; eight ⅜ x 6-in. carriage bolts, nuts, washers (for optional handrail)

1 Make the Support Beams. Each of the three beams is made with two 2x8s nailed together. Most long boards have a slight *crown*, as shown in the illustration. You can best determine which edge is crowned by looking down the length of each board. Attach and install the boards with the crowns facing up.

Make sure that the boards are all the same length; trim if necessary. Stack two 2x8s on top of each other; align the edges; and fasten with 8d nails, about 10 on each side, spaced and staggered as shown.

2 Position the Posts. Place three 4x4 posts on each side of the pond, stream, or depression. Extend the posts 1 ft. above grade. For a bridge with a railing, extend the four corner posts at least 4 ft. above grade. (See "Install a Handrail," on the next page.) Center the two sets of posts no more than 7 ft. apart. Measuring from the center of the middle post on each side, set one corner post 2 ft. on center and the other 2 ft. 6½ in. on center.

Measure and stake the locations of the posts. Then dig 8-in.-diameter postholes at least 6 in. below the frost line. If frost is not a problem in your area, dig the holes at least 30 in. deep. Add 6 in. of gravel. Tamp the gravel.

Install the posts. Center the 4x4 posts in each hole. Brace the posts so that they are plumb. Mix and pour concrete an inch or so above grade at the support posts. Tamp the concrete with a piece of wood so that it completely surrounds each post. Slope the concrete away from the posts for good drainage. Let the concrete set undisturbed for at least a day.

3 **Install the Beams and Decking.** Set the beams against the posts. Study the illustration for proper beam placement. The two outside beams should be installed on the insides of the corner posts. Align the beams so that they overhang the posts equally on both sides of the bridge. Check the beams for level in both directions using a spirit level. For temporary support, attach the beams with one 20d nail into each post. With the beams leveled and temporarily attached to the posts, trim the posts flush with the tops of the beams. (Do not, however, trim the corner posts if you are installing a handrail.)

Secure the beams. At each post, drill two ⅝-in. holes through the posts and beams. Secure the beams to the posts permanently with ½-in.-diameter, 7½-in.-long carriage bolts, nuts, and washers.

Cut the 10-ft.-long 2x6s in half. Fasten the decking across the tops of the beams with 10d nails. The decking should overlap the outside beams by about 4½ in. on each side. Keep the decking square by starting at one end, installing the first 2x6 flush with the ends of the beams. Leave a ¼-in. gap between each board (a ¼-in. diameter bolt makes a handy spacer). If nailing causes the boards to split, first predrill a hole slightly smaller than the diameter of the nails.

Doubled 2x8 Beams

4x4 Posts

2x6 Decking

8'

5'

4 **Install a Handrail.** If building codes require, you'll need to install a handrail. A single or double handrail provides an extra measure of safety for bridge crossers and also provides a feeling of security. (The local building code may require one and specify how it is to be constructed.)

For a handrail, extend the 4x4 corner posts 3 ft. above the decking surface or to the height required by local codes. Attach a 2x6 handrail, 3 ft. high or to the height specified by the local code, narrow edge up. Handrails should be bolted with a minimum of two ⅜-in.-diameter 6-in.-long carriage bolts at each post.

Affix the bolts securely with washers and nuts. Note: you may add one more board (a 1x3), turned on its side, to the very top of the handrail. This will provide a wider surface area.

2x6 Handrail

4x4 Post

4x4 Post

2x6 Decking

A low bridge over a shallow pond offers different views of the garden.

Stepping-Stones

If you want to provide a means for crossing your pond but don't want to block the view of the other side, stepping-stones can be both a practical and an attractive solution. They can lead either all the way across the pond or simply a few feet out into it for observing or feeding fish. For formal pools, use square or rectangular cast-concrete slabs, large quarry tiles, cut stone, or similar geometric shapes. For informal ponds, use irregularly shaped flat rocks or flagstones. No matter the style, stepping-stones usually look best in a zigzag or random pattern rather than in a straight line.

If the pond is shallow enough, you may be able to use large rocks or stone slabs set directly in the pond. If these aren't perfectly flat on the bottom, however, they can shift dangerously; you may need to embed them in a nest of concrete. In a deeper pond, build up a layer of mortared flat rocks, or construct piers of poured concrete, brick, or block to support the stones. Cardboard tubes sold for making concrete piers are easy for amateurs to use as molds.

If you've installed a flexible liner or preformed shell, you'll need to provide a suitable concrete footing to support the stones and piers if you've used them. Stepping-stones need a firm foundation under a liner or shell, especially if the combined weight of the stone

Concrete stepping-stones need a strong foundation under the pond liner or shell.

Stepping-stones

Brick Masonry Stepping-stone

Masonry Footing

Boulder Stepping-stone

Extra Underlayment Material

Stone Masonry Stepping-stone

Masonry Footing

A variety of materials may be used for pond stepping-stones: brick, large flat boulders, flat stones, quarry tiles, and concrete slabs. A stable footing should be placed under each one.

and its support is more than 100 pounds. The best solution is a poured-concrete footing as large or slightly larger than your supporting pier. Protect the liner or shell by sandwiching it between layers of pond-liner underlayment—one between footing and liner and another between liner and support pier or stepping-stone.

You can risk adding stepping-stones later without the footing if you are sure the soil under your liner is firm. Protect the liner with an extra piece of liner between it and the stepping-stones, and use the lightest stones possible. Make sure each stone is large enough to provide a stable footing, and place the stones close enough together so that people can walk across the pond without hopping. (A gap of 12 to 15 inches between stones is comfortable for most people.) The surface of the stones should be high enough above the water so that they stay dry; wet rocks are often slippery, and if they're constantly wet, they can develop algae or moss that makes them even more dangerous. For that reason, avoid placing your stepping-stones near a waterfall or fountain, where they are likely to have water splashing on them continuously. Porous rocks such as sandstone are more prone to develop moss than nonporous rocks such as granite. Check your rocks regularly for any slick buildup, and scrub it off with a stiff brush. Walking across the stepping-stones from both directions on a regular basis will alert you to any looseness or stone movement that could contribute to someone's fall.

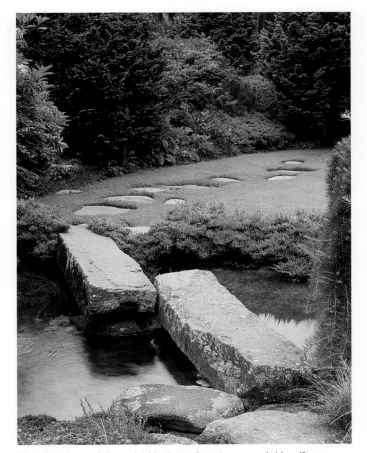

Massive stone slabs make ideal stepping-stones or a bridge. If you can handle their sheer weight and bulk, you can build this style of bridge quickly.

Even the smallest urban garden can hold wetland plants at the pond's edge.

PART 3

Wetland and Rain Gardens

Bordering your pond with plantings that grow in damp areas is one way to make your water feature look as though nature created it. Once a liability for the gardener, wet areas today are places to grow unusual varieties of flowers, grasses, ferns, and shrubs. Rain gardens, too. In its most basic form, a rain garden is a depression in the ground that's filled with sand, topsoil, and compost and planted with native perennials, non-natives, and grasses with deep roots that let water slowly permeate the ground. Besides addressing flooding, putting water back into the soil helps to recharge underground aquifers and reduces surface runoff (and pollutants) to streams and rivers.

CHAPTER 8

Natural Swimming Pools, Pondside Wetlands, and Rain Gardens

A wetland or rain garden can be a narrow strip, a sprawling bed, a simple edging of a few sedges and cattails, or an elaborate planting with native wetland species. If you don't have a naturally wet or low area, consider creating a spot that can capture runoff from the roof to create a rain garden.

If your goal is a natural-looking pond, an adjoining wetland will make it look realistic. Wetland plants include some of the flowers most attractive to hummingbirds and butterflies, such as bright red cardinal flowers and towering joe-pye weed. In nature, ponds are surrounded by wet meadows, marshes (where soft-stemmed plants grow), or swamps (which may be home to shrubs and trees). These wetlands act as filters for ponds and streams by absorbing silt and pollutants. In your home garden, a wetland can absorb water that overruns your pond due to a heavy rain.

In this chapter, the term wetland garden refers to an artificial marsh in which the soil never dries out. The plants are not, however, growing in standing water. Appropriate plants include moisture-loving perennials and many grasses, ferns, and shrubs.

Although some gardeners and water-garden suppliers may refer to these specialized gardens as "bog gardens," a true bog is a more specialized habitat where the soil is highly acidic and low in oxygen and nutrients. If you mimic the conditions of a true bog, you can grow fascinating carnivorous plants such as pitcher plants, Venus flytraps, sundews, and terrestrial orchids. Keep in mind that they are not winter hardy in cold climates and must be brought indoors. Plants that thrive in shallow-water spots between a natural pond and a marsh or swamp are called "marginals." In garden ponds, these plants are grown inside the liner or the pond shell in containers.

If you have an area in your yard where the soil is saturated with water, consider using it as a site for an informal wetland garden. Lacking that, you can create a natural-looking bog garden using a flexible liner.

A low spot in the garden is a natural place for moisture-loving plants.

Natural Swimming Pools

What better than to swim in a pond surrounded by water lilies in the comfort and privacy of your garden? Natural swimming pools offer a pool that looks and acts like a swimming pond in your backyard, without the harmful effects of chlorine and other chemicals. With a natural pool, you get a recreational pond, while having lower maintenance costs than traditional and chemically treated pools.

Natural swimming pools (or ponds) are a throwback to the days before manufactured pools. People swam in local ponds, lakes, or streams. Today, the "natural" swimming pool can be a feature for a larger back yard. Natural swimming pools stay clean by having clearly defined swimming areas and constructed wetlands. Bacteria and microbes keep the water pure, clean, and healthy for swimming. In general, half the pool is plant free for swimming and the other half is for regeneration and keeping the water clean.

The regeneration zones have small, energy-efficient pipes that circulate the water, breaking down impurities. The regeneration zones have specific aquatic plants that extract excess nutrients in the water to keep the pool clean. Water from the swimming zones pumps through natural, biological filters made up of microorganisms, plants, and small life forms to purify the water. Each natural pool has overflow channels, which collect debris in the water.

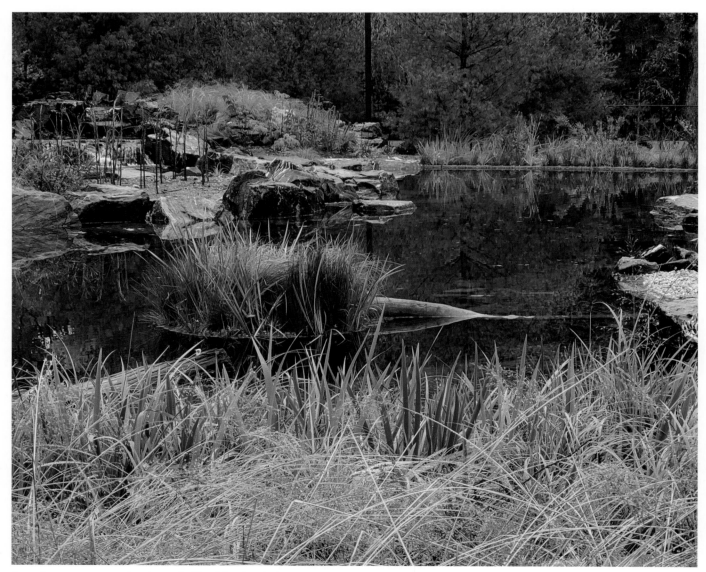

A pond can serve as a swimming pool without the chemicals.

Pondside Wetlands

If you want to have a natural-looking pond, you'll need to create a wetland garden along one or more sides of it to establish a smooth transition into the rest of your landscape. If you plan the wetland (or bog) garden before you build your pond, it will be easy to create both at the same time.

Visit natural ponds in local parks or gardens to study the way that plants are grouped. Try to resist amassing a collection of individual specimens. Instead, concentrate on several representatives of a few species that occur together naturally. A trip to a native-plant nursery in your region or a good book on regional plants (known as a "flora") can help you (Creative Homeowner's Regional Home Landscaping Series, for example).

You must make the wetland watertight. You can do this either by extending your pond liner or by using a piece of liner cut from an unused corner. If you use a scrap, seal the gap between it and the pond liner with liner tape to minimize leakage from your wetland.

To keep soil from washing from the wetland garden into the pond, you must create a division between them. This can be a solid division, in which case you'll need an independent source of water to keep the garden area wet.

An attached wetland with a "leaky" division allows the pond to provide water for the wetland. If you don't have time to check and water the wetland frequently, this second option is probably better. Keep in mind, though, that a large wetland or bog garden connected to a pond can lower the pond's water level if water is allowed to seep out too readily. Most experts advise against the connected option for a true bog garden because it might allow chemicals or nutrient-rich fish wastes in the pond water to upset the bog's chemistry.

Independent Wetland Garden

To create an independent bog or wetland, simply leave a mound or berm of soil along one edge of your pond higher than the planned water level (usually the same level as the rest of the edge). Run the pond liner over the mound and into the wetland area.

Ensure good drainage for the top few inches by puncturing holes around the sides, about halfway down from the top. Follow the directions under "Creating a Wetland Environment," on page 142, for installing perforated pipe to maintain soil moisture. Camouflage the liner with whatever you use as edging material or with large stones.

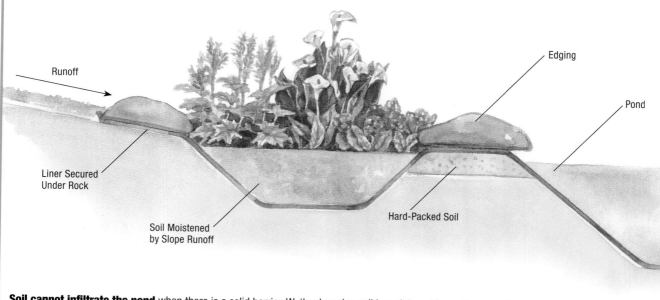

Soil cannot infiltrate the pond when there is a solid barrier. Wetland garden soil is moistened from slope runoff.

Attached Wetland Garden

To create a connected wetland, make the berm between your pond and garden a little lower than the expected water level. Then, on top of the solid berm, create a semipermeable barrier that extends a little above the eventual water level. There are several different ways you can go about creating this barrier, which will serve as an automatic-watering device for your wetland. You may find that one of the following options allows better control of water flow for your particular design or is more aesthetically pleasing than the others.

■ Stones are a popular option. Some people find that they get enough control of the water flow by stacking stones on the mound and letting pond water seep between and under them.

■ Mortar some of the stones together to reduce the gaps for seepage if too much water flows through. Or combine stones with the sod option, described next. This is very easy to put in place.

■ Sod, stacked in layers, is another popular material for the semipermeable barrier. Top the mound with pieces of sod turned upside down; hold them securely in place; and hide them with large stones or other edging.

■ Stones with two or three pieces of perforated pipe run between them and into the soil in the wetland area is a more involved option. Mortar the rest of the stones together so that water flows only through the pipe.

Now you're ready to add your planting medium. (See "Filling Your Wetland Garden," on page 145.) For attached wetlands, add the soil mix gradually, saturating it as you go and testing the amount of water that's running between pond and wetland. Wait to plant until you're satisfied that you have the right amount of water seepage.

Edging

Stones or Sod
to Allow Seepage

Pond

Liner Secured
Under Rock

Soil

Liner

Hard-Packed
Soil Berm

A semipermeable barrier allows pond water to seep into the wetland garden and moisten the soil.

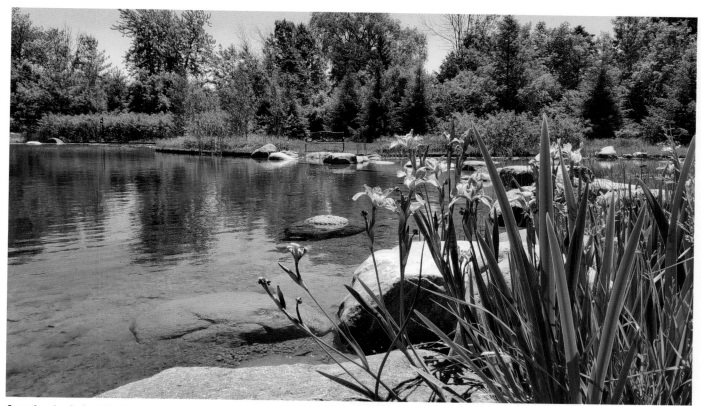

A contractor helped the homeowner create a beautiful and functional swimming pond.

A Freestanding Wetland Garden

A wetland garden surrounding a pond creates a smooth transition to the rest of the home landscape. Consider including a wetland, bog, or rain garden as you plan your pond so you can create them at the same time. Natural ponds in local parks or public gardens can provide inspiration for plant groupings. Selecting a few plant species that occur together naturally, especially local, native, water-loving plants, will ensure your success. Rain gardens and wetland areas are important tools to bring sustainable practices to our home landscapes.

Although many people place wetland gardens next to their ponds, you don't need a pond to create a wetland. If your yard already has an area that's always soggy, stop trying to grow grass there and instead transform it into a home for a whole array of wonderful plants that thrive in constant moisture.

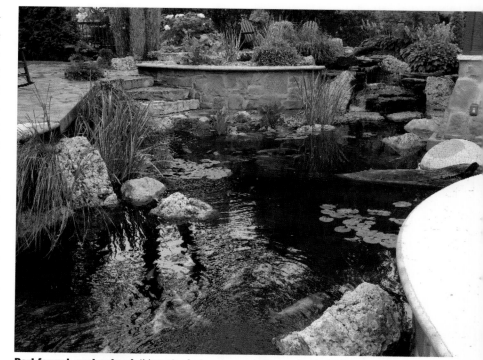

Part formal, part natural, this water feature connects the garden to the house.

If you're starting from scratch, design the wetland or bog so that it will blend in with its surroundings. If it's not next to a pond, situate it next to an area of dense, informal planting. If you want to locate it next to a woodland or much taller plants, be sure to put it on the south side so that it will get enough sun.

Try to visually tie it in with an existing dense planting. If that's not possible, try to echo the shape of another bed in your garden that you've filled with typical dryland perennials or shrubs. Any of these options will help make the wetland garden appear as though it belongs rather than looking like an afterthought.

Access to water is crucial so that the wetland will never dry out. Many people locate wetland gardens where the plantings can capture runoff from rooftops. This is helpful if you are trying to mimic a true bog, in which case you want to avoid the chemicals and alkaline minerals often present in tap water. (The quality that makes rainwater soft is its acidity. Tap water that's hard is too alkaline for bog plants; commercial water softeners fix the alkalinity but make the water too saline for bog plants.)

Keep in mind the sun requirement of the plants you want. A number of moisture-loving perennials thrive in partial shade, and shade will reduce the need to water the wetland garden. But carnivorous plants and many other wetland species require full sun to flower and grow well.

CREATING A WETLAND ENVIRONMENT

Wherever you place the freestanding wetland garden, the basic mechanics are similar. Your goal is to keep the soil at the bottom of your excavated area from ever drying out, while at the same time keeping water away from the crowns of the plants (the point where the stems or leaves meet the roots) so that they don't rot.

Building a wetland or bog garden in the ground is

Freestanding Wetland Garden

A reliable water source to keep the soil moist is of utmost importance. A perforated pipe (end-capped) connected to a hose is a good solution.

Hose

Edging

Liner

Gravel

Perforated Pipe

Plugged End

A half barrel is a good choice for containing a freestanding wetland garden.

similar to building a pond—you dig a hole and make it watertight with a pond liner, but then you fill it with soil instead of water. Just as a large pond requires less maintenence than a small one, a large wetland or bog garden won't need watering as often as a small one. Dig the hole at least 2 feet deep; 3 feet is even better. You can make the sides of the wetland hole much less steeply vertical than those of your pond; the gradual slope will help keep them from caving in.

Calculate the size of your liner in the same way that you would for a pond. (See the example on page 69.) Liners for wetland gardens don't need to be completely wa-

tertight, so there's no need to buy the same high-grade PVC or rubber you bought for your pond. Look for a sheet of heavy-duty polyethylene large enough to cover the bottom and sides in one piece.

After you've centered the plastic sheet and let it settle into your excavation, ensure good drainage for the crowns of your plants by puncturing drainage holes around the sides, about halfway down from the top.

At this point most wetland gardeners install perforated pipe to help keep the soil evenly moist. Here are several options that will help you deliver water throughout the planting area during a drought.

WETLAND OR BOG GARDENS IN CONTAINERS

You can create a small wetland or bog garden in a watertight container such as a half barrel, a trough, or even an old bathtub or child's wading pool. A wooden or plastic container is best, especially if you live in a cold climate because other materials will crack when they freeze in winter. Fill it with the same growing medium described in "Filling Your Wetland Garden," opposite: half compost, half garden loam for wetland plants; half peat moss, half sand for specialized bog plants.

You might want to install an automatic watering system to irrigate the container garden if you'll be away on vacation. A simple homemade device is a plastic gallon jug with a nailhole punched in the bottom; when filled with water, this will drip slowly until the jug is empty. A more elaborate option is to connect a line running from an automatic drip-irrigation system to your container.

As with any water garden, wetland and bog gardens in containers need special care in the winter. If you're growing plants at the northern edge of their hardiness range, sink the container into the ground in winter before mulching, or move the container to a protected place such as a garage. Check moisture levels periodically to make sure the soil doesn't dry out.

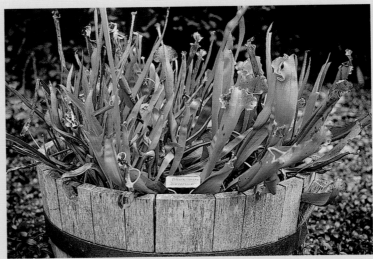

■ **Run one or more perforated pipes vertically** down the side of your wetland or bog, stopping a couple of inches above the bottom of the excavation and leaving 1 to 2 inches of the pipe above the soil surface. Block the bottom end of the pipe to ensure that the water seeps out slowly and to keep the drainage holes from getting clogged with dirt. You can camouflage exposed piping with plants.

■ **Use one pipe inside another** for even more gradual seepage. Garden writer C. Colston Burrell suggests using two perforated pipes, one larger than the other (the larger at least 10 inches in diameter), inserting the smaller into the larger, and filling the space between with gravel. When you need to water, place the end of a hose or the spout of a watering can into the inside pipe; the water will slowly seep through the gravel into the soil. Again, camouflage exposed piping with plants.

■ **Run a length of rigid perforated pipe horizontally** across the bottom of the wetland. Join it to a vertical length of solid (not perforated) PVC pipe with an elbow connector. If you choose this option, lay 3 to 4 inches of gravel around and on top of the horizontal pipe to help keep soil out of the drainage holes. Again, remember to block the end of the pipe, and disguise the exposed inch or two with plants.

■ **Purchase flexible leaky hose**, or soaker hose. Intended for subsurface irrigation, flexible leaky hose is less likely to plug up with soil than regular leaky hose. Drape the hose around the bottom of your wetland so it forms almost a complete loop. Cap or plug the far end and attach the other to a hose at the surface.

Filling Your Wetland Garden

After the area is excavated and lined, you're ready to fill the "wetland" or container with soil or growing medium, such as a mixture of compost and good garden loam. The idea is to provide organic matter that holds moisture for plant roots. If your soil is currently sandy or has heavy clay, it will need to be amended. If you're considering adding true bog plants, they require a mix that is typically described as "sterile," a mix of half peat moss and half sand. (Here, "sterile" describes a mix that is almost completely lacking in nutrients and therefore unable to support ordinary plants and soil organisms.) Some growers use as much as five parts peat to one part sand, so don't skimp.

After the wetland is filled to the surface with growing medium and is thoroughly damp but not soaking wet, it's time to plant. By planting densely (placing plants a bit closer than the tag suggests), you will reduce soil surface exposed to evaporation. Close planting also reduces weeds. Some plants, like swamp milkweed, prefer moisture—but not standing water all the time. Set the plants in the soil so that their crowns (the spot where the stems meet the roots) are at or just slightly below the soil surface.

In areas with cold winters, a mulch of leaves or pine needles will keep plants from pushing out of the ground during freeze-and-thaw periods. A summer top-dressing of compost reduces weeds and retains moisture in the soil. In larger settings, a wetland planting next to a pond makes a smooth transition to the rest of your landscape.

Rain Gardens

Flooding is a problem in many areas of the country. If you live close to a river or where housing has been built where there was no consideration for drainage, flooding may be a regular occurrence during thunderstorms. With ongoing building of homes, roads, shopping centers, and industrial sites there is simply less permeable space for water to enter the ground.

A one-inch rainfall on an acre produces about 27,000 gallons of water. Some of it runs off onto beds, borders, and grass, but that's problematic, too. Lawn really is impervious because the roots are only three to four inches deep. Water will eventually permeate the soil, but when it's dry, the water runs right off and into streets, sewers, or neighboring property.

In its most basic form, a rain garden is a depression in the ground that's filled with sand, topsoil and compost and planted with native perennials, non-natives and grasses with deep roots that let water slowly permeate the ground. Besides addressing flooding, rain gardens put water back into the soil and help to recharge underground aquifers and reduce surface runoff (and pollutants) to streams and rivers.

A rain garden is simply a low spot in the ground where water can gather and infiltrate. It can be collected from the home's roof so that it will soak into the ground within 24 hours. It's not a place that's always moist. If that was the case, instead of a rain garden, it would be a wetland garden. Because rain gardens and wetland gardens collect water runoff, they should be sited so they do not overflow into your pond.

While planning your water feature, consider a wetland garden adjacent to it. It makes a smoother transition to the rest of the landscape.

A wetland garden on one or more sides of your pond is a natural-looking enhancement.

SPECIALIZED PLANTS FOR BOGS

Growing true bog plants takes a special commitment. Not only must you make sure that their soil never dries out, but you also need to water them with distilled water or rainwater. Tap water can make the soil too alkaline or introduce chemicals bog plants can't tolerate. Nor is the bog garden flexible about sunlight. You'll need to find a location with at least six hours of sun each day throughout the growing season.

Once your bog garden is established, it can only host a limited range of plants. A true bog lacks in soil nutrients and is too highly acidic for most moisture-loving perennials and shrubs that would grow in other gardens. Nevertheless, the array of fascinating and beautiful plants that grow in bogs has made this type of gardening an obsession for many, with its own international plant society and numerous Web sites and specialized nurseries.

Bog plants don't send their roots deep, so an excavation of 12 to 18 inches is enough in this case. After you add your peat/sand mix, wait three to four weeks for the pH to adjust and the medium to settle.

Remember that a bog is a nutrient-poor environment. Never fertilize it. And your carnivorous plants don't need any artificial food for their traps, either. *Little Shop of Horrors* and other popular images to the contrary, these species didn't evolve eating hamburger. Passing insects will suit them just fine. It's another matter if there is limited insect life in your area. Provide some bugs only if absolutely necessary.

In winter, carnivorous plants go dormant and don't need insects. But they do need protection from fluctuating temperatures; give bog plants a loose, acidic mulch of insulating pine needles or a mixture of oak leaves.

POPULAR CARNIVOROUS PLANTS

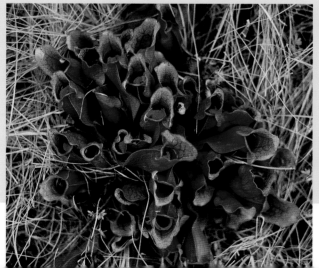

Carnivorous plants are not particularly hard to grow as long as they have three things: a good six hours of sun a day, a very acidic growing medium high in organic matter, and constant moisture. Carnivorous plants fail to grow as houseplants both because they don't get enough sun and because they aren't allowed to go dormant in winter.

American Pitcher Plants (*Sarracenia* species). There are eight species of native pitcher plants, some of which can reach 3 feet tall. They get their common name from modified leaves that form trumpetlike hooded "pitchers." These showy pitchers, often speckled and veined in different colors, trap insects attracted to the plant's nectar. They open shop after the unusual, droopy dogs-ear flowers (either yellow or red) finish their two-week bloom in spring. Most pitcher-plant species (some endangered) are native to the southeast United States and are cold hardy to Zone 7. An exception is the common or purple pitcher plant, *S. purpurea,* native as far north as Canada. It holds its pitchers low to the ground, growing only 6 inches tall. It traps insects by drowning them in rainwater collected in its leaves. There are many natural hybrids and several easy-to-grow named varieties.

Venus Flytrap (*Dionaea muscipula*). The only species in its genus, this carnivore can grow to 18 inches tall. Its insect-trapping mechanism looks like a clam with spikes along the edge of each "shell." Pink inside, it has three tiny hairs that serve as triggers: when an insect brushes against them, they cause the plant to slam the two halves shut. The Venus flytrap is native to parts of the Carolinas and is cold hardy to Zone 8, although some strands have been established in New Jersey.

Sundews (*Drosera* species). There are some 130 species of these fascinating plants, found from Alaska and Siberia to New Zealand and South America. Hairlike tentacles on a sundew's leaves are brightly colored. At their tips, a drop of gluelike nectar sparkles in the sun like dew, luring various unsuspecting gnats and similar tiny bugs. The insect's thrashing causes the sundew's tentacles to curl further inward, trapping its victim ever more securely. Sundew flowers vary widely in arrangement, although most

American Pitcher Plant. The modified leaves, left, often colorful with speckles and veins, trap insects seeking nectar.

are round and flat with five pink or white petals. Love-nest sundew (*D. intermedia*) has maroon foliage and white flowers and is hardy in Zones 6–9. *D. limearis*, which also has white flowers, does best in Zones 3–6. Both grow to approximately 6 inches tall.

Bladderworts (*Utricularia* species). There are more than 200 species of this highly advanced, somewhat bizarre perennial. Hobbyists grow them for their orchidlike flower. Harder to see are the bladderlike traps, some no bigger than a pinhead on their stems or roots. They can capture tiny organisms in 10 thousandths of a second. The easiest aquatic bladderwort to grow is *U. gibba*, which has ½-inch yellow flowers with a hood, curving spur, and tongue with red veins. It's not cold hardy, so you'll need to keep it in a container.

Butterworts (*Pinguicula* species). This genus of about 70 species from throughout the Northern hemisphere gets its name from its greasy leaves with glands that trap insects such as gnats and fruitflies; their struggles stimulate other glands to secrete digestive juices. From rosettes a few inches across, temperate species produce cone-shaped, two-lipped flowers with long spurs and beards, most often purple, violet, or white. Some you might find in cultivation are *P. caerula* (violet with a yellow beard, Zone 8) and *P. grandiflora* (deep blue violet, Zone 3), and *P. vulgaris* (violet with a white throat, Zone 6).

BOG ORCHIDS

Most people think of orchids as exotic plants that grow only in rainforests. But North America is home to more than 200 species, many of which make their homes in bogs. They include the fringed orchids (*Platanthera* species), with frilly flowers in magenta, orange, and yellow. But because orchids are difficult to propagate, few nurseries sell them. Many species are threatened by development and should never be collected in the wild. They rarely survive transplanting to home gardens because they depend on the presence of particular fungi in the soil.

'Chadds Ford' (*Spiranthes odorata*). A native orchid that is both widely available and fairly easy to grow is a selecion of the fragrant ladies'-tresses orchid. Fragrant little waxy, white flowers spiral around its stems, which can grow to 18 inches tall. Ladies'-tresses aren't as particular about their growing conditions as most of the carnivorous plants, as long as they are grown in well-drained soil that remains constantly moist. They are hardy in Zones 5–8.

Venus Flytrap. Insects are trapped, left, by the plant's hair-like triggers.

Sundew. The plant's tips are covered in glue that snares insects, below.

'Chadds Ford'. This fragrant ladies'-tresses orchid, above, is available from nurseries and is relatively easy to grow.

This garden offers an array of plantings that are suitable to grow in and around water.

RESPECTING NATIVE BOG PLANTS

In recent years, nongardening catalogs and even hardware stores have offered the Venus flytrap, a carnivorous bog species, as a novelty: a plant that behaves like a pet by eating insects. But there are two things wrong with this scenario. First, carnivorous bog plants demand special conditions and quickly die when they are treated as ordinary houseplants. Second, this and many other bog species are being collected from the wild, further depleting the populations of those that have managed to survive the draining of wetlands for development, agriculture, and other uses.

Fortunately, some nurseries are making an effort to propagate, or breed, their own carnivorous plants rather than buying their inventory from people who collect from the wild. Two North Carolina horticulturists,

Larry Mellichamp and Rob Gardner, went a step further and developed two new pitcher-plant hybrids, 'Ladies in Waiting' and 'Dixie Lace', for home gardeners. "We thought that man-made hybrids that do especially well in cultivation might offer more enticement to grow them, and ease some of the pressure to collect them," says Mellichamp. Because these two pitcher plants don't grow in the wild, you can be assured that they've been propagated by a nursery, wherever you buy them.

'Ladies in Waiting' grows up to 16 inches tall. Its color is deep maroon with white spots; its hood has a scalloped edge. 'Dixie Lace' is smaller and has dark red veins on a light yellow background; the edge of its hood is wavy. Mellichamp believes that the new hybrids will grow to Zone 5 with some winter protection.

'Ladies in Waiting' hybrid

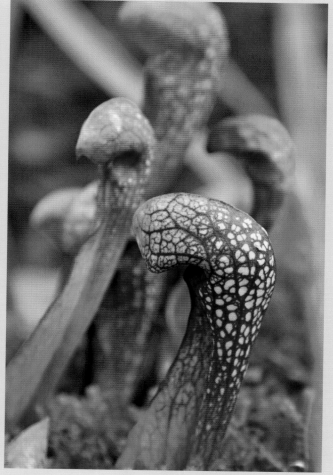

'Dixie Lace' hybrid

CHAPTER 9

Pond Critters

Wildlife—from fish, frogs, birds, and other animals—brings delight to the pond owner. Water attracts birds, especially during spring and fall migration. And, surprisingly, many people who have never seen a frog, toad, or turtle suddenly find them attracted to the pond. You can make these wildlife wonders feel at home (or in some cases, encourage them to seek accommodations elsewhere)!

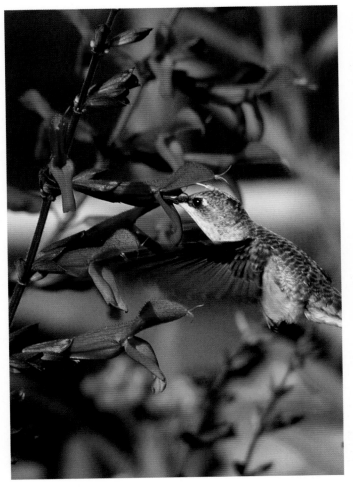

Fish

Watching the casual movements of fish can be hypnotic and relaxing. They have a calming effect in a pond whether they are rare, colorful koi or common minnows. Feeding time is a pleasure as you watch them race to gobble food or chase each other. Not only are they captivating, but fish help control insects as well as provide nutrients for plants. They can be an integral part of a pond's thriving ecosystem.

Introducing fish adds new challenges. You may have to protect them with netting over the pond to prevent predators such as raccoons or herons from grabbing one or two for dinner. Their waste may cloud the water, or they might nibble your prize plants. Before you build a pond, decide whether you want large fish, such as koi. They need ample room to swim and extra depth for hiding and for surviving winter temperatures in cold climates. If the pond isn't sited in partial shade, you may need to introduce floating plants to cover roughly half of the pond's surface. Predators are wily! Fish need hiding places such as overhangs on the pond's edge, terra-cotta drainage tiles, or drainpipes weighted on the bottom where they can hide.

Before you buy any fish—expensive or not—discover what they need. Like any other pets, fish can become ill or die without proper care. They are outdoor pets in an environment that will never be completely natural. Make that environment as healthy for them as possible and they will bring new enjoyment with their movements and colors.

Ruby-throated hummingbirds are found east of the Mississippi River, but there are many other species throughout the United States.

Colorful koi add a new dimension to pond life.

Birds, butterflies, bees, and dragonflies will enjoy visiting the pond.

Choosing Your Fish

If you have an existing pond, you will have to select the species and number of fish appropriate to those conditions. If you're still in the planning stages, check the entries in this section to see whether the fish you want need deep or shallow water, and make the pond large enough to accommodate them. A common rule for stocking your pond is that 1 square foot of well-balanced pond water can support 2 inches of fish. Thus in an area of 6 square feet, you could have four 3-inch fish or two 6-inch fish. (Koi are an exception to this rule; they need 25 square feet each.) In addition to the size of your pond, there are several other factors to consider when choosing among available fish species. Tropical fish species will need to be removed from the pond each fall and kept in an indoor aquarium, which can become a demanding chore if the fish become numerous. Other species are quite sensitive to high temperatures and will get sluggish or even die during hot summers. Some feed at the surface, skimming insects off the water and even jumping out to gulp them. This is entertaining but can make the fish more obvious to predators. Bottom feeders can hide better, but they have an annoying habit of churning up bottom muck and may be harder to see from the surface.

Overstocking a pond is a sure route to failure. Avoid buying more fish (or larger fish) than your pond will support. Fish often take care of overstocking themselves, by eating their own spawn or not spawning at all. If you hope to increase your stock for yourself or friends, choose fish that breed easily in a pond situation, and take measures to remove the fry.

If you want to create a wildlife pond, you may want to

A healthy environment that includes well-balanced water and adequate space is essential for fish.

focus on native fish. Expect a natural pond to attract nature—which means fish-eating raccoons and birds—and native fish are usually quite a bit less expensive to replace. In addition, some exotic fish have caused problems after escaping to natural waterways. (Refer to "Keep Pond Creatures in Their Place," below.)

When you start out, buy small fish of less expensive breeds. This will allow you to get comfortable with the routine of fish care, to observe any problems with your water supply or potential predators, and to see how your fish adjust to their new home. The following pages show some of the most popular and readily available fish for home ponds.

KEEP POND CREATURES IN THEIR PLACE

Never dispose of your fish, snails, or other pond life in nearby waterways or sewers. Animals outside their natural environments, just like non-native plants, can upset the healthy balance of waterways. Water creatures that have caused the most trouble have been introduced by commerce: zebra mussel in ships' ballasts, tilapia to raise for food markets, trout for sport. The bullfrog has been taken beyond its native range in the eastern and central United States by connoisseurs of frog legs, and in their new homes these amphibians are wiping out small native frogs. These animals don't just dominate native species by eating them or their food but can also spread diseases for which native animals have no resistance. The common carp—a relative of koi—carries some 130 different parasites.

GOLDFISH (*Carassius auratus*)

This group of fish, which originated in China, is a favorite for either aquariums or ponds. Members of the carp family, they're colorful and tough, and they feed at all levels, so you'll have no trouble seeing them. All goldfish breed easily, although if you have more than one kind, they'll interbreed, and their distinguishing characteristics can be lost.

Common Goldfish. This popular fish, most often reddish orange, usually grows to about 6 inches long but can get bigger in a large pond. Goldfish can tolerate shallow, somewhat stagnant water and survive water temperatures up to 95°F for brief periods. They can overwinter outdoors where pond water won't freeze solid, and they can learn to recognize their feeder.

Comets. These specially bred goldfish have long, deeply forked caudal fins (tails) that can be as long as their bodies. Gold comets can grow more than a foot long. While they need a depth of 30 inches or so for wintering over, they can take even more extreme temperatures than their common cousin, down to almost freezing and up to 104°F. Sarasa comets, which have red-and-white markings on a silver base, do best in water that remains cooler than 70°F.

Fantail. Goldfish in this group have wider, more transparent fins and tails. This makes them slower swimmers and more vulnerable to predators, and their ballroom finery can soon look like Cinderella's rags. Only about half as long as the common goldfish, they have roly-poly bodies and are considerably less flexible about extreme temperatures. The Japanese strain is reddish orange, and the calico strain is mottled.

Shubunkin. This goldfish, developed in Japan, also grows to a robust 12 inches or longer with a long, flowing tail that is almost plumelike. Its most unusual multicolored body distinguishes the shubunkin, which is available in blue, purple, black, red, and brown. It prefers temperatures over 45°F and lower than 70°F.

Moor. This is a special type of fantail, easily recognized by its extremely dramatic black color, although the shadowy garb makes it especially difficult to observe in a pond. Slightly larger than other fantails, at 4 to 5 inches long, it also has a double caudal fin and may have comical *pop eyes.*

Common goldfish. These are highly recommended for beginners.

Comet. This fancy type of goldfish is very popular.

Fantail. Their hardiness makes maintenance fairly easy.

Shubunkin. "Calico" colors and black spots distinguish this fish.

Moor. These fish must overwinter indoors.

KOI (*Cyprinus carpio*)

Like goldfish, koi are members of the carp family. But while goldfish are easy, koi and most other carp relatives are more demanding and often unsuitable for smaller ponds. These big fellows aren't as tolerant of temperature extremes as goldfish are. They become listless if the water temperature approaches 70°F, although they can overwinter where the bottom of the pond remains unfrozen. The common carp, from which koi were first bred, really needs a lake to dart around in because it stirs up mud in which to hide from enemies. Most carp also have a tendency to nibble or uproot pond plants.

Of the carp sometimes mentioned in water-garden books, only koi are widely available and worth trying to include in a home pond. These fish, with a natural life span of several decades, are so revered in Japan that their image appears on flags and windsocks on Boys' Day, May 5, as a symbol of strength and loyalty.

Little "whiskers" (barbels) lend personality to their faces, and they will eat out of your hand or even learn to jump through hoops. Those that have been carefully bred for specific color patterns can cost into three figures, but a small common koi can cost as little as $5. All can grow 2 to 3 feet long and have hearty appetites that will include your prized water lilies. That means you'll need to protect underwater plants with mesh; raise other plants high in the water, where koi rarely trespass.

Koi need water at least 3 feet deep, and each needs 25 square feet of pond to call its own. Their preferred temperature range is 39° to 68°F. Because of their hearty appetites, they also create a lot of waste, and so you'll probably need a pond filter to keep them happy and healthy. Butterfly koi, available from mail-order suppliers, are smaller and have longer fins and tails. They are costlier than common koi (although less expensive than collector koi) and hardier as well.

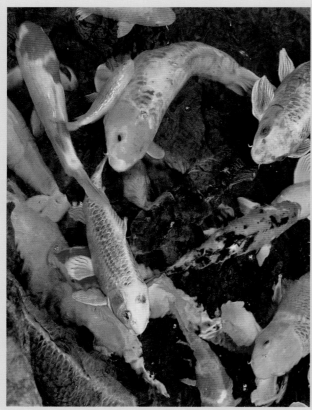

Koi. Members of the carp family, koi need room—25 square feet per fish. Some of the elaborately patterned specimens are costly.

Butterfly koi. If you don't have a big enough pond for other koi, try this small type called "Butterfly," which is surprisingly hardy.

OTHER FISH

In addition to various types of goldfish and koi, there are other fish that you may want to consider for your pond. Here are some examples.

Orfe (*Leuciscus idus***).** This slender fish is a good choice if your pond is well oxygenated, not subject to runoff that contains any toxins, and at least 40 square feet. Not only is the orfe large (18 inches in length), it's also a schooling fish that needs friends to bring out its natural friskiness—a half dozen is ideal. (A 40-square-foot pond will accommodate the school of six.) The orfe will reward you by nibbling on floating insects and sometimes jumping out of the water for airborne ones. It needs a gravel area in which to spawn. (The depth of this area isn't critical.)

Rudd (*Scardinius erythrophthal-mus***).** This surface-feeding fish with reddish fins can be gold or silver. Although no more than 10 inches long, the rudd nevertheless needs some space in which to frolic as well as a generous amount of underwater foliage where it can hide and lay eggs. Native to Europe, the rudd can handle a wide range of temperatures, including a maximum of 102°F. The golden rudd (*S. e.* var. *aurata*) is bronze colored.

Tench (*Tinca tinca***).** Once called the *doctor fish* because it was thought to cure pondmates of disease, the tench spends most of its time cleaning waste matter from the bottom of the pond. Look for the golden tench, which is bright enough for you to see it even when it's on the bottom. It usually grows about 18 inches long and is relatively tolerant of both temperature swings and occasional dips in oxygen. Its adaptability makes it a good choice for many different parts of the United States.

Orfe. Orfe, a frisky schooling fish, will entertain you by leaping from the pond for insects. It can grow 18 inches long.

Rudd. Although it is a compact species, the rudd needs a spacious pond as well as a lot of submerged plants to encourage breeding.

Tench. A school of tench is like having a professional sanitation crew at work. They're always cleaning the bottom of the pond.

FISH FOR WILDLIFE PONDS

If you're creating a wildlife pond, you are probably doing so out of respect for the natural environment, with a goal of balancing the plants and animals so that they'll need relatively little care. Native fish, like native plants, will do better than imported species—if you've taken care to create a habitat that's as much like their natural one as possible. They'll be able to get much of their food from the plants you've chosen, and they'll survive winter in the pond. They'll even look more appropriate in your pond.

Your wildlife pond is bound to attract predators that will eat some of your fish; if you buy native fish such as minnows, it will be less financially painful to lose some of them.

Minnow (*Pimephales promelas* **or** *Cyprinodon variegatus***).** The common name *minnow* is used for several different small fish. These fish can grow to 6 inches long but are usually half that. Minnows like water that is shallow but also clear and well oxygenated. They need other minnows because they are schooling fish; they also need an area of clean sand or fine gravel in which to lay eggs.

Mosquito Fish (*Gambusia affinis***).** If you live in a semitropical area, this fish can be a good investment because it has a prodigious appetite for the larvae of mosquitoes and midges. It is native to roughly the southeastern portion of the United States. Silvery blue-gray, mosquito fish grow to 2½ inches and breed quickly.

Three-Spined Stickleback (*Gasterosteus aculeatus***).** The 2- to 3-inch stickleback is unusual not only for the triad of spines for which it's named but also for its fascinating behavior in spawning season: the fry are housed in a volcano-shaped underwater nest, to which the red-flushed male will return them by mouth when they wander. Sticklebacks can live for three years. The three-spined stickleback is a northern species, native as far south as New Jersey. A related four-spined stickleback (*Apeltes quadracus*) is native farther south, into Virginia.

Minnow. Several species of small fish go by the common name minnow. Because all of them are schooling fish, you'll want to buy several.

Mosquito fish. Even the smallest pond can use a population of mosquito fish to gobble the larvae of mosquitos and midges.

Three-spined stickleback. A northern fish, the three-spined stickleback has a 4-spined cousin that is available for those south of New Jersey.

Don't be surprised if your pond attracts fish-eating raccoons or birds.

WATER QUALITY

To keep fish healthy, pond water needs to stay within certain parameters. These include moderate temperatures, a sufficient oxygen content, a relatively neutral pH (a measure of the water's acidity/alkalinity), the absence of chlorine compounds, and minimal amounts of nitrites and ammonia (which come from both fish waste and fertilizer runoff).

Some chemicals used to purify water are toxic to fish. If your water comes from municipal or county sources, you'll need to check with local authorities to determine what chemicals are used to purify the water supply. If your water contains only ordinary chlorine, uncompounded with other chemicals, the chlorine will dissipate within 24 to 48 hours after you fill the pond. If your water supply contains chloramine (a compound of chlorine and ammonia) or chlorine dioxide, you'll need to treat the water with a dechlorinating agent, available from water-garden suppliers. Even if your water is free of these substances, it's a good idea to hold off introducing fish until the plants have had a couple weeks to become established, algae has cleared, and the pond's normal population of beneficial microscopic creatures has built up.

To monitor the water-quality parameters most important for fish, you will probably want the following items.

■ **A thermometer.** This is not so important for goldfish, which tolerate a broad range of temperatures, but it is crucial for some other fish that can't survive water temperatures above 70°F.

■ **A kit for testing pH.** Fish need a pH level near neutral, between 6.6 and 7.5. You should test your water supply to see whether it falls within this range; test the pond again after it's filled with plants and animals. You should also re-test the water periodically to make sure the pH stays within the recommended range, especially after adding more than 20 percent new water or after introducing new fish and plants to your pond.

Water from some wells is naturally alkaline; if your water is hard, it will probably be alkaline too. (Both calcium and magnesium, often the cause of hard water, also cause alkalinity.) If you use a water softener or a water conditioner, don't use the treated water for your fish (or plants). If you don't already have a direct line for outdoor or garden use, install an outdoor faucet that connects directly to the water supply and bypasses the water conditioner or softener. Water can become alkaline if your pool is concrete, from contact with mortared edges, or if you use concrete blocks to raise water plants. Algae can sometimes change the pH level. You may also want to have products for adjusting pH on hand.

A healthy environment for fish means monitoring water quality to prevent problems.

■ **A kit for testing ammonia and/or nitrites.** Some water-testing kits will also test for ammonia and nitrites, which can build up from fish waste when a pond is overpopulated. If your test kit doesn't, you'll need to buy a separate testing kit. (See "What's in Your Water," Chapter 10 on page 181 for how to correct excess ammonia and/or nitrites.)

■ **Dechlorinating formula.** This is essential if your water supply contains chloramine or chlorine dioxide. You'll need it especially during the summer, when it's important to keep ponds topped off with water. You can safely add up to 5 percent of pond volume once or twice a week without using a dechlorinator; if you add more, you'll need to retreat the water. Adding water with a spray or sprinkler will help dissipate ordinary chlorine as well as add some oxygen.

■ **Rock salt or pond salt.** Fish have a coating of mucus that protects them from disease but that can be lost when they are stressed. Periodic treatment of the pond with rock salt (not iodized table salt) at the rate of 2 pounds per 100 gallons will restore this protection. Salt corrects the electrolyte balance of the fish and helps prevent the loss of fluids. Salt manufactured especially for ponds includes beneficial trace elements. It's not good for plants, though, so it should be added to the pond as far away from plants as possible. If you prefer not to add salt to the pond water, you can give fish a salt bath. (See the aquarium discussion, above right.)

■ **A parasite treatment or preventive.** Use this when you add new fish—especially if they haven't been treated by the dealer—or when you spot the symptoms of parasites. (See "Common Fish Diseases," on page 165 for a discussion of various parasites.)

■ **An aeration kit.** The oxygen content of your pond can decrease rapidly in thunderstorms or during a sudden change in air temperature. (Warm water doesn't hold oxygen as well as cooler water does.) This kit may be needed to restore the oxygen level for your fish. Also, fish may suffer from an oxygen deficit at night, when plants release carbon dioxide, so it's usually a good idea to leave your waterfall, fountain, or other aeration device operating all night. (You can also help aerate the pond by splashing water in with a hose or even by stirring it.)

■ **One or more plastic buckets for transporting fish.** For medium-size fish, a 5-gallon bucket is a good size; for large fish, get a short, wide bucket.

■ **A soft net (on a pole) for guiding fish into the bucket.** Lifting fish out of the water in a net is stressful to them, so you should use the net only to steer them into the bucket.

■ **An aquarium.** You'll need to use an aquarium as a "hospital tank" for treating sick fish, as a holding tank to inspect new fish before adding them to your pond, or as a winter home for the fish if you live in a cold climate. Consult an aquarium dealer about what size to buy. Obviously, size isn't as important if one or two fish will be in the tank for a few hours as it will be if you bring all your pond residents indoors for several months.

The aquarium should be filled with water from the pond, unless you have reason to believe something is wrong with the water quality. It should be connected to an aeration device of some kind, as sick fish will be additionally stressed by a lack of oxygen. Medications in the water also increase the need for aeration. Where you put the tank is a matter of practicality, as long as it's kept out of the sun so that the water doesn't heat up; indoors is best, because some treatments might take as long as two weeks.

If you don't want to add rock salt to your pond as discussed earlier, use the aquarium for a salt bath and then return the treated fish to your pond.

Maintenance. Kits to test for oxygen, ammonia, nitrites, and other substances are necessary to help keep fish healthy. Pond salt and a transfer net are two of the tools you will find useful.

Bringing Fish Home

Don't buy your fish until the water temperature in your pond consistently stays at least 50°F, which is the temperature at which most species become active in spring. If you have a reputable pond supplier in your area, it's worth driving out of your way to buy fish there. The salespeople will be more knowledgeable; they will probably offer a guarantee; and when they slip your new fish in a plastic bag for the ride home, they will inject the bag with oxygen.

Certain mail-order water-garden suppliers ship fish over long distances, although spending a day or two in the belly of a plane at a variety of different temperatures will stress out even the most well-packaged creature.

Fish from a pet store may have a harder time making the transition from indoors to out. But if buying fish this way seems your only option, study the list of fish diseases on page 165 so that you can identify a sickly fish. Ask the store staff whether they guarantee the fish's health for a length of time, and if they can treat the fish for parasites before you take them home. On the ride home, keep the fish in a cool, dark place. A picnic cooler with a lid is a handy way to transport them. Don't put them in the trunk or keep them in a closed car while you run other errands.

Lower the bag into the pond, and add some of the pond water. Doing this over a period of 10 to 15 minutes will

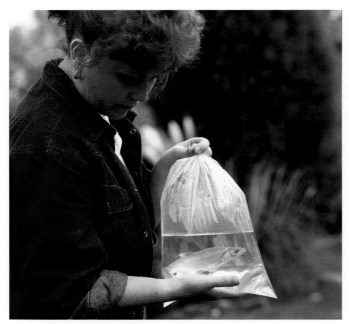

When bringing new fish home or when moving them around, handle with care. They are easily stressed and do better with a gradual transition.

ease the transition to a different temperature and different water quality. It's best not to add the water from the bag to the pond, on the chance that it contains parasites. Instead, ease the fish out with your hand or, less desirably, a net.

Watch the fish for an hour. Fish are apt to try to jump out of a new pond. If they continue to jump out or gasp, check the water. Move them to an aquarium to fix the problem. Feed the fish sparingly for the next couple of days.

SPAWNING

Fish play their mating game in late spring and early summer, usually when the water has warmed to between 54° and 60°F. Males get tiny white bumps on their gills, and some become brighter colored. Females take on a slightly pregnant look because their ovaries are bulging with thousands of eggs.

A frantic morning chase around the pond convinces the female to lay her eggs, usually on an underwater plant, after which the male fertilizes them with his sperm, or milt. Babies, known as fry, hatch about a week later and spend the first day clinging to the plant or the side of the pond or hanging vertically in the water, absorbing their egg sacs for nutrition.

Fish fry are vulnerable not only to pond insects and other predators too small to bother adult fish but also to other fish species and even to their own parents. If you want to save as many fry as possible, buy a spawning mat (not unlike a crude welcome mat) to put on the pond bottom. Remove it to an aquarium when you see eggs on its surface. The young fry need a high-protein diet of flakes, brine shrimp, or daphnia.

FISH DISEASES

Even a novice can spot many of the changes in behavior or appearance that mean a fish is ill. A sick fish may act lethargic or huddle against the edge of the pond, gasp for air, swim frantically and bump the pond edge, or be bullied by other fish. It might clamp its fins against its body or develop red veins or fins, or its dorsal (spine) fin may be droopy.

If you see unusual symptoms, check the water temperature, pH, and levels of ammonia and nitrites to determine whether any of these is stressing the fish. Correct any water-quality problems, and see whether your fish improve.

FEEDING YOUR FISH

In a well-balanced pond, fish theoretically do not need to be fed at all. But supplemental feeding is usually necessary. You'll enjoy watching them scurry after their food and hurry to the water's edge to greet you.

Fish need supplemental food in spring and fall. They become active as soon as the water has reached 50°F in spring, but this early in the season not many plants will have leafed out yet, nor will there be many insects and other little creatures for them to feast on. At this time, don't feed your fish protein. Instead, choose wheat germ or other similar high-carbohydrate foods, which are easy for fish to digest. Once the water has warmed another 10°F or so and their activity level rises dramatically, they need more protein in the form of chopped worms, daphnia (also called water fleas), or some frozen or freeze-dried fish foods. (Daphnia can be seen as pale pink clouds in the water and will help keep the pond clean by eating free floating algae.) Most fish-food products on the market contain around 40 percent protein, which should be adequate in a balanced pond.

These supplements come in sticks, pellets, or flakes. All of these forms float, which allows you to net out uneaten food and keep the pond clean. A granular form, although often less expensive, will sink; you'll save money, but you can't be sure how much is turning into waste at the bottom of your pond. This waste is a potential cause

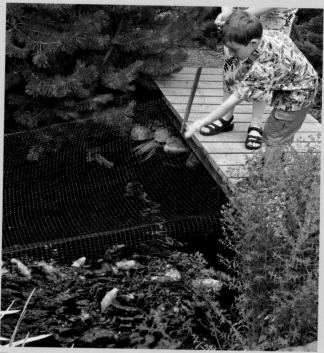

The water temperature should be above 70°F for young koi to properly digest and metabolize their food. (Note the net to keep predators away from the fish.)

of disease, so avoid overfeeding your fish.

Feeding Schedule. Feed your fish once or twice each day when spring first arrives; then gradually decrease your feedings to every other day or so. They should survive quite well without feeding if you take a short vacation. Never feed them more food than they can eat in five minutes, and use a net to remove any food that remains. Avoid feeding them late in the day. Their metabolism goes up after they eat, so they then need more oxygen. Because plants give off carbon dioxide at night, less oxygen will be available to the fish then. Cut back gradually on food as temperatures drop in autumn and fish become less active. Stop feeding for the winter once water temperatures fall below 50°F. Your fish will survive the winter by living off the fat they have stored. They will use these resources slowly because their metabolism has slowed.

Sometimes diseased fish will benefit from a change of diet; try a different brand of fish food, and see if your fish improve. Members of the carp family will also eat worms as well as vegetables, such as lettuce scraps and peas.

Always select reputable name-brand commercial fish food. The floating type lets you easily remove any leftovers.

When fish become ill remove them from the pond using a net. Nurse them back to health in the aquarium water.

COMMON FISH DISEASES

If fish are clearly ill, it's often best to remove them to an aquarium, where you can treat them with a medicine or salt bath and keep the disease from spreading to the rest of the pond inhabitants. Handle the fish as little as possible to minimize additional stress. Net each fish underwater, guide it into an underwater bowl or bucket, and then lift out the bowl and lower into the aquarium water.

Some of the more common fish diseases are described below. Consult your supplier or a veterinarian for more specific treatments.

Anchor Worm. This isn't a disease but a tubelike parasite, about ¾ inch long, which attaches under the fish's gill with its hooked head while it produces two eggs at its nether end. The main symptom is a swelling where the parasite is attached. Catch the fish, and remove each anchor worm with tweezers; then treat the spot with an antiseptic such as merbromin or iodine (from a drugstore).

Dropsy. This ailment, most often caused by bacteria, has such a telltale symptom that it's sometimes called the pinecone disease: the fish swells, and its scales bristle away from its sides, making it look like a pinecone. Fish will also get bug-eyed. Dropsy is hard to cure, although a salt-bath treatment may help.

Finrot, or Bodyrot. The fish—often a fantail or a shubunkin—develops a white line on its caudal area (where the body joins the tail), and this area becomes inflamed. The tissue disintegrates and needs to be gently removed with a sharp knife; then the fish is put on treatment with a special antibiotic. Antibiotics can be administered in fish food, in water in an aquarium, or on the affected area directly. It's always an excellent idea to consult a veterinarian before you administer antibiotics, just to make certain that you're using the correct medication and dosage.

Flukes. There are both gill and skin flukes; in either case they are microscopic, parasitic flatworms. When they prey on fish, you'll see excess mucus plus irritated puffy patches or loss of color, and the fish will act irritated, banging against objects, twitching their fins, and opening and closing their mouths rapidly. A salt bath may help.

Fungus. When fish are stressed and their protective mucous layer breaks down, they become susceptible to fungi normally present in pond water. Instead of tolerating these fungi, the fish sprout cottony growths. Most fish suppliers sell fungicides that can treat the problem.

Lice. These flat, gelatinous creatures are only ¼ inch long but have clearly visible legs and eyespots. The tissue damage they cause by attaching themselves to the fish, often on the fins and gills, can eventually prove fatal to the victim. Remove lice deftly with tweezers, and treat the fish with an antiseptic such as iodine.

Tuberculosis. This is a highly contagious bacterial disease that can cause rapid weight loss, as the human version does. Fish may lose color and develop raw swollen patches, and fins may waste away. It is almost always fatal. To prevent the spread of this disease, remove any fish from the pond as soon as you suspect it is tubercular.

Ulcers. Bacteria common to pond water will cause stressed fish to develop ulcers, popped eyes, bloody patches, and ragged-looking fins. Treat with an antibiotic for fish, and test the water to determine what's stressing the fish.

White Spot. Fish with this disease (technically, ichthyophthiriasis, or "ich" for short) will have spots like grains of salt, similar to those that males develop on their gills during the mating season. But these will be all over the fish's body, and because they itch, the fish may bump against the sides of the pond. White spot is caused by the parasitic protozoan *Ichthyophthirius multifilis*, hence the disease's tongue-twisting technical name; consult your dealer or veterinarian about a cure.

Fish tick or lice is a tropical-fish parasite that can be removed with tweezers.

Keeping Fish Healthy

- Test water quality regularly. If you have a lot of fish, be particularly vigilant about ammonia and nitrite levels.
- Be prepared to remove fish quickly. Have an aquarium or other hospital tank available should they display any signs of distress or illness.
- Be aware of predators. Install protective netting or fencing if you see birds or animals lurking around your pond.
- Find a reliable expert. Have a contact number handy for a trusted supplier or veterinarian whom you can call for advice.

WINTER CARE OF FISH

If you've made your pond at least 18 inches deep (2 feet deep in cold climates), goldfish and other hardy fish should survive winter there because the water in your pond won't freeze all the way to the bottom. But it's also crucial to keep the surface of your pond from freezing solid. If that happens, the normal exchange of oxygen and carbon dioxide can no longer occur, and poisonous methane released by any decaying organic matter will be trapped in the water. You can't just bang a hole in the ice, however, because the shock waves will carry through the water and can injure or kill the fish. An electric pond heater is the most reliable way to keep a hole open in the ice, but you can also use a pan of boiling water. Some northern gardeners erect greenhouses over their ponds to keep them from freezing. (See Winter on page 191 of Chapter 11, for more details and other ideas for protecting and maintaining your pond.)

FISH PREDATORS

Even if you live in a city, don't assume that your fishpond is safe from natural predators. In the heart of Washington, D.C., the owner of a rooftop pond has seen blue herons swooping overhead (although she hasn't caught them landing) and had to have a raccoon removed by animal-control officials. Because effective ways to protect fish from predators can be unsightly, you may have to forgo either finny friends or aesthetics.

BIRDS AND BEASTS

You can discourage or slow down terrestrial predators such as raccoons with dense plantings of grasses around the pond edge. Don't fret too much about cats, which love to watch fish but are rarely able to catch them (and hate to risk taking a swim). Retrievers and other water-loving dogs don't harm fish, but they make themselves a nuisance by knocking over planters and puncturing liners with their sharp nails.

Herons. These entertaining birds, which goose-step with backward-jointed knees, are plentiful along the coast as well as inland waterways. The great blue heron can grow 6 feet tall; the green heron and related egret are smaller but equally skilled fishers. Because they walk to the water, rather than swooping down like seagulls, they can be discouraged with fishing line strung around the pond about 6 inches off the ground. Statues of herons may deter them—these birds like to dine alone—but usually not for long.

Heron. Although herons are great fun to watch, they need to be kept away from your pond. Trip them up with a "fence" of fishing line.

Kingfisher. Belted Kingfishers go after prey by taking a vertical plunge. Remove any high perch from which they can dive.

Gull. Because gulls are divers, defeat them by to installing netting over the pond. This will make them move on to easier foraging.

Belted Kingfisher. This is another great bird to watch—for its spiky punk hairdo, distinctive loud crick call, and ability to plunge after fish in a vertical dive. Kingfishers kill fish by beating them against their perch, tossing them in the air, and swallowing them headfirst. Since you don't want this happening to your fish, avoid any kind of tall perch located conveniently near your pond.

Gulls. Compared to herons, gulls rarely fish in ponds. They're happier hunting around larger bodies of water or scavenging garbage dumpsters. If diving birds become a problem, the only solution is to suspend a fine net just above the pond.

Raccoon. Of all pond predators, raccoons are the most feared. But while they love water, always washing their food fastidiously, they like to enter the water at their own pace and won't appreciate a sheer drop off the side of a pond. In short, they're looking for the most graceful entrance possible. Where raccoons are common, design fishponds with steeply vertical sides and no shallow plant ledges. In addition, plant the perimeter thickly with grasses and other dense marginal plants. This type of barrier will put a real dent in their fishing efforts. If problems with raccoons become overwhelming, don't give up on keeping fish. Instead, call your local animal control agency or your state's fish and

Raccoon. Considered Pond Enemy Number 1, raccoons will often be deterred by a pond with steep sides.

game department for savvy ideas or assistance. Avoid direct contact with raccoons, which can be fierce fighters when cornered. If you see one out during the day, this may mean it has rabies.

TROUBLESOME INSECTS

There are a number of insects that you should be on the alert for if you see them in or around your pond. Some are fascinating to watch while others can be nuisances, preying on your fish. Following are some examples of troublesome bugs you may see hanging in or around your pond.

Diving Beetle (*Dytiscus* **species and** *Acilius* **species).** These dark brown or green oval beetles are native throughout North American waters and can range from 1/16 to more than 1½ inches long. Although they usually live on water insects, mites, and larvae, they will also attack small fish, frogs, and tadpoles. The great diving beetle, which is dark brown with golden trim, is especially fierce; it will attack fish and suck their body fluids.

Water Boatman and Backswimmer (*Corixa* **and** *Notonecta* **species).** Somewhat elongated, these beetles are dark gray-brown, often with darker bellies marked with triangles. You can see the bellies of some species because they are swiming upside down, using their legs like oars. They are only capable of wounding larger fish but can claim their fair share of newborn fry.

Giant Water Bug (*Lethocerus americanus***).** Some-times more than 2 inches long and 1 inch wide, this brown bomber skulks around in bottom vegetation. The bug uses hooked front legs to grab its prey, injects fluids that paralyze it and dissolve its innards, then sucks it dry. Victims of giant water bugs include other insects, tadpoles, and small fish.

Dragonfly (*Order Odonata***).** Who doesn't love to watch dragonflies and damselflies flitting colorfully and hovering among the water plants? During their aquatic nymph stage, though, some species will eat small fish.

Water Scorpion (*Nepa* **species).** These 1-inch-long insects lie in wait among submerged plants and, like the giant water bug, grasp their prey with their feet before biting it and sucking it dry. They will wound, although not kill, fairly large fish.

Whirligig Beetle (*Dineutus* **species and** *Gyrinus* **species).** These black oval beetles, less than ¼-inch long, are endless fun to watch because of the way they spin around on the water surface. They need air to breathe and can blow themselves a submarine bubble for diving underwater. They usually eat other aquatic insects but will sometimes eat fish fry. You can net them off the surface if you want to protect your fry.

Diving Beetle. These oval beetles are well-equipped predators that usually live on insects but have been known to snack on fish, frogs, and tadpoles.

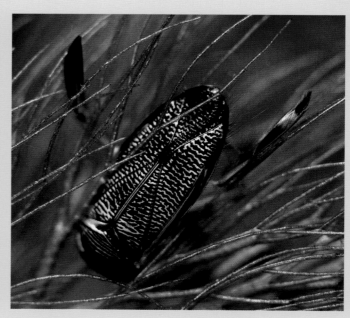

Water Boatman. Entertaining swimmers, water boatman beetles will do the backstroke across your water surface and will keep down your fly population.

Giant Water Bug. This 2-in. water bug would be easy to spot if it didn't hide in bottom vegetation. It paralyzes and sucks dry its prey.

Dragonfly. Much like helicopters, dragonflies dart around on their gossamer wings to the delight of on-lookers. In their nymph stage, they may eat small fish.

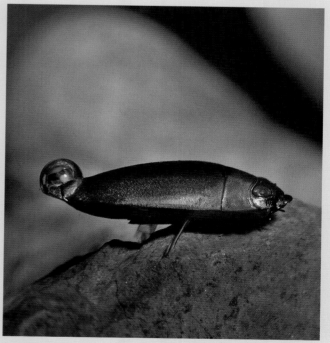

Water Scorpion. A ferocious predator that can wound large fish and kill smaller ones, the water scorpion lies in wait, then pounces, grasping prey with its feet and sucking out the victim's innards.

Whirligig Beetle. Usually more amusing than harmful, a whirligig beetle spins like a top on the pond surface. It sometimes supplements its diet of other aquatic insects by eating fish fry.

OTHER WATER-LOVING CREATURES

In addition to fish and some members of the insect community, there are other creatures who enjoy the water. Here are some to consider.

Frogs (*Rana* species) and Toads (*Bufo* species). Toads are land dwellers but, like frogs, lay their eggs in water and spend the first part of their lives as tadpoles. Tadpoles are beneficial for ponds, acting as scavengers and cleaning up algae and spent vegetation. Toads will eventually hop away from water to live on land and will help keep your garden free from slugs and bugs. Frogs remain in and near water; they eat primarily insects, although bullfrogs (which can grow to 6 inches long) are capable of eating good-size fish. In winter, frogs hibernate in mud near the pond; in spring, they may move away from your pond to find a new mate at another one. Wildlife experts advise not buying bullfrog tadpoles, which have voracious appetites, but instead waiting for smaller, sometimes endangered, native frogs to colonize your pond.

Mussels and Clams. You may want to introduce these bivalves into your pond as natural filters—unless you have koi, which will eat them. They'll need a shallow tray of coarse sand to burrow in. Avoid the zebra mussel (*Dreissena polymorpha*), which has become a serious problem in our country's waterways. Look for the brown swan mussel (*Anodonta cygnea*), which requires a large pond, or the freshwater clam (*Elliptio crassidens*). Be sure to remove any dead mussels immediately, as they decompose with a strong unpleasant odor and can pollute your pond.

Newts (*Notophthalmus* species). These lizardlike reptiles spend the first few months of their lives as aquatic larvae. Most then spend a couple of years on land hunting insects, crustaceans, and worms; unlike salamanders, adult newts eventually return to water and again become aquatic. Males develop showy crests during the spring mating season.

Snails. Water-garden suppliers often sell snails to help keep ponds clear of algae, decaying vegetation, and wasted fish food. Those most commonly offered are the ramshorn snail (*Planorbis corneus*), which has a spiral shell, and the black Japanese or trapdoor snail (*Viviparus malleatus*). The latter is the more desirable of the two because it won't snack on your prized plants. Trapdoors bear live young; other snails

Frog. Frogs will serenade you with their nighttime chorus, but males will often abandon the pond in search of a mate.

Mussel. Provide a little sand for them, and mussels or clams will obligingly serve as natural water filters. Be aware, though, that koi and raccoons both love to eat them.

Newt. A cousin of the salamander, the newt starts out life in the water, has a two-year hitch on land, and then returns to water.

Snail. Working hard as the pond's cleanup crew, snails take care of algae, decaying vegetation, and uneaten fish food.

lay eggs in jellylike masses on the undersides of leaves. Different species of snails may show up in your pond and will serve the same useful function, but they'll munch on live plants if they multiply too rapidly. Don't tolerate the presence of the great pond snail (*Lymnaea stagnalis*). Shaped like a 1-inch ice cream cone, it will quickly overpopulate your pond. You can attract snails by floating a lettuce leaf on the pond—remove the leaf when enough snails have boarded it. To further keep their numbers in check, wipe egg masses off of leaf undersides. Stock eight to ten small snails or six to eight large snails per square yard of water surface area.

Turtles (Order *Testudines*). A turtle that does laps in your pond will also add its waste to the water. But you may need to learn to coexist, as many turtles are endangered; moving them to another habitat is illegal in many states. Fortunately, snapping turtles—the ones most likely to cause problems—are not endangered, and it's legal in some areas to hunt them. Discourage turtles by making sure they don't have an easy way into your pond.

Snakes. You shouldn't have to worry about snakes moving into your pond unless you live near another body of water where aquatic snakes are at home. The most common are the water snakes (*Nerodia sipedon* and other *Nerodia* species), nonpoisonous snakes native to the eastern United States and into Canada. Other species, such as garter snakes, may stop for a drink and eat your fish when they do. The dangerous water moccasin, or cottonmouth (*Agkistrodon piscivorus*), is native to the southern states. It holds its flat head well above water when it swims (unlike other water snakes); fortunately, it's rarely active during the day. If you have any reason to suspect that the snake in your pond is a water moccasin, call your local animal-control official. Snakes can eat your fish and frogs. With the exception of the aggressive water moccasin, snakes you'll find near water are afraid of humans and will try to retreat, unless they feel threatened. If you encounter one, always leave the snake an exit.

Turtle. Because they need air to breathe, turtles may avoid your pond if they don't have an easy way in and out. They are destructive and can harm both plants and fish.

Snake. Most snakes, such as this banded water snake, are harmless and should be tolerated in your garden. Aquatic snakes aren't likely to visit your pond unless you live near water.

Attracting Birds

A water feature of any kind or size can be a magnet for birds. The most irresistible will be those that provide a shallow area where birds can drink or bathe with ease. Birds are especially drawn to moving water, even if it's only a tiny trickle.

Birds need two other things if you want them to hang around for any length of time: food and shelter. You can provide food by putting bird feeders near your pond and by growing food-bearing plants. Feeders are easy but do have disadvantages. Some people feel that feeders can make birds lazy about looking elsewhere for food, so they become dependent on you to keep them fed. Feeders can also be a source of bird diseases. You need to keep them clean. (Scrape out old seed, or wash out hummingbird feeders, before refilling them.) Sterilize them yearly with one part bleach to nine parts water.

BIRD FOOD

If you want to attract a variety of species whether you have feeders or not, you should fill your garden with plants that offer seeds and berries. In summer and fall, birds will flock to seeds of sunflowers (*Helianthus* species), black-eyed Susans (*Rudbeckia fulgida* or *R. hirta*), purple coneflowers (*Echinacea purpurea*), and many ornamental grasses. Garden staples such as zinnias (*Zinnia* hybrids) and marigolds (*Tagetes* hybrids) are also good seed producers.

Some good berry plants include eastern red cedar (*Juniperus virginiana*), black cherry and chokecherry (*Prunus serotina* and *P. virginiana*), mulberry (*Morus rubra*), hollies of all types (Ilex species), dogwoods (*Cornus* species), and viburnums (*Viburnum* species). The larger, more prolific berry producers such as red cedars and mulberries should be kept a good distance from your water garden so that scooping up uneaten berries won't add to your pond-maintenance chores. This is rarely a serious problem with smaller trees and shrubs; just try to find a leftover of something you might also like to eat, such as a juicy blueberry or black cherry!

Birds appreciate a garden that's a bit untidy. Among good sources of berries are many "weeds" such as sumac and Virginia creeper (both of which are gaining in appreciation as garden plants), wild blackberries, wild grapes, and even poison ivy. A slightly overgrown garden will harbor more insects, which is good news if you want to attract insect-eating birds. Branches or stumps along the water's edge, or a rock jutting out of the water, let birds land and possibly hunt small water insects.

Berries can attract songbirds in fall and winter.

When this rudbeckia finishes blooming, its seeds will feed birds in the fall.

PROVIDE NESTING SPOTS

Shelter is just as important as insects and seeds if you want to attract birds. Dense plantings of leafy shrubs or evergreens provide places where birds can hide from predators or build their nests. Some birds, like wrens, chickadees, sparrows, and bluebirds will nest in birdhouses. Choose one made from wood (not metal, which heats up). Many birds rely on insects to feed their young, So, by attracting them, they'll help to reduce bug populations in your garden. If you own cats that go outdoors, consider adding a collar with a bell to warn visiting birds

Shelter. A birdhouse may persuade feathered friends to stay. Plant shrubs and tall grasses where they can hide from enemies.

AVOID CHEMICALS

Pesticides will not only kill "bad" bugs, but will eliminate beneficial insects that many birds eat, including worms and grubs in the lawn. Birds, too, may be harmed by pesticides on insects and plant parts that they eat. Herbicides used to control lawn weeds will harm plants if they wash into the pond. Even common fertilizers, if they get into your pond, will upset the healthy balance needed for plants and fish. Seek out nontoxic control options for garden pests. If you must fertilize near a pond, use as little as possible and try organic or slow-release products to reduce runoff. You will be rewarded with the songs of colorful winged wonders on summer mornings and at dusk, as well as new species every spring and fall during migration.

Visiting Foragers. The red-winged blackbird may drop by to forage. Avoid garden chemicals, which kill bugs that birds eat.

PART 4

Water Feature Maintenance

Afew routine tasks will keep your pond or other water feature flourishing. Maintaining water quality is critical to a healthy pond. Clear pond water is not only important for fish and plants, but it will also be more attractive. Other tasks involve seasonal maintenance and troubleshooting. We'll start by addressing water quality, which is one of the greatest challenges in water gardening.

CHAPTER 10

Ecological Balance

Factors that affect the ecological balance of your pond include its size and depth, the amount of sun it receives, water temperature and movement, pollutants from runoff, and the kind and number of plants and fish you have. Because of this complicated ecological interplay, your pond can take anywhere from several weeks to several months to achieve an ideal balance. Then the pond can stay balanced indefinitely unless any of these factors changes appreciably.

How Your Pond Works

Your pond or water garden is a small, self-contained ecosystem. When you introduce aquatic plants, they draw nutrients (especially nitrates and phosphates) from the water and, if they're potted, also from the soil. These nutrients, combined with sunlight, are what nourish plants, enabling them to grow and thereby release oxygen into the water as a result of photosynthesis.

When fish are introduced into this ecosystem, they consume the oxygen produced by the plants. Fish derive other benefits from plants. Surface plants such as water lilies help keep water from overheating by providing shade from the hot summer sun. Plants also give fish a place to hide from other fish, cats, raccoons, birds, and other predators.

In turn, fish provide gases and nutrients that plants need in order to grow: carbon dioxide from their breathing, and nitrogen and other chemicals from their wastes. Fish also help control populations of plant-eating insects. To some measure, they likewise consume some of the plants and thus keep excessive plant growth in check.

When the numbers of fish and plants in the pond reach a stable relationship (not too many of one or the other), the pond is in biological balance. The reason balanced ponds are relatively clear is because plants and fish in tandem help control the algal growth that can turn the water cloudy. Scavengers such as snails and tadpoles also help balance the pond by consuming algae and organic debris.

Water Problems. The most common water problems are caused by having too many fish or feeding the fish too much. A buildup of dead plant material, having too many living plants covering the surface, prolonged hot weather,

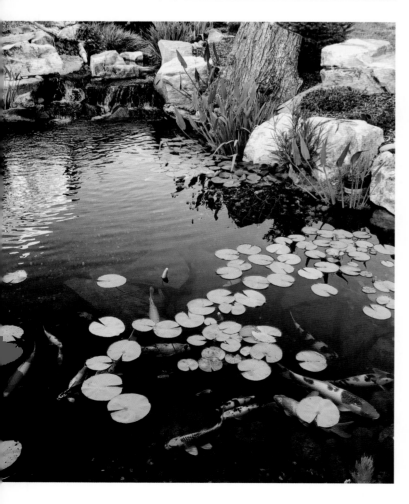

A waterfall (left) maintains the water quality and keeps the pond aerated.

An algae-free surface (right) can prevent oxygen depletion.

or an excess of algae can deplete oxygen and lead to more problems. Your water may also contain pollutants from pond-building materials and toxic chemicals that may have been washed or blown into the water from outside sources.

Incorporating a waterfall or a fountain in your pond design will promote good water quality. Either of these features will aerate your pond and help ensure that fish have all the oxygen they need. Lack of oxygen will bring fish to the surface, gasping for air. This sometimes happens with little warning after long periods of hot, dry weather. But it can also occur in stormy weather, when water may turn and decrease available oxygen in the pond's top layer, or when prolonged cloudy weather disrupts photosynthesis by your pond's plants. You can rescue gasping fish quickly by oxygenating the pond with spray from a garden hose. Or you can have on hand a separate aeration kit that includes an air pump. If the need for aeration arises, you simply place the pump about an inch below the water surface, screening the pump's intake so that it doesn't suck in small fish or other tiny pond creatures while in operation. When fish behavior returns to normal, these measures can be discontinued.

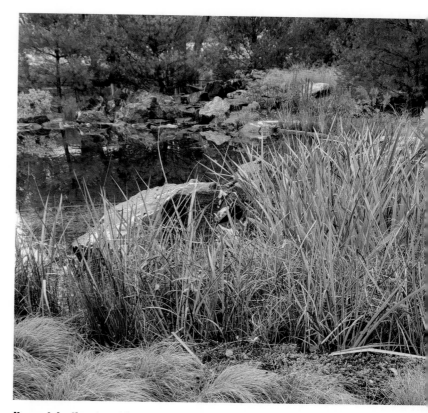

It may take time to get the water, plants and fish to coexist in a balanced environment.

Nitrogen Cycle

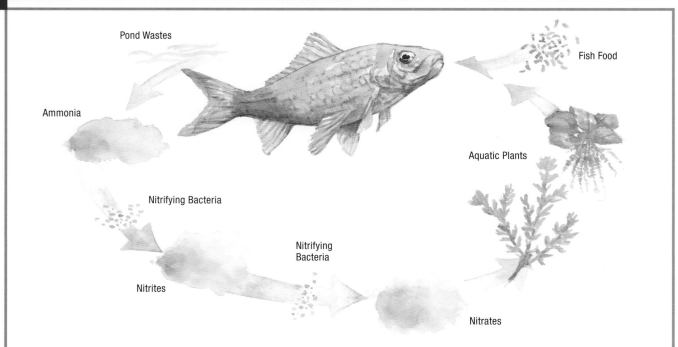

Pond Wastes

Fish Food

Ammonia

Aquatic Plants

Nitrifying Bacteria

Nitrifying Bacteria

Nitrites

Nitrates

Ammonia from pond wastes can be fatal to fish. Bacteria in biological filters and some algae convert ammonia first to nitrites (also harmful), then to nitrates that plants can consume.

ALGAE: FASCINATING AND SOMETIMES HELPFUL

Algae may look unappealing in your pond, but they can be beautiful under a microscope. Under magnification, their usual colors of green, brown, and yellow can give way to reds, blues, oranges, and other hues.

Algae lack flowers and the leaves, stems, and roots that circulate nutrients in "higher" plants. They range from the single-celled forms that can cloud your pond to sea-dwelling kelp more than 200 feet long. The type that turns a pond murky is called planktonic, a term that covers all forms that are suspended in water. Under a microscope, you would see that these algae have threadlike "tails" (flagella) that allow them to move through the water.

Planktonic algae thrive when it's warm and sunny. When the weather cools in fall, you might see more filamentous algae—the type that forms long, hairy-looking strands. Some of these algae are yellow or gold. *Spirogyra*, the melodic name of which derives from its spiral

bands of chlorophyll, consists of long strings of cells that attach themselves to the pond bottom and other surfaces.

Not all algae live in ponds. One called *Haematococcus* prefers shallow water such as birdbaths. (You might see its telltale reddish color if you have the Japanese water basin called a *tsukubai*.) Others grow on moist stones or even in soil. Some of these soil dwellers are the blue-green algae, or cyanobacteria, that have become such a popular item in many health-food stores.

Mosslike algae that grow on the sides of the pond are beneficial and a sign of good pond health. Because they harbor the same kind of bacteria found in an artificial biological filter, they help to remove toxic chemicals from your water.

CONTROLLING ALGAE

When you first fill your pond, the water will be crystal clear. After a few days, however, the water will turn murky and take on a greenish tinge. This is caused by microscopic, single-celled, free-floating algae. Their presence is to be expected until aquatic plants have established themselves. Submerged (oxygenating) plants eventually starve the algae by outcompeting them for available nutrients. Floating plants and water lilies likewise help starve the algae; they not only consume nutrients but cut off the sunlight that algae need to grow. To a lesser degree, fish, snails, and accidentally introduced algae eaters such as water fleas also help.

Algal Concentration. You can expect to have some algae in the pond, even after it's balanced. At a level that causes only a slight discoloration, algae are not harmful to fish or plants; they help conceal the artificial-looking liner or shell as well as any planters or pump on the pond bottom. As the pond matures, most of the free-floating algae will eventually be replaced by various visible forms of filamentous, mossy, and slime algae growing on the sides and bottom of the pond, as well as on plants, rocks, and any other convenient surface.

When algal growth becomes excessive, however, it's worse than unsightly. Not only do algae consume the pond's oxygen in the process of decaying, but in excessive amounts they will cut off sunlight to oxygenating plants below the surface, reducing the oxygen supply even further. Algae can also coat the floating leaves of water lilies and other plants so that they lose their ability to help balance pond gases. When pond water is depleted of oxygen, fish begin to gasp for air and eventually die.

Natural Control. Make every effort to control algae naturally with oxygenating plants and pond scavengers such as tadpoles and snails—or mechanically. Algae that forms a scummy mat on the surface, sometimes called filamentous algae, can be removed with a fine-mesh net or by twirling it around a long-handled brush or rake as you would twirl spaghetti on a fork.

Chemical Control. You can buy chemicals called algicides to kill algae. Many people use algicides for initial algal control after they install a pond or to control the algal blooms that tend to occur in spring. But like any garden chemical, algicides are just a temporary remedy and not a cure. Moreover, they can cause other problems. Some algicides are toxic to fish, and those sold in pet stores for use in aquariums, in particular, will affect the growth of other water plants. (Always check the package label.) Furthermore, these products do not guard against the growth of new algae, which is inevitable. A much better, long-term solution, in addition to the natural controls mentioned above, is adding one or more filters to your system. (See "Filtration" on page 182.) If algal growth continues to be a problem even after some type of filtration has been installed, consult a pond specialist.

Algae removal. Excess algae is unsightly and unhealthy for your pond. It's easily removed with a stick, rake, or long-handled brush.

Balancing a New Pond

Once you've done all the hard work to install your pond, you'll be eager to populate it with plants and fish. But a bit of patience now will pay off with fewer problems later. Do your homework by calling the local water authorities so that you will know what chemicals your water supply contains; then you can obtain test kits and any chemicals you will need to correct chlorination or any other anticipated imbalances. (See "What's in Your Water" on the next page.) Follow the steps below to create a natural biological balance in your brand-new pond.

Rinse and Fill the Pond. If you've used pool paints, wood stains or preservatives, pipe-joint glues, or similar wet materials on your pond, let them dry thoroughly, because otherwise they can contaminate pond water and poison fish and plants. Treat mortar, concrete, and cement with an acidic solution to prevent lime from leaching from these materials, which would make the pond water too alkaline. (See "Constructing a Lined In-Ground Pond," Step 6 on page 71.) After you've rinsed the solution off, drained the water, and rinsed out any debris remaining from pond construction, fill the pond with fresh water. If you've installed a filter, run it continuously for the first few days before introducing plants. Depending on your situation, you may have to drain and refill your pond several times.

Test the Water. When you first fill the pond, the water may contain chemicals and minerals that are toxic to fish and plants. Well water may contain hydrogen sulfide (also produced by decaying organic matter and detectable by a slight rotten-egg smell), which requires extra aeration. Tap water from public supply systems may contain chlorine, chlorine dioxide, chloramine, or ammonia; well water won't. Allowing tap water to stand for a few days will get rid of most free chlorine, but chlorine dioxide and chloramine require chemical treatment. (See next page.)

After filling the pond but before introducing plants or fish, test the water. You can buy kits from pond dealers, garden suppliers, and pet shops to test for most problems. The kits usually include instructions for correcting any problems you find. Some pond dealers and pet shops provide water-testing services and can advise you on proper treatment.

Correct Water Conditions. Follow instructions included with the test kits to correct any problems that have been detected. Some fish and plant dealers recommend

INTRODUCE FISH TO THE POND

Two to three weeks after you've introduced plants and corrected any adverse water conditions such as the presence of chloramine (next page), it's safe to add fish, snails, and tadpoles. The size and number of plants and fish a pond will support will vary with the amount of available oxygen and sunlight and the water quality. A pond with good water circulation and filtration will support a larger population of fish than will a stagnant pond with no filter.

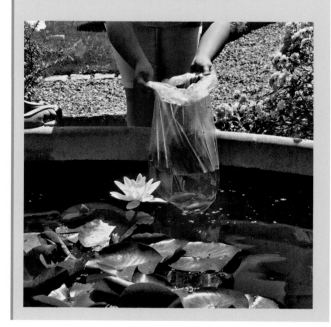

giving the pond a dose of a general-purpose water conditioner before adding fish or plants, just to be on the safe side. But just as you shouldn't use chemicals in the rest of your garden unless there's a good reason, you shouldn't use water conditioners in your pond unless tests show that they're actually needed. Even if you use a conditioner to achieve your initial water balance, try to determine the source of the pollution to prevent future problems.

Introduce Plants. Once water tests show that you've removed chloramines and that other measures are within a safe range—and the danger of frost is past—you can add plants. The sooner you add them, the sooner they can begin their balancing act of helping to prevent algal buildup, and providing oxygen and food for fish. The pond water will likely start to turn green right then, but it will probably clear up in a few weeks as plants become established.

WHAT'S IN YOUR WATER

Water-garden suppliers offer kits you can use to test water for potentially harmful chemicals or unhealthy situations. Here's a quick explanation of what you might find. (For more on monitoring contaminants, see "Water Quality" on page 160.)

■ **Ammonia.** Ammonia is present in fish waste, so the usual explanation for high levels of ammonia is having too many fish. But some public water supplies contain ammonia if they've been treated with chloramines. Decaying organic matter will also contribute to ammonia levels. Ammonia will stress your fish, and too much will kill them. Clean out the pond bottom, and change at least 50 percent of the water. The best control for an ongoing problem with excess ammonia is having a biological filter installed.

■ **Chlorine.** The most common additive in municipal water supplies, chlorine is also fortunately the easiest to deal with as it dissipates within 24 to 48 hours. If you are adding chlorinated water to an existing pond, however, avoid adding more than 20 percent of the pond volume at one time to keep from harming the fish.

■ **Chloramine.** Also used to purify municipal water supplies, chloramine is a combination of chlorine and ammonia. It's more toxic to fish than chlorine and does not dissipate on standing. Find out from local water suppliers whether it's used in your tap water. If so, always have on hand the chemicals needed to neutralize it.

Fish need a pH level that is near neutral—between 6.6 and 7.5—so you should test the water periodically.

■ **Nitrites.** Resulting from the breakdown of ammonia, and so are most likely to be present when there are too many fish, nitrites suffocate fish. Control nitrites by changing half the water and treating it with 2½ pounds of dissolved pond salt per 100 gallons of water. (Dissolve the salt in a small amount of water first, and remove as many plants as possible.) You can make emergency filters by putting an absorbent substance called zeolite, sold by water suppliers, into mesh bags and dragging this around the pond.

■ **Nitrates.** Harmless compounds that result from the breakdown of ammonia or nitrites, nitrates serve as nutrients for plants. Their presence can show that your pond is going through a healthy process of converting those harmful compounds into the harmless form that plants can use. An excess of these nutrients can feed algae, however, and may indicate the need for more submerged plants (oxygenators) and other plants. In general, you won't need to test for nitrates.

■ **pH.** Short for "potential hydrogen," pH is a measure of acidity or alkalinity. The scale ranges from 1.0 (highly acidic) to 14.0 (highly alkaline), with 7.0 being neutral. Healthy pond water ranges in pH from 6.5 to 8.5. Tap water is more likely to be within this range than well water in some areas. Alkaline water can be caused by leaching from concrete or limestone rocks; fish tend to raise acidity. You can buy commercial products to adjust your pond water's pH, but use them carefully because a rapid change in pH is harmful to fish.

■ **Hardness.** Hard water, which has an excess of minerals, is not in itself harmful, but it can affect pH. If your tap water is hard, it may be alkaline; if your tap water is very soft, it's probably somewhat acidic. While there are kits available for testing hardness, you won't need them. If you suspect hard or soft water, just test the pH.

■ **Oxygen.** Maintaining high levels of oxygen in your pond keeps everything in balance. You might want to test for dissolved oxygen before adding fish or if the fish you have seem ill. If oxygen levels test low and you already have a waterfall or a fountain, add an aerating device to provide more oxygen. Oxygen can be depleted by having too many fish.

Filtration

If your goal is to have a small ornamental pond with a few plants and fish and you don't mind slightly cloudy water from time to time, you may not need a filter. If on the other hand, you have a large pond with many fish and want clear water for viewing them, a good filter will certainly help. Koi ponds, particularly, require clear, relatively pure water.

There are two basic types of filters: mechanical and biological. Mechanical filters trap algae and other particles, while biological filters convert chemical pollutants into harmless substances. When you're shopping for any type of filter, it's a good idea to seek out the advice of an independent dealer who carries several brand names.

Filters require pumps to move water through them. If the pump will be used for filtration only (and not also for a waterfall or fountain), arrange the system so that the pump intake is at one end of the pond—preferably the deepest—and the discharge is at the other. This will produce a slight current across the bottom of the pond, which will aid in recirculating the water to remove sediment and other water impurities.

A skimmer removes leaves and other large debris before they fall to the pond bottom and start decomposing.

STOCKING FORMULA FOR A BALANCED POND

It will take time and experimentation to achieve a balance between plant and animal life. For starters, use the following formula for stocking your pond. More detailed information is provided in "The Roles Plants Play" (see page 202) and "Pond Critters" (see Chapter 9, page 152).

■ Two bunches of submerged (oxygenating) plants per square yard of pond surface.

■ One medium to large water lily for each square yard of surface area, or enough water lilies, lotuses, or floating plants to cover 50 to 70 percent of the pond surface during the summer months. Most water plants go dormant during the winter months and then reestablish themselves during the spring. After they are established, you will have to divide or prune water lilies and other water plants occasionally to prevent them from overcrowding the pond.

■ Two inches of fish (length) for each square foot of pond surface in a pond 18 to 24 inches deep, or one koi for every 25 square feet in pond surface. When you are stocking your pond, keep in mind their eventual size, rate of growth, and the possibility that they will produce fry.

■ Eight to ten small snails or six to eight large snails per square yard of pond surface.

MECHANICAL FILTERS

Don't confuse mechanical filters with the filter screens and prefilters attached to pumps. Those screens are meant only to keep debris from clogging the pump impeller and fountain jets; they won't have any effect on water quality. Debris- or algae-filled water will be hard on your pump, however. (And a good mechanical filter will keep the screen or prefilter from clogging with mats of algae.)

The primary purpose of a mechanical filter is to trap large particles of suspended matter that can cloud water. This material includes fish waste, decaying organic matter, floating algae, and leftover fish food. Mechanical filters are less expensive than biological filters, and they start filtering your pool immediately, whereas biological filters are not effective for several weeks. Their main drawback is that they require frequent cleaning—at least once a week, and usually daily during the summer. Some mechanical filters (suction filters) are plumbed into the pump inlet, while others (pressure filters) are plumbed to the pump outlet. Some go inside the pond, and others are placed outside. An in-pond cartridge-type filter is sufficient for most small ponds (those with a capacity of less than 1,000 gallons). These devices use a corrugated polyester filter medium, which looks and works much the same as an automobile oil filter. Other small filters strain the debris through screens, foam, or woven fiber pads or wraps. Some let you add activated charcoal or a mineral called zeolite to remove ammonia and other chemical impurities from the water. None of these filter media has any particular advantage over another. The effectiveness of the filter depends more on its overall size, which is usually expressed as the surface area of the filter medium (in square feet) and the amount of water pumped through it (in gallons per hour). Manufacturers generally provide performance capacities for their filters—for example, "for ponds up to 300 gallons."

Pump and filter. The choices of mechanical filter and pump kits are numerous. They are generally rated for pond duty by the number of gallons in the pond.

Very large ponds (1,000 gallons or more) require more substantial filters. Options include a diatomaceous-earth filter or a high-rate sand filter, like those used in swimming pools. These large filters must be placed outside the pond and require a large pump and extensive plumbing.

Skimmers. A variation on the mechanical filter, called a skimmer, removes debris before it can sink to the bottom of the pond, holding it in a bag that you remove, much like a vacuum cleaner bag, a couple of times a month. Water gardeners with numerous deciduous trees find them indispensable. Skimmers are installed in the ground at the perimeter of the pond. Dealers recommend that they be run with a separate pump so that all of the water, not just that on the surface, is circulated regularly.

To be effective, a mechanical filter needs a high flow rate. The filter should be combined with a pump that can circulate all of the water in the pond once every two hours. If you've installed a fountain or waterfall, be sure you have a pump large enough to operate that feature and still provide sufficient circulation through the filter. Your water-garden dealer can advise you. If your budget allows, select a filter that exceeds the minimum requirements for your pond. The larger the filter, the less often you'll have to clean it. Fortunately, cleaning generally takes only a few minutes: you simply remove the filter pad, cartridge, or screen, and wash it off with a garden hose.

BIOLOGICAL FILTERS

The main function of biological filters is not to remove debris or even algae but to convert organic pollutants into relatively benign substances. Primarily this means converting ammonia from fish wastes (and to a lesser extent, from decaying plant matter and uneaten fish food) into nitrates, which can be absorbed by plants as a nutrient. If you have an excess of nitrates, however, you are more likely to have algae. To avoid this situation, be sure to include a sufficient number of oxygenating (submerged) plants. (See page 207 for descriptions.) They are particularly good at absorbing nitrates.

How They Work. Biological filters contain two or more layers of gravel or other medium that harbor large concentrations of beneficial nitrifying bacteria naturally found in ponds. As water slowly flows through the medium, these bacteria break down toxic ammonia (and nitrites, which result from the partial breakdown of ammonia) into nitrates. Other specialized microorganisms feast on single-celled algae passing through the filter. More complex types of biological filters may incorporate mechanical prefilters or compartments filled with activated charcoal, zeolites, or other media.

Look for a filter that includes an aeration tower, which provides additional oxygen for beneficial bacteria. Dirty water is pumped from the pond through the aeration tower to the bottom of the filter, where it slowly percolates up through the gravel filter medium (giving the bacteria a chance to eat their fill). It exits near the top of the filter and through a return pipe to the pond. (The return pipe can be hooked up to a waterfall.)

You can grow submerged plants in the top layer of gravel to provide additional oxygen for the bacteria and to absorb nutrients. The layers of gravel also serve as a crude mechanical filter to trap some suspended particles in the water, further clarifying it. If you still have problems with debris, add a mechanical filter to the filtering system.

Cleaning. About once a month, drain the filter by opening a drain valve at the bottom to remove accumulated silt and sediment. (You can use this to fertilize garden beds.) Then lightly rinse the filter medium to dislodge trapped particles. Don't use heavy sprays of chlorinated tap water, as that would tend to dislodge or even kill the beneficial bacteria in the filter medium; a small bucketful of rainwater is better. Give the filter a more thorough cleaning at the end of the season. (The bacteria won't survive below 55°F anyway, so once it gets cold, you don't have to worry about chlorinated water.)

Unlike mechanical filters, biological filters do not require a high flow rate to operate efficiently. The pump needs to turn over the total water volume only once every four to six hours. So even though they are initially more expensive than mechanical filters, they use less electricity. Biological filters need to be run constantly and don't start working efficiently until several weeks after they are installed—unless you give them a dose of "starter" bacteria, purchased from your water-garden supplier. Most of them are large, unsightly tanks placed outside the pond above water level and will need to be disguised somehow, such as behind a shed or under a deck. Several manufacturers have recently introduced small in-pond biological filters, but their capacity is limited to ponds of 300 gallons or less.

Basket for Additional Plants

Anchored Lava Rock

Filter Media

Filter Media

Water Passages

Waterfall box and biological filter. This upflow biological filter is used to convert organic wastes into nontoxic forms. As water flows through various media, harmful substances are broken down and rendered harmless.

OTHER WATER-CLEANING DEVICES

Mechanical and biological filters will be sufficient for most ponds. Where algae or fish diseases are an ongoing problem, consider adding one or more of the following devices.

Ultraviolet Sterilizers. Ultraviolet (UV) water sterilizers and clarifiers are sometimes used along with a biological filter. Plumbed into the inlet side of the filter, they use an ultraviolet bulb encased in a transparent, waterproof sleeve, which in turn is placed inside a tube plumbed into the system. When exposed to concentrated ultraviolet light, harmful microorganisms, algae, bacteria, viruses, and certain fish parasites are destroyed. The light also encourages minute organic particles to clump together so that they can be trapped in the filter. UV sterilizers usually aren't needed if you have a good biological filter. If you're constantly dealing with fish diseases or parasites, they may help.

Ozone Generators. An ozone generator converts oxygen from the air into ozone, infusing it into the water, where it breaks down chloramines, ammonia, nitrites, and phosphates into harmless gases that escape the pond. They purify water and reduce bacteria and fish parasites. Like UV light, ozone promotes the clumping of minute toxic waste particles, which then are more easily trapped by other filters. Ozone generators have been used for years to treat swimming pools and wastewater due to their powerful disinfection properties. Although they can be costly, they may be a good investment if you want a crystal-clear fishpond with few or no plants to remove nitrates from your water.

Natural Plant Filters. Another option for ponds with few or no plants, a natural plant filter is nothing more than a separate small pond or a large tub densely planted with such plants as water hawthorn, watercress, water lettuce, or water hyacinth placed between a biological filter outlet and the main pond. Because the plants consume nitrates and other nutrients produced by the biological filter, they reduce the formation of algae in the main pond. They can also be incorporated as an attractive part of the overall landscape design. Using natural plant filters to remove excess nutrients is a low-tech, relatively inexpensive option—especially for the beginning pond enthusiast.

In addition to lily pads, which are natural oxygenators, your pond needs an efficient filter system.

Preventing Disease Transmission

Fish are not the only ones susceptible to water-borne diseases. Mosquitoes are disease-carrying pests that lay their eggs in standing water—whether it's a pond, birdbath, or a fountain. The insects can transmit malaria, Zika virus, dengue fever, West Nile virus, yellow fever, dog heartworm, and more. By preventing or eliminating mosquito larvae, you minimize the chance of bites from infected mosquitoes.

Fish and frogs will eat some of the mosquito larvae in a pond, but when there are too few natural predators, you may want to consider using products with Bti (*Bacillus thuringiensis* subspecies *israelensis*), a bacteria used to control mosquito larvae. Bti comes in many forms, including dunks, tablets, briquettes, pellets, granules, or liquid. According to the US Centers for Disease Control (CDC), Bti can be added to standing water and to containers that cannot be emptied, covered, or turned over every week, such as rain barrels, fountains, ornamental ponds, and pools that are not in use. When used as directed, Bti can be applied safely to standing water where mosquitoes lay eggs. The CDC also notes that Bti is not harmful to people, honeybees, animals, and the environment when used as directed. Bti is an insecticide registered by the Environmental Protection Agency (EPA). EPA-registered insecticides have been studied for their effectiveness and safety when used according to label instructions. Always follow label instructions to ensure that the product is being used correctly.

CHAPTER 11

Routine Tasks

Once your pond is established, it needs cleaning and maintenance on a regular basis. There are many time-saving devices, and pond maintenance can be a pleasurable pastime, allowing you to closely observe the plants and the fish that swim there.

Fish are susceptible to stress after their winter fast. Give them a closer look, right, if they show any signs of illness.

Fertilizing and removing spent flowers or dead leaves will keep your plantings looking good.

Season to Season

The summer months are a time when ponds need the most attention. Plants are growing and fish are active. Even during warm weather, when your pond requires the most attention, it shouldn't take more than an hour or so to keep it in good shape. The larger the pond, the more time it may take.

Depending on where you live, your pond will go through seasonal cycles. If you live in a more temperate climate, you will likely need to be more vigilant year-round when it comes to pond care. But the sequence of routine maintenance tasks is the same everywhere, whether you live in California, Texas, New Hampshire, or Florida.

In cold climates, winter offers a respite from routine maintenance.

SPRING

The advent of warmer weather is a time for inspection and remediation. Early spring, before plants have leafed out, is a good time to check your pond's edges for any settling or shifting and repair them if needed. Grounds softened (but not soggy) by spring rain make landscaping easier. Check your electrical connections, lights, and pumps; repair any loose connections. Make sure ground-fault circuit interrupters are working by hitting the "test" button. If you stored your pump and filters for the winter, bring them out, reconnect them, and make sure they're in working order.

Clean out any pond debris that accumulated over the winter. Start biological filters once the water temperature remains above 50°F. When you put a biological filter back in service, it will take several weeks for the beneficial bacteria to reestablish a presence in the filter medium. You can buy starter bacteria from a water- garden supplier to speed up the colonization process.

As the weather warms, you may notice excessive algae (called an "algal bloom"). This problem will usually take care of itself once water lilies and other aquatic plants leaf out and begin providing shade and consuming nutrients.

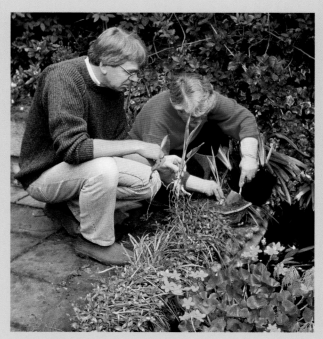

Spring is the traditional time to add new plants to your water garden and to transplant or tidy up existing ones.

Chemical Adjustments. Spring is a good time to check pH and water chemicals. If tests indicate that your water is polluted, you should replace a third of the water volume. Don't do this if the pond is undergoing an algae bloom, however, as that could make the problem worse. If you make the water change, do it over a few days. If you add more than 5 percent of your pond's volume in a week, then dechlorinate the tap water.

Late spring is the time to introduce new aquatic plants and to remove any dead foliage from existing ones. If you overwintered tropical water lilies, put the tubers in a shallow pan of water on a sunny windowsill about two months before the expected last frost in your area so that they can begin sprouting. Don't put them back in your pond before the water temperature reaches 70°F.

Divide water lilies, lotuses, and marginals with roots that are filling their pots. The best time to do this is after danger of frost has passed and before rapid growth resumes. Start giving lotuses fertilizer pellets twice a month; water lilies, once a month. Weed and mulch peripheral beds.

Frogs will begin singing and laying eggs. Fish, at first lethargic and weak from winter hibernation, will start to feed as the water temperature climbs toward 50°F. In the middle of the day, when their digestion is most active, offer them small amounts of high-carbohydrate foods containing wheat germ. Koi will like fresh salad greens.

Weather Changes. If the weather turns hot before water lilies have leafed out to provide shade, create temporary shade at one end of the pond with a tarp, or other fabric held down with rocks. Because the fish have gone many weeks without food, they have a heightened susceptibility to stressors of all kinds. That means they're more likely to become ill, so check them frequently for unusual symptoms. Watch for blotchy or discolored skin, missing scales, or lethargic or erratic behavior. If you treat your pond with a fungicide because your fish are ill, do so before starting a biological filter because fungicides will also kill the beneficial bacteria that make the filter work. In mid- to late spring, you may see fish bumping and chasing each other because it's spawning time. To assist the process, you can buy spawning mats to place in the pond.

SUMMER

As fish become more active in warming weather, you can give them high-protein foods such as chopped worms and daphnia (water fleas). In established and well-balanced ponds, they may get all the protein they need from insects and other small water creatures. Never overfeed fish: the rule of thumb is to give them no more food than they can eat within five minutes.

Oxygen. Because flora and fauna will be flourishing and multiplying, you should inspect the pump once a week and clean it as often as necessary. As the water heats, it's a good idea to run the pump continuously. Oxygen levels will drop, especially at night or during a thunderstorm. If you have fish, it's worth investing in a kit to test for dissolved oxygen. Blackened water, a foul smell, or fish gasping at the surface of the water is a sign that the oxygen level is dangerously low. For emergency aeration, you can spray the pond with a garden hose or use a separate aerator, which many pond owners find to be a worthwhile investment.

Spend a few minutes each day snipping off faded blossoms and keeping plants trimmed; such maintenance chores can be relaxing and give you additional quiet moments to enjoy your water garden. Insects will start to appear on plants, but avoid the use of insecticides in or near the pond. Handpick larger insects and dispose of them. Use a garden hose to spray aphids from water lilies, or wipe plant leaves with a damp cloth periodically. Once the water temperature reaches

In summer, you'll need frequent access to water for aerating the pond, topping it off, and spraying pests off plants.

75°F, increase your fertilizing of water lilies to twice a month. Blanketweed, a filamentous alga, may be a problem in hot weather; if you twirl a long stick under it, it will wrap around the stick like cotton candy for easy removal.

Evaporation. As the weather becomes hotter, water evaporation will increase, so you'll need to top off the pond every day or two. It's best to add a little water each day rather than a large amount once a week. Otherwise, if you use tap water, you'll need to dechlorinate it. You may find it helpful to store tap water in rain barrels, since chlorine will dissipate from the stored water. You can also set out plastic barrels to capture rainwater for topping off your pond. Remember to check it for pH, though, because rainwater can be highly acidic. Be vigilant about testing your pond's water quality at least once a month, or more frequently if you suspect a problem.

Heat brings greater incidence of fish diseases caused by bacteria, fungi, and parasites. Check fish regularly for signs of illness. (If you think you might forget, schedule a routine weekly check.) Immediately move sick fish from the pond to an aquarium, and treat them with the appropriate fish medicine. Seek treatment advice from a book on fish or from your aquarium supplier.

Warmer weather means lower oxygen levels. Consider buying a kit to test for oxygen levels.

AUTUMN

Keep falling leaves from collecting in your pond or they'll decay and pollute the water. If the pond is under a tree, stretch netting over the pond and weigh it down with bricks or rocks. If leaves tend to blow in from one direction, you may be able to keep them out with a line of netting or other temporary fencing. Scoop up floating leaves and other debris with a net. Remove any leaves that sink to the bottom of the pond with a soft plastic rake, pool sweep, or spa vacuum. (A pool sweep circulates water from your garden hose, so it may require you to dechlorinate your pond.)

Autumn is a good time to rein in rampantly growing oxygenating plants, which should be thinned and cut back severely. Don't remove the turions, or overwintering buds, from plants such as frogbit. Cut back other aquatics as they go dormant; water lilies can be trimmed to about an inch above the container. Do not cut marginals below the water level. Remove tropical water lilies and other tender aquatics and discard them or store them in their containers for the winter. If your pond has several depths, move water lilies to a level where the water will not freeze. If your pond might freeze below their crowns, you'll need to overwinter them in a frost-free place. Cattails and many of the ornamental grasses are beautiful in winter; don't cut them back until early spring.

Fish Food. As fish metabolism slows in preparation for winter, you should switch back to fish foods containing wheat germ. Gradually taper off the feedings to once every two to three days. Cease feeding as the fish become more lethargic and the water temperature drops to 50°F. When the water temperature drops below 45°F, fish become inactive and stop eating; you won't need to feed them again until the following spring. Refrain from feeding if fish become active during brief warm spells. In warmer climates (where water temperatures remain above 50°F), continue to feed fish all year, or as long as they remain active. As floating plants and water lilies die back, the fish will lose cover from predators, so lay down some sections of 4-inch drainpipe where they can hide. (Black plastic is less visible than drain tiles, but it may need to be weighted down with a rock.)

A well-maintained pond won't need an annual stem-to-stern decontamination. But if yours is filled with grit and debris or tests show it to be polluted, autumn is the best time to drain and clean it. As days shorten and temperatures drop, most water plants are on their way to dormancy and the increasingly drowsy fish are less likely to be stressed by a temporary relocation.

If you won't be running the pump during the winter, remove it from the pond, and clean all parts before storing it. Drain all pipes to keep them from cracking. Even if you'll be using your pump to keep the water from freezing as suggested on the next page, detach and clean fountain nozzles. External pumps should also be removed and tended. To avoid damage to a biological filter, drain, rinse, and store it.

In autumn, installing a net over the pond will keep out falling leaves that can decay and pollute the water, which will cause more work next spring.

WINTER

If you live in a warm climate where freezes are rare, your pond duties won't change much in winter. Anywhere else, your main concern is to keep your pond from freezing for long periods. When ice forms on the pond, it can cut off oxygen to the fish and trap toxic gases beneath the surface. If the pond is frozen for more than a few days, fish may suffocate. (You should never break the ice, however, because the vibrations can injure your fish.) Ice can crack a concrete pond and may also damage inexpensive shells or the vertical sides of lined ponds.

Ice. Raised ponds are particularly susceptible to freezing. Plants and fish can't survive the winter in aboveground ponds except in frost-free areas. Protect a raised pond from ice damage in short freezes by covering it with boards and a tarp or similar heavy material. You can also keep ice from exerting pressure on the sides of the pond by floating something in it—rubber balls, wooden planks, a couple of milk jugs. This will work for in-ground ponds, too, where freezes are infrequent or of short duration.

In mild climates, where ice is a temporary condition, you can place a pot of boiling-hot water on the ice to melt a hole in it. Use a pot with a hole in the handle and run a heavy string through the hole so you can retrieve the pot if it melts clear through the ice.

In moderately cold climates, raise a circulating pump off the pond bottom (so it doesn't circulate cold water into the bottom where fish and plants are keeping warm) and direct the outward flow up with a short tube or pipe; this will keep ice from forming in that part of the pond. The easiest way to keep a pond ice-free, and the only way in extremely cold climates, is to buy a floating pond deicer to keep a hole open in the ice all winter. These devices are controlled by a thermostat, so they run only when needed, and (of course) should be plugged into a circuit with a ground-fault interrupter. Keep snow off the ice surface so light reaches the bottom of the pond.

Planning. Use winter downtime to your advantage. Make observations about your pond's microclimates; consider planting shrubs to block stiff cold winds; or figure out where to move slow-growing water lilies so they get more sun. Winter is the traditional time to order plants for the coming spring. Also replenish your supply of snails or tadpoles if necessary, and any testing kits or plumbing supplies you expect to need. Suppliers will wait to ship plants and animals until it's safe to put them outside in your area.

Many types of fish can spend winter in your pond as long as the surface doesn't freeze solid. Ice cuts off their oxygen and traps toxic gases. A pond deicer is the most reliable solution.

In climates where freeze-ups are relatively brief, balls or other floating objects will keep ice pressure from damaging the sides of your pond.

Troubleshooting

Your ability to observe and respond to small changes in the pond environment—whether it's a different color to the water, altered behavior in your fish, or a slight shift in your edging—can save you more expense and heartache down the line. The solution to serious problems may involve emptying the pond of water and quickly refilling it with the least amount of trauma to its inhabitants.

MAINTAINING THE POND

A well-maintained pond should only need cleaning every three or four years. You should avoid cleaning wildlife ponds if possible, because the microorganisms and small creatures in the water are all important to the ecosystem you want to maintain. It can take many months to reestablish a good balance.

But if the water is choked with algae, filled with sediment, or severely polluted, you may have to completely drain the pond, scrub it down, and refill it with fresh water. Draining may also be necessary to find and repair a leak in the pond liner or shell.

The best time to clean the pond is during late summer or in early autumn. If you clean the pond in the spring, you might disrupt spawning fish and amphibians or destroy the eggs, or damage emerging plant shoots. And cleaning a pond in the middle of summer is like trying to make a bed with people still lying in it; it's much harder, in addition, it upsets the sleepers!

Quick Guide to Common Problems

PROBLEM	SOLUTION
Pond stays green into summer	Remove debris from bottom Add more oxygenating and floating leaved plants
Fish gasping at surface	Add more oxygen to water with garden hose or aerator
Fish act frantic	Spring: this is normal spawning behavior Other seasons: check for diseases (see page 165)
Fish disappear	Suspect predators (see page 166)
Water level drops after topping	Suspect a leak (see page 196)
Water level turns black, smells unpleasant	Oxygen is low: aerate quickly with garden hose or aerator Add more submerged plants to prevent in future
Lotuses don't bloom	Climate too cold; choose a more appropriate plant
Water lilies don't bloom	Not enough sun; look for shade-tolerant varieties

Make it a daily habit to snip off faded blossoms. This "chore" can actually be a way to relax and enjoy your water garden.

Drain and Clean the Pond

howto

DIFFICULTY LEVEL: MODERATE

When it's time to clean your pond, arrange to do it when you can drain and refill it as quickly as possible. Although it's important to do a thorough job, you don't want to leave a flexible liner exposed or aquatic plants out of the water any longer than absolutely necessary. Be sure to run the pumped-out water into a nearby garden that can benefit from the water's nutrients.

Tools and Materials: holding tubs (plastic wading pool or trash can); plastic buckets; fish net; newspaper or burlap (for water plants); plastic dustpan; aquarium air bubbler (for lengthy cleaning/repairs); garden hose and adapter for pond pump (if available), or sump pump; soft-bristled brush (optional); water purifier or dechlorinating agent; thermometer

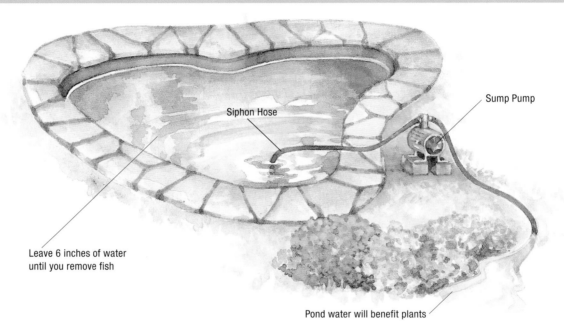

Sump Pump

Siphon Hose

Leave 6 inches of water until you remove fish

Pond water will benefit plants

Remove the water. Use a siphon hose, the pond pump, or a high-capacity sump pump to drain the pond.

1 Drain the Pond. Before you start, prepare one or more holding tubs for your fish. You'll need about a gallon of water for each inch of fish (for example, one 5-in. fish in a 5-gal. bucket). If you have a lot of fish, a children's plastic wading pool or 50-gal. plastic trash can works well. Place either in the shade; fill with some of the pond water; and add a few bunches of oxygenating plants to the tank.

Drain the pond to about 6 in. above the bottom; then carefully net out the fish and put them in the holding tub. If the fish will be out of the pond for more than a few hours, place an aquarium air bubbler in the tank to provide additional oxygen. If your property slopes and your pond is situated slightly uphill, you can use a garden hose to simply siphon out the water to a lower area of your yard. Otherwise, you can use your pond's pump to pump the water out.

Garden hose adapters are available for many pond pumps. If you can't get an adapter for your particular pump, or if you can't use the pump to remove the water for some other reason (it's a slow process, and it may be that you simply can't spare that much time), you can rent a high-capacity sump pump at most tool rental shops or home centers.

Run the pumped out water into a nearby garden area; the nutrients it contains will benefit your plants. Don't allow the pump to run dry, or the motor will burn up. At this point, you will be glad if you have followed the advice to create a sump area when building your pond. (See page 60.) It will ensure that your motor does not run dry before you have most of your water pumped out, and will also leave you a smaller area of water and muck to bail out by hand. To avoid damaging your liner or shell, always use a plastic bucket to bail out any remaining water.

Capture
Fish Gently

Wrap or
Submerge Plants

Preserve fish and plants. Place fish, snails, and other pondlife in tubs filled with pond water. Aerate the water. Submerge or wet-wrap plants as appropriate.

2 Remove the Wildlife. You'll have to take measures to preserve the fish and plants. All of your oxygenating plants will have to be submerged in holding tanks or buckets; it's often easiest to make new bunches of stems and repot them in fresh soil. Water lilies and marginals need to be kept moist and out of the wind. Wrap them in wet newspapers or burlap sacks; put them in a shady location; and spray them occasionally with a garden hose.

When the pond is drained, sift through the silt, and pick out as many snails as you can find. (You probably won't get them all.) Put these snails in the holding tank with the fish. Use a plastic dustpan to shovel out the silt on the pond bottom.

Soft Bristled Broom

Clean pond gently. Use soft tools that won't damage your liner or shell.

3 Clean the Pond. Carefully scrub the sides and bottom with a soft-bristled brush or a strong jet of water from a garden hose; don't use chemical cleaners; and be careful not to tear or puncture the liner or pond shell. Rinse and drain the pond several times in order to remove any remaining muck. Once the liner is completely clean, inspect it carefully for leaks. This is a good time to make liner repairs.

Refill with Water,
then Dechlorinate
if Needed

Refill pond. Treat any water imbalances; reintroduce plants; then add fish when water warms.

4 Add Fresh Water. Refill the pond with fresh water. Unless you are using well water, add a dechlorinating agent or water purifier. Pour a few buckets of the original pond water back into the pond to help establish the biological balance. Reintroduce your plants now, but don't put the fish back into the pond until the water temperature returns to within 5 deg. of the temperature in the holding tank. Don't forget: as with new ponds, you can expect increased growth of algae until the ecological balance is reestablished in the pond.

how to

Repair a Pond Foundation

DIFFICULTY LEVEL: MODERATE

If you've been careful installing a liner or shell, not introduced a 200-pound statue with no footing, and avoided wading across the pond in your golf cleats, the chances are good that your foundation will meet or exceed its life expectancy. But accidents happen to even the most careful pond keepers: big branches fall, big dogs drop by for an uninvited romp, big rocks tumble from the edging. Here's what to do if your pond is leaking.

Flexible Liners. If flexible liners develop punctures or tears before the end of their life expectancy, it's worth repairing them with patching kits available from water-garden dealers. The kits usually contain a small can of adhesive and a piece of liner for making patches; some come with double-sided tape rather than adhesive.

Tools and Materials: scissors or utility knife; milk or food coloring; buckets (for fish); wet newspaper (for wrapping plants); sand; liner underlayment; cloth; utility paint brush; liner patch material; liner adhesive; weight (sandbag, etc.)

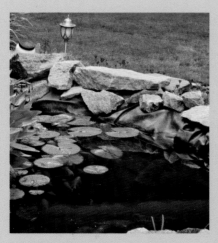

A flexible liner can develop tears or leaks, which can usually be repaired.

Use Food Coloring to Find Leak

1 Locate the Source of the Leak. Eliminate a leak in a waterfall by shutting it off, topping off the pond, and seeing if the level goes down. If not, check along the sides of the waterfall or in the tubing. Then check the pond's edges to make sure a spot hasn't settled lower than the water level. Add water to just above this level. Squirt milk around the edges of the pond; it will form a line toward a leak. Drain water to below the leak. Cushion the area behind the tear with damp sand or liner underlayment.

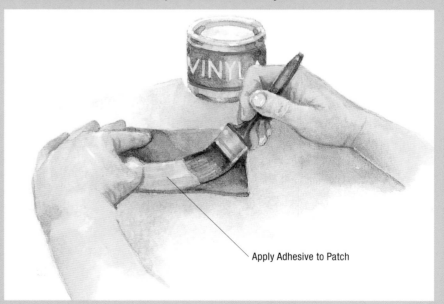

VINYL

Apply Adhesive to Patch

4 Coat the Patch. Apply a coat of adhesive to the back of the patch, making sure you cover it completely. Allow the adhesive to become slightly tacky (about 2 to 3 min., or as recommended on the label directions).

Clean and Dry Leak Area

Apply Adhesive
to Liner

2 **Wipe off the Leak Area.** Make sure the tear or puncture is completely clean and dry. This is important because otherwise the adhesive you will be using on the liner material and the patch will not adhere properly.

3 **Brush on Adhesive.** Cut a patch from the same material as the liner (PVC plastic or rubber) that is about 2 in. wider and longer than the tear. Apply a thin, even coat of adhesive over and slightly beyond the torn area.

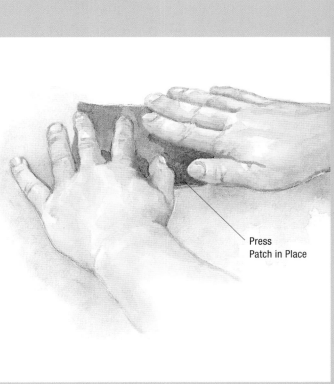

Press
Patch in Place

5 **Adhere the Patch.** Firmly press the patch down, and smooth it to remove wrinkles. If possible, weight the patch with a bag of sand. Allow the adhesive to dry thoroughly.

Rigid Ponds. Leaks in rigid pond shells usually indicate an uneven base (in which case you will find the leak along the rim) or a sharp stone under the shell (in which case you'll find a leak farther down). You can repair the leak with a fiberglass-boat repair kit, which has resin and a catalyst you will have to mix.

After locating the leak, drain the pond and either level the shell bottom or remove any object that may have caused the puncture. You can patch the shell before or after returning it to the hole, whichever seems easier. Using sandpaper, roughen the area round the leak so that the patch will stick. Spread the adhesive mixture on the patch, and apply the patch to the leak. Follow the manufacturer's directions for drying.

Concrete Ponds. You may be able to patch a few small cracks with a caulk and neoprene rubber coating. Or install a flexible liner on top of the concrete. Sand down rough spots; fill deep crevices; and install an underlayment before lining.

PART 5

Plants, Plants, and More Plants

Selecting plants for in and around your water feature is one of the fun elements of gardening. From trees and shrubs to annuals, perennials, ornamental grasses, and tropicals, there are countless plants that can enhance your outdoor paradise. The design possibilities range from a very formal garden to one that's wild and carefree. The Plant Encyclopedia that follows will help you get started.

CHAPTER 12

Plant Encyclopedia

Any pond with an area of stillwater can be home to a few water lilies or an elegant lotus. There are plants that float, plants that grow in pots underwater, and marginal plants—those that grow at the water's edge. Some ponds contain all three types of plants. A formal water feature might boast a few elegant, but simple, water lilies. Choosing plants is like choosing furniture. The plants you choose should complement the style of the pond, whether it's informal and casual or formal with very rigid lines. Clump-forming plants are more well behaved than aggressive spreaders. A little homework before making a purchase will go a long way to growing healthy, attractive, and lower-maintenance plants.

What's Your Style?

Is your water feature and garden informal or formal? The design of your outdoor space affects the way you arrange and place plants. Formal gardens tend to emphasize straight lines, angles, and circles in balanced proportions. There may be a main axis divided by paths or lawn. Plants are often repeated and there is a sense of symmetry throughout the garden that results in a sense of order. To complement a formal water feature, limit your choices to a few plants. It could be a single dramatic specimen—a solitary bonsai on a pedestal, or a weeping cherry tree.

The informal garden features flowering, organic lines rather than symmetry. Curving borders and an assortment of plants with contrasting colors, textures, and heights add to the informality. An informal pond calls for a planting area with sweeping curves and a relaxed mix of plants in a variety of shapes, textures, and colors.

Pickerel weed's tiny blue flowers grow on spikes and bloom from late spring to autumn. It thrives in full sun and in water up to 5 in. deep or alongside a wetland or pond.

A simple stone fountain can be enhanced with plants.

The Roles Plants Play

There are four basic categories of water garden plants.

■ **Submerged plants** are those that grow below the water surface. Called oxygenators, they act as natural filters to keep the pond in biological balance, making it more hospitable for fish and less inviting to algae. If you want fish and don't invest in a biological filter, submerged plants are a necessity.

■ **Floating plants** drift freely on the surface, or they're rooted in containers under the water and send up leaves that float. They discourage the formation of algae by shading the water and keeping it cool. Floating plants include lotuses and water lilies.

■ **Marginal plants** are those that prefer to grow in shallow water or at the wet edge of a pond. They can be planted in containers that are raised on shelves or blocks underwater to their preferred level. Marginal plants are useful for creating the look of a natural pond and they help conceal the edge of a flexible liner or shell.

■ **Moisture-loving and bog plants** include most any plant that likes very moist to slightly soggy soil (more moisture than is typical in the average garden, but not standing water). In a natural environment, a lake, pond, or stream will be surrounded by a zone of relatively wet soil that supports an array of plants. True bog plants are a subcategory of moisture lovers. They require a more specialized environment of acidic soil and low oxygen.

Most water gardeners choose a combination of submerged, floating, and marginal plants.

Successful design means both varying and repeating textures and shapes.

Waterlilies are not only colorful, but the leaves protect fish and discourage algae.

Water Garden Planting Profile

Moisture-Loving Plant
(very moist-to-slightly
soggy soil)

Floating Leaved Plant

Marginal Plant
(1-6 in. water)

Free-Floating Plant

Moisture-Loving Plant
(very moist-to-slightly
soggy soil)

Select an interesting mix of plants for your pond
from among the four basic categories: submerged; floating; marginal; and moisture-loving.

Filtration Pump

Submerged Plant
(oxygenator)

Lythrum salicaria

Eichhornia crassipes

Hydrilla verticillata

Myriophyllum spicatum

Beauty or Beast?

There are many plants that are considered invasive. According to the U.S. Department of Agriculture, an invasive plant "has the ability to thrive and spread aggressively outside its native range. A naturally aggressive plant may be especially invasive when it is introduced to a new habitat."

Invasive species are costly, disrupt natural ecosystems, and consequently threaten native species. Some invasive plants grow into dense stands that quickly outcompete native plants. They can degrade large areas of highly productive wetlands. As a result, they reduce habitat diversity and have a negative impact on wildlife.

Some plants, like some animals and insects, were first introduced as beneficial for landscapes, agriculture, wildlife, or livelihood. Others landed here by accident or chance. Many have become pests, invading wetlands, prairies, pastures, and woodlands. The landscape-swallowing kudzu vine, introduced in 1876 as an ornamental and crop plant, has twined its way from the South into the Midwest.

Nearly all of them originated in other countries and have no natural controls in their new home. They reproduce in an uncontrollable manner and escape to natural areas, where they compete for soil, light, and moisture with more delicate native plants, and as a result, diminish food sources for birds and other animals. Some interfere with boating and other water sports by clogging waterways. Many of these species have succeeded with their takeover because they are aided by wind, birds, or other animals, which spread their seeds from gardens to parks or along waterways, where they can be carried for many miles.

Miscanthus grass, (aka Chinese silver grass) was introduced to the U.S. more than a century ago. By 1906, The Garden Magazine ran a story, "Beauty in Garden Grasses," in which *Miscanthus sinensis* (then called eulalia grass) was considered "an excellent substitute for tender pampas grass. The silvery plumes adorn the garden after the foliage has fallen from the trees." According to the U.S. Forest Service, by the early 1940s, Chinese silver grass occurred along roadsides and railroad tracks in some eastern states. Like many other plants, miscanthus has come in and out of vogue. It roared back into popularity in the 1980s, along with many perennials, and breeders created dozens of showy cultivars.

In the eastern U.S., *Miscanthus sinensis* is a problem, while in the Midwest, it's *M. sacchariflorus*, which spreads by aggressive rhizomes. *Miscanthus x giganteus* is a natural (and sterile) hybrid of these two species and has been studied as a possible candidate for renewable energy. It can grow to 12 feet tall and spreads by slower-growing rhizomes. While growers continue to educate themselves and be stewards of the landscape in a manner that balances what is good for business and what is good for the green industry, consumers in every state should be aware of potential invasive plants before they bring them home.

The plants pictured here are considered pests in various regions of North America. Plants that pose serious problems in one region may be harmless in another. For more information on invasive plants, visit the websites of the

Myriophyllum spicatum

U.S. Department of Agriculture, the U.S. Department of the Interior, The Nature Conservatory, your state university extension service, or a local native plant society or arboretum.

An example of a serious invasive perennial is purple loosestrife (*Lythrum salicaria*), an attractive perennial imported from Asia. It bears magenta flower spikes in mid to late summer. Its ability to spread by prolific amounts of seed and by roots has allowed it to choke out other native wetland species in the Northeast and Midwest. It has no food value for animals, and research shows that even purple loosestrife cultivars that were thought to be sterile (and as a result, seedless) will also spread. There are other non-invasive and native perennials that can substitute for this aggressor.

Water hyacinth (*Eichhornia crassipes*) looks like a floating orchid. A native of South America, this plant chokes waterways in the Gulf States, California, and other warm areas across the globe. Although it is touted as "safe to use" in gardens north of Zone 8, those gardeners living in Zone 7 near waterways should avoid it. There are better, less invasive plants like water lilies or pickerel rush that make good substitutes.

Two other very troublesome plants are hydrilla (*Hydrilla verticillata*) and Eurasian water milfoil (*Myriophyllum spicatum*). Millions of taxpayer dollars are spent trying to eradicate both plants to keep them from spreading into waterways where they make the areas unusable for boating or swimming.

The lovely yellow flag iris (*Iris pseudacorus*) has made the least-wanted lists in the Mid-Atlantic states. That is the trouble with many invasive plants: they are lovely to look at but pose a big problem. If you live in one of those states, consider other species or hybrids such as Louisiana or Japanese irises for your garden.

Another rapidly spreading invasive plant is common reed (*Phragmites australis*). It moves into "disturbed" areas and is very difficult to eradicate. It is found in ditches, wetlands, and alongside waterways, where it displaces native plants to the detriment of local wildlife.

It is not only invasive perennials that are a problem, but some woody plants like imported trees and shrubs are pests as well. Melaleuca (*Melaleuca quinquenervia*) is taking over the Florida Everglades. In western states, tamarisk trees (*Tamarix* species) are invading riverbanks and draining precious water resources, increasing the salinity of the soil and displacing important native plants that support local wildlife.

Iris pseudacorus

Melaleuca quinquenervia

Phragmites australis

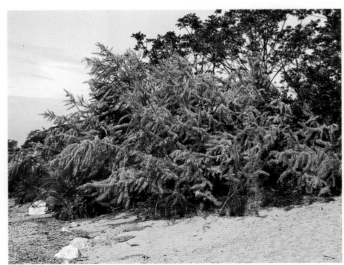

Tamarix species

THE SIX PLANT CATEGORIES

Each of the six plant categories here include proven performers, some with outstanding features such as wonderful fragrance, colorful flowers, dramatic leaves, long bloom period, etc. Plants are listed alphabetically by botanical name (genus and species, which appear in italics in parentheses). If the plant has a common name it appears in capital letters above the botanic name, and the cultivar name, if there is one, appears in single quotes.

A genus is a group of related plants, and genus names are often derived from Latin or Greek words. The species part of the name describes one kind of plant within the genus. Some plants are listed by the genus and nonspecific species, for example Ludwigia species, to indicate that several species of Ludwigia are worthy of consideration.

Water lilies belong to the genus Nymphaea and are listed alphabetically by species or cultivar name. Similarly, all lotuses belong to the genus Nelumbo and are also organized by species and cultivar name.

Submerged Plants (Oxygenators)

Submerged aquatic plants are often referred to as "oxygenators" because, during the day, they produce oxygen that helps support fish and tadpoles. Submerged plants also remove mineral salts and fish wastes that promote undesirable algae. Some of these plants produce flowers above the water. But the main reason to buy these plants is for their oxygenating and filtering ability. Before you introduce fish, place the plants in the water a few weeks before so they can establish and start working.

When it comes to your pond and the minimum and maximum temperatures in your locale, availability and cold hardiness will dictate your plant choices. The climate zones provided in the plant descriptions are a general guide. All the plants described here are efficient oxygenators, and you can plant one species or several. When buying plants, the general rule is that you need one bunch (six stems) of submerged plants for every one to two feet of pond surface. You can plant two or three bunches of plants in a pan one foot in diameter.

PLANTING OXYGENATORS

Submerged plants obtain their nutrients from the water. You can plant them in sand or gravel and they will never require fertilizing. Oxygenators don't need containers. Bundle a half dozen plants and weigh them down on the bottom of a pond with a rock!

Don't plant oxygenators in rich soil, manure, or compost. The nutrients will leach out and disturb your pond's ecology. If you use containers, fill them with sand to the rim of the pot. Poke each plant stem an inch or two into the sand. Plant one stem for each inch of pot diameter. For example, a 12-inch-wide pot would have 12 stems.

To hold the sand and plants in place, top the sand with clean gravel. Then, water the container to remove air bubbles. If you have koi, you can protect the plants with mesh that is available from aquatic suppliers.

When placing pots into the pond, allow one to two feet of water over the roots of the plants. For deeper ponds, set the containers on blocks to ensure they get enough sun. If sunlight is blocked by too many floating plants or by algae, the plants will not thrive and may die. Pots should be kept away from the pump, as most pond plants don't like agitation.

Oxygenating plants do need to be kept in check, especially if you don't have fish to control them. Some oxygenators can grow three feet long and may choke a pond by robbing it of oxygen. Fish do an efficient job of controlling plant growth. If you don't have fish, inspect the plants periodically and trim them if they get too large. Algae and decaying plant material floating in the pond can cling to submerged plants and eventually smother them. If you see this, pull the pots out of the water and hose them off.

RECOMMENDED OXYGENATORS

Water hyssop
(Bacopa caroliniana)
Native to coastal areas of southern and central North America, water hyssop has a stiff, round stem 2 feet long that is covered with fine hairs. Egg-shaped leaves are about an inch long and hairy underneath. Light blue tubular flowers about ½ inch long appear above the water in the leaf axils (where leaves are attached to the stem). **Zones 8–10.**

Fanwort Carolina
Water Shield
(Cabomba caroliniana)
This plant is native to ponds and streams from Michigan to Texas and south to Florida. Underwater, its leaves are feathery, in a fan shape 1½ inches across. Leaves that grow above water are linear, pointed, and ¾ inch long. Flowers are usually white with yellow spots. **Zones 6–11.**

Hornwort
(Ceratophyllum demersum)
Hornwort develops stems 1 to 2 feet long, clothed in whorls of forked leaves, which remain completely underwater. Like some other aquatic plants, it reproduces from turions, buds that drop to the pond bottom in winter. You can pot up these turions when they start to grow in spring. **Zones 6–9.**

Anacharis
(Egeria densa, also sold as *Elodea densa* or *Anacharis densa)*
This is a widely available submerged plant, but suffers from name confusion. It goes by many botanical names, and its common name may be used for Canadian pondweed. Sometimes it is called Brazilian waterweed. This plant is semi-evergreen and produces branched stems up to 3 feet long. In summer it has small but pretty white flowers above the water surface. **Zones 6–11.**

Hair grass
(Eleocharis acicularis)
You can use this aquarium plant to create an underwater lawn. (And it will never need mowing.) Pale green needle-like leaves grow to 8 inches tall and spread to form a mat that looks like prairie grass or green hair. Flowers are little brown spikes. Avoid using it in earth-bottomed ponds, where its vigorous roots can quickly turn it into a nuisance. (Other species of *Eleocharis* that need water only a few inches deep are described under "Marginal Plants," starting on page 225.) **Zones 7–10** (but often hardier; some northern gardeners report that it usually winters well in ponds that freeze over).

Canadian pondweed
(Elodea canadensis)
Whorls of translucent leaves on each stem are dense and curl downward. Found in Quebec, it will also grow in the Deep South. In fact, it's so obliging that it can become a pest where it can spread out, but it may be a good choice for a water gardener who has trouble growing other oxygenators. Some catalogs call this anacharis because of its resemblance to *Egeria densa*. **Zones 5–11.**

Milfoil
(Myriophyllum species)
Some of the milfoils are extremely invasive, and others aren't winter hardy. Avoid *M. spicatum*, which is a waterway pest in states from Wisconsin to Massachusetts and down to Florida. *M. aquaticum* ('parrot's-feather'), which you'll find with marginal plants starting on page 225, can grow in or out of water but is hardy only to **Zone 9.**

Farther north, substitute myriad leaf (*M. verticillatum*), which has 3-foot-long graceful stems with whorls of bright green leaves; above the water the leaves are little comblike tufts. In summer, it bears 6-inch spikes of tiny yellow flowers.

Floating Plants

The leaves of floating plants drift on the water's surface and provide shade. They make the pond less hospitable for algae, cool the water, and give fish a place to hide and lay eggs. Floating plants are not typically used in a water feature that has a fountain or waterfall that churns the water because it creates too much movement for them.

Most floating plants prefer full sun but tolerate partial shade. As a rule, water lilies need at least six hours of sun a day to bloom. Lotuses are less particular about the amount of sun they receive than they are about temperature. They will bloom in partial shade if they have a sufficient stretch of warm weather.

For most floating plants, all you need to do is drop them in the water. They receive nutrients through roots suspended from their leaves. When floaters become too vigorous, they reduce light to submerged species, which in turn reduces the filtering and oxygenating functions of underwater plants. Floating plants should not cover more than 70 percent of the water's surface. A large pond of 1,000 square feet or so should be only half covered by floaters. Excess floating plants should be placed in a compost pile.

Water lilies are aptly described as floating-leaved plants. Plant them in containers of heavy garden soil and put the pots on a shelf or block anywhere from a few inches to two feet under the water's surface. Some water lilies can live either submerged or in shallow water near the pond's margins. Containerized plants need monthly aquatic fertilization. Remove spent plants to keep the pond clean.

Some of the plants featured here are not winter hardy in most of North America. You may want to experiment with growing them as annuals or over-wintering them in an aquarium. That way, you can start a new crop the following spring.

RECOMMENDED FLOATING PLANTS

Water hawthorn, Cape pondweed
(*Aponogeton distachyus*)
Tropical gardeners can try this South African perennial with 8-inch elongated oval leaves. Heavily scented flowers, which bloom in both spring and fall, are held on a double spike; their purple-brown anthers look like freckles on the rows of white petals. Give water hawthorn a container 1 foot across and start it about 4 inches below the surface of the water, lowering it to 1 to 3 feet. **Zones 6–9.**

Mosquito fern
(*Azolla caroliniana*)
Often called by the more charming name of fairy moss, this tiny fern with inch-long fronds floats freely on the water surface, each plant above its own little root. The dainty green snowflakes turn burgundy in autumn or in strong sunlight. Their delicate appearance is deceptive, though. This native of subtropical America has naturalized in North America and Britain and easily becomes invasive. It can be useful if you need quick cover for a new pond and are willing to thin regularly. **Zones 7–10.**

Water hyacinth
(*Eichhornia crassipes*)
This is one of the most beautiful yet one of the most noxious water-garden plants. One of the worst pest plants in California, Florida, Georgia, and Louisiana, it can't be shipped across state lines anywhere. (If you want to grow it, you'll have to buy it from a supplier in your state.) Nevertheless, it is considered safe to grow as an annual in **Zone 7** and north because it can't survive freezing temperatures. Its shiny round leaves bob in the water, supported by buoyant stems. The free-floating plants are topped by 6-inch spikes of exotic-looking lilac flowers. Each plant has a foot-long root and spreads by stolons. Be prepared: this rampant beauty can take over your water garden if you don't thin it regularly.

Frogbit
(*Hydrocharis morsus-ranae*)
This free-floating species from Eurasia has shiny, 1-inch-diameter leaves shaped like a water lily's and handsomely veined. Delicate cup-shaped white flowers have three yellow petals near the base. New plants form on runners; in fall, turions (winter buds) drop to the pond bottom to overwinter. Frogbit is a good choice for gardeners who don't have the time to do a lot of thinning. **Zones 6–10.**

Water poppy
(*Hydrocleys nymphoides*)
A Brazilian native, water poppy is worth growing as an annual for its 3-inch pale yellow flowers with red-and-brown centers. The three petals overlap slightly to form a shallow cup just above the water. Thick, glossy leaves are also about 3 inches across and look a lot like a water lily's. Plant it in rich soil and in shallow water, 6 to 9 inches deep; it likes acidic water. **Zones 9–11.**

Common duckweed
(*Lemna minor*)
This free-floater is the water gardener's crabgrass. Each one of its light-green oval leaves has a root hanging beneath it, but plants will cluster in large communities. It is a nutritious food for goldfish. **Zones 3–11.**

Ludwiglia species. Taxonomists have made a serious muddle of this group of aquatic plants. Some of the plants are free-floaters and others are better adapted to the margins of a pond. The most attractive is probably tropical *L. sedioides*, which has red stems and floating diamond-shaped leaves that form kaleidoscopic patterns. Place it so its crown sits 4 to 12 inches under the water. **Zone 11.**

Water clover
(*Marsilea* species)
These plants are technically ferns, but they look like four-leaf clovers. The most colorful is *M. mutica*, from Australia; its quartet of 3-inch leaves has two shades of green separated by a dark band. The hardiest is *M. quadrifolia*, from Europe; its new leaves are downy. Water clovers can be grown in up to 12 inches of water, in which case their leaves will float. They can also be grown as marginal plants with only an inch of water above their crowns, and then their stems will stand a few inches above the surface. **Zones 9–11.**

Bogbean
(*Menyanthes trifoliata*)
In spring, bogbean produces a foot-tall spike of 10 to 20 white-fringed, star-shaped flowers that unfold from a pink bud and remain pink on the outside. Full sun produces more flowers. It has three-part leaves and can form a clump 3 feet or more in diameter. Bogbean will grow in a container 6 to 9 inches below the surface as well as in mud at the water's edge, where it will camouflage pond edges by creeping into the water with its spongy rhizomes. It likes the acidic environment of a true bog; it will grow better if you mix peat moss in the soil to increase acidity. It may not flower in the warmer parts of its range. **Zones 5–11.**

Pond lily, spatterdock
(*Nuphar* species)
These plants make a good substitute for water lilies where water is shaded, gently moving, or acidic. Globe-shaped flowers are followed by oval berries. Plants develop long thick roots—divide them in spring. *N. lutea* bears 2-inch flowers. Its translucent submerged leaves can be a

foot long, while the 16-inch floating leaves are leathery and slightly more pointed. **Zones 5–11.**
The best choice for an average-size water feature is *N. pumila*, which can be grown in water only a foot deep. **Zones 4–8.** Japanese pond lily (*N. japonica*) has arrow-shaped leaves and flowers blushed with red; a variegated cultivar, 'Variegata', is suitable for small ponds and another, 'Rubrotincta', has reddish orange flowers. **Zones 6–9.**

Floating heart
(*Nymphoides* species)
These plants are often compared to water lilies. Unlike water lilies, all thrive in relatively shallow water—plant them 3 to 12 inches deep in a container 18 inches across. The ¾-inch white or yellow flow-

ers are usually fringed. Two native species are *N. aquatica* (banana plant), which bears ½-inch white flowers and forms tubers that look like tiny bananas, and *N. cordata*, which varies only in its tubers; both are hard to find. **Zones 6–9.**
N. peltata (water fringe, yellow floating heart), a European species that has naturalized in the United States, has rounded, 3-inch leaves with brown splotches and holds bright gold, fringed flowers several inches above the water all summer; it needs a large pond. **Zones 6–11.**
N. cristata has fragrant white, yellow-centered flowers. **Zones 7–11.**

Water lettuce, shellflower
(*Pistia stratiotes*)
It's easy to see where this subtropical free-floater got the name "water lettuce." Shaped like romaine, the 8-inch leaves are undulating, velvety fans that stick up from the water, near white on base and

undersides. Little green flowers are negligible, but the roots—which mature from white to purple to black—hang 18 inches and make a great fish nursery. It is a noxious weed in southern states (it can't be shipped to California, Texas, Louisiana, or South Carolina); grow it as an annual north of **Zone 8.**

Butterfly fern
(*Salvinia* species)
Hairy, 1-inch paired leaves of these free-floating aquatic ferns inspired the name, looking like a butterfly at rest. In this genus they're grouped again into whorls of three, ranging from light green to brownish purple. Happy in even an inch of water, they reproduce fast and are pests in warm regions. **Zones 10–11.**

Water Lilies

Although it's quite possible to have a stunning and soul-satisfying water garden without water lilies, most gardeners plant at least a few. These plants are prized not just for the blossoms that open day after day, but also for the shiny pads that serve as landing strips for frogs and dragonflies. While not as colorful as the flowers, these floating leaves have a fascination all their own. When they first unfold, they are often purple or copper and show pronounced splotches and streaks. Some retain this mottling as they age. Most lily pads are roughly round, but some are more egg shaped. The edges are sometimes serrated, similar to a bread knife. All pads have an indentation, or sinus, which can be wide open in a triangle or closed so that the two lobes overlap. In some   cases, one or both of the lobes may turn up, showing a flash of burgundy on the leaf's underside.

Adding to the visual interest of many water lilies are plant parts in colors that contrast with petals. These include the sepals, which while in many plants are unexciting green structures that simply protect the bud, in others such as water lilies develop another color as the plant matures. Providing color in the center of the water lily flower are the stamens (the male reproductive organ) and anthers (the part that holds pollen). They are most often yellow and orange, but in some water lilies can be white or

ANATOMY OF A WATER LILY

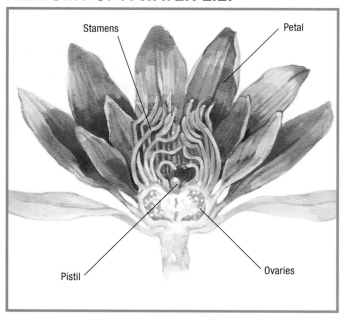

Stamens

Petal

Pistil

Ovaries

GUIDE TO WATER LILY ENTRIES

All water lilies belong to the genus *Nymphaea.* They are listed here alphabetically by their cultivar name or by their species name, within one of three categories: *Hardy Water Lilies; Tropical Varieties: Day-blooming; Tropical Varieties: Night-blooming.*

■ Hardy Water Lilies, page 214
■ Tropical Varieties: *Day blooming,* page 218
■ Tropical Varieties: *Night blooming,* page 221

bear touches of red or pink.

The flowers also vary in shape. They are usually described as either cup-shaped—with the petals held upright and close together—or star-shaped—with the petals opening wider and flatter. Many open cup-shaped and then become star-shaped. They can also range from single, with a few elegant petals, to fully double, with so many petals that they look like floating peonies.

There are biological arguments for planting water lilies as well. They discourage algae and protect fish. To achieve both of these goals, you need to cover about half of your pond surface; in a small pond, up to 70 percent. If you're meeting these goals with water lilies alone, plant at least one water lily for each 10 to 20 square feet of surface. Water lilies vary in the surface area they will cover, from a single square foot to 10 or 12. Some are demure enough to grow in a small patio tub, whereas others are too frisky for anything smaller than a lake.

Water lilies are classified as either hardy, meaning that they will survive winters into Zone 4 as long as the pond doesn't freeze down to the level of their roots, or tropical, meaning that they can be left in your pond all year only if you live in Zone 10 or 11.

CHOOSING WATER LILIES

You can find hardy water lilies in white, pink, yellow, and red as well as the so-called changeables, which go through an array of sunset colors. Hardies open around 9 A.M. in midsummer and close between 3 and 5 P.M.

Tropical water lilies also come in blues and purples, shades that are unavailable in hardy water lilies. Tropicals are further divided into day bloomers, which close around dusk; and night bloomers, which open at dusk and close late the next morning. The flowers of the tropicals are bigger and more fragrant than those of hardy water lilies; they bloom two to three times as heavily, and their leaves are more heavily textured.

If you're a 9-to-5 worker, bloom time may be important. A few day-blooming water lilies reliably stay open a couple of hours later each evening, giving you a short time to enjoy them when you arrive home. The hardies' day-blooming habit is a good argument for having at least one night-blooming tropical, even if you have to replace it every year.

Your chief consideration when choosing a water lily is likely to be the spread of its leaves. Some varieties that get no more than 2 to 3 feet across will even restrict their growth further in a tub or patio water garden. Others will quickly zoom to 10 feet across, covering all the surface in a small pond and limiting options for other plants in a medium-size pond.

A medium-size pond is generally considered to be one about 100 square feet (10 x 10 feet) in area. Keeping this in mind, here's a rough rule for choosing the maximum size of your water lilies: tub, no more than 3 feet in diameter; small pond, 6 feet; medium-size pond, 9 feet; large pond, 10 or more feet.

GROWING WATER LILIES

Water lilies like full sun, at least six hours a day, and calm water. Although it's possible to build permanent beds for them on the floor of your pond, most water gardeners use plastic tubs. Water-garden suppliers sell specially-made baskets, but you can recycle plastic dish pans, trays sold for mixing concrete, or other containers. If you live in frost-free Zone 10 or 11, you can plant water lilies any time of year. Elsewhere, plant hardy water lilies when the danger of frost is past in spring, up until a few weeks before the first expected frost in fall (although if you plant them early in spring, you'll get to enjoy their flowers the first year). Plant tropical water lilies once the water in your pond has warmed to 70°F.

Keep your hardy water lilies moist and cool until you plant them. Tropicals should be planted as soon as you receive them from the nursery. Suppliers will ship mail-ordered water lilies at the appropriate time for planting in your area.

The container you use needn't be deeper than 6 to 8 inches, but most water lilies need a diameter of 12 to 18 inches; vigorous hardy water lilies and tropicals need more width. Err on the too-big side and you may be able to divide the plants less often—but then they will be more difficult to lift from the pond.

Heavy garden soil—even clay that's not good for other plants—is the ideal planting medium for water lilies. Lighter soil may float away, and manure or compost may foul the water. Fill your container about half full of soil and lay the water-lily rhizome on top. The rhizome can be either a "pineapple" type, with growth coming from the top, or more similar to an iris rhizome, with growing tips running along the rhizome's length. In both cases, add soil around the rhizome until just the growing tip appears above the soil surface.

Potted Plants

Top with an inch of gravel to hold the soil. Now lower the container into the pond, so the first few lily pads easily reach the surface. If your plant has already unfurled leaves, put the container on bricks or blocks so leaves can float. (Avoid concrete blocks, which can make water more alkaline.) Otherwise, place so the growing tip is about 6 inches below the water surface. As leaves grow taller, lower the container gradually to a maximum depth of 18 inches.

A 1- to 3-gal. dishpan or special container lined with burlap and filled with heavy garden soil

Gravel (1-in.)

To keep your pond clean, your only ongoing chores will be to remove dead foliage and fourth-day flowers (which usually stay underwater) and fertilize the container once a month in spring and fall and twice monthly in midsummer. Fertilizer tablets sold by aquatic dealers are the most convenient way to feed your water lilies without polluting your pond or breaking the plants' fragile growing tips.

Divide water lily pads every two to three years, and possibly every year in the Deep South. Spring is the best time to do this. Gently upend the container and pull the rhizome from the soil. Cut the rhizome into sections 3 to 6 inches long, using a clean knife, and replant.

TROPICAL WATER LILIES: NYMPHAEA SPECIES AND CULTIVARS

Flowers of almost all tropical water lilies are fragrant and stand above the water. They should bloom for at least a short time anywhere in North America except for the Northwest, where summers don't get hot enough. They need air temperatures over 65°F.

Some tropical water lilies are viviparous, meaning that they develop perfectly formed baby plants on their leaves. All you have to do to have more plants is pull off the babies, press each into a container of garden soil, and lower the containers gradually into your pond to a depth that allows the first leaves to reach the surface.

WINTER CARE

If your pond doesn't freeze entirely, you can leave your hardy water lilies out all winter. If your pond is very shallow or your climate is cold, you need to winter over your hardies by lifting their containers from the water and storing them in a cold place such as a garage. Put containers in plastic bags, and make sure they don't dry out completely.

Although most people just let their tropical water lilies die and buy new ones the following spring, you can try storing them for the winter. Lift each container, pull the rhizome out, rinse it, and let it air-dry for a couple of days. Brush off remaining dirt and pull off excess roots; store the rhizome in a container of distilled water in a cool but frost-free place. In early spring—a couple of months before you expect your pond water to reach 70°F—pot up the rhizome and place the pot in a pan of water in a sunny window to start the growth process.

Most water lilies on the market are hybrids that are sold under a cultivar name often without indicating a species. However, in a few cases, you will find species offered.

Little Lotuses

Plantlet

Some lotus plants are vivaparous, meaning that fully formed baby plants form on the leaves of mature plants. They can easily be removed and potted.

Hardy lily pads growing above the water need to be divided.

HARDY WATER LILIES

Nymphaea cultivars

'Arc-en-Ciel'

Described as a "moderate" bloomer, this beauty would be worth having even if it never flowered at all. Developed at the turn of the twentieth century by the great French hybridizer Joseph Bory Latour- Marliac and named for the rainbow, it has foliage that rivals that celestial phenomenon: deep and pale pink, purple, yellow, green, cream, and bronze. The fragrant flowers are soft pink and have slim petals. **Flowers 5 inches, light pink, fragrant; leaves 9 inches, variegated; spread 4 to 5 feet.**

'Attraction'

These flowers are among the biggest of the red hardies. Opening in a cup shape and spreading to a star, they are a deep, rich garnet red with slightly paler outer petals, set off by orange stamens. Blooming is vigorous. Oval leaves often have one lobe raised. This, like other dark red water lilies, can burn in intense sun; it tolerates a little shade and in the South even benefits from it. **Flowers up to 8 inches, garnet red; leaves up to 12 inches; spread 4 to 5 feet.**

'Charlene Strawn'

Kirk Strawn, a hybridizer at Texas A&M University, named this deliciously fragrant water lily after his wife. Large, star-shaped yellow flowers with long pointed petals are held several inches above the water surface. Leaves often keep some of their purple markings as they age. 'Charlene Strawn' is a generous bloomer with a longer flowering season than most water lilies. **Flowers up to 8 inches across, yellow, fragrant; leaves 9 inches; spread 3 to 5 feet.**

'Chromatella'

Sometimes listed as *N.* x *marliacea* 'Chromatella' or 'Golden Cup', this reliable water lily is small enough for a tub only 2 feet across and 1 foot deep; it will take some shade as well. The broad petals of the canary yellow flowers curve up at the edges; anthers in center are slightly darker yellow. **Flowers 6 inches, semidouble, canary yellow; leaves 8 to 9 inches; spread 3 feet.**

'Chrysantha'
(formerly **'Graziella'**)

This changeable cultivar has spoon-shaped petals, and its little flowers remain cup shaped. Their color alters from an apricot-yellow to a reddish orange; the overall effect is a steadily deepening apricot. Olive green leaves remain splotched with maroon. 'Chrysantha' flowers freely and will work in a tub, but it doesn't like hot summers. **Flowers 3 to 4 inches, apricot to red-orange; leaves 6 inches, mottled; spread 2 to 3 feet.**

'Comanche'

This is one of the largest changeable water lilies. First a cup-shaped golden yellow, it spreads to a rosy apricot star that turns deep coppery orange with redder inner petals and pale yellow tips. The leaves change, too, from bronze to olive green. 'Comanche' is a bit more susceptible to crown rot than some other changeables. **Flowers 5 inches, gold to copper; leaves 12 inches; spread 4 to 5 feet.**

'Darwin' (formerly **'Hollandia'**)

This cultivar starts life with pink inner petals and white outer petals, all becoming pinker as it ages—usually for more than the standard three days. Profuse flowers are fully double and goblet shaped with a tidy habit. Fragrance is slight, but 'Darwin' makes good cut flowers. **Flowers 7 inches, double, pink, lightly fragrant; leaves 11 inches; spread 4 to 5 feet.**

'Ellisiana'

Looking for a fragrant, bright red water lily for a small pond? 'Ellisiana' will stop blooming in hot weather, but if you garden in **Zones 3–7,** it may be perfect. Its star-shaped flowers are a rich purple-red hue. The mid-green leaves have open sinuses. **Flowers 5 inches, purple-red; leaves 8 inches; spread up to 3 feet.**

'Escarboucle'

If you miss seeing your water lilies bloom during the work week, this one will cut you some slack by staying open a couple of hours longer than most. A vivid vermilion red with white-tipped outer petals, yellow anthers, and dark orange stamens, it offers a spicy fragrance, too. Flowers change from cup- to star-shaped. Leaves age from copper to deep green. **Flowers 6 inches, white-tipped red, spicy fragrance; leaves up to 11 inches; spread 4 to 5 feet.**

'Firecrest'

The name was inspired by the flaming orange-and-yellow center, which contrasts strikingly with the soft lavender-pink petals. From spring until fall, stems hold blooms just above the water; the outer petals hang down like a bed ruffle, while the central petals form a perky egg cup. Leaves are dark purple when they unfold and keep some dark purple specks as they turn dark green. Give it a container at least 2 feet across and 1 foot deep for lots of flowers. **Flowers 6 inches, lilac-pink; leaves 9 inches; spread 4 feet.**

'Froebelii'

This little gem can handle water a mere 6 inches deep. Burgundy flowers perch jauntily above the water; contrasting stamens are orange-red. It first looks almost like a tulip and flattens to a star. Leaves mature from bronze to pale green and have open sinuses. Like 'Ellisiana', it does best where summers are relatively cool. **Flowers 4 inches, burgundy; leaves 6 inches; spread 3 feet.**

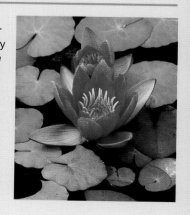

'Gladstoniana'

Sometimes sold as 'Gladstone', this vigorous water lily is for large ponds. It is as interesting for its foliage as for its large flowers, which are pure white and semidouble. Leaves are somewhat waxy looking and have crinkly margins. **Flowers to 7 inches, semidouble, white; leaves 12 inches; spread from 5 to 8 feet.**

'Gloriosa'

The many red petals of this cuplike flower get redder with age and sometimes have darker flecks. The white sepals are flushed with pink; stamens are orange-red. Oval leaves mature from a dark-blotched light purple to bronze-green. 'Gloriosa' is susceptible to crown rot, one of the few diseases to trouble water lilies. But you'll still see it on lists of the best water lilies because of its abundant flowers. **Flowers 5 feet, red, fragrant; leaves 8 inches; spread to 5 feet.**

'Gonnere' (also sold as 'Crystal White' and 'Snowball')

This pure white cultivar has two to three times as many thick, curved petals as most others. The flowers stand out among the relatively small, light green pads, are fragrant, and stay open late into the afternoon. 'Gonnere' can adapt to small, shallow ponds, but it doesn't do well in the summer south of **Zone 7. Flowers 4 to 6 inches, white, fragrant; leaves 6 to 9 inches; spread 3 to 4 feet.**

'Helvola'

(sometimes listed as *N.* x *pygmaea helvola* or 'Yellow Pygmy')

Want to enjoy a water lily on your patio after work? This gem opens late in the afternoon and stays open later, too. Plus it can be grown in a tub only 6 inches deep. It produces clear yellow, semidouble flowers and mottled oval leaves. **Flowers 2 to 3 inches, semidouble, clear yellow; leaves 5 inches long; spread 2 feet.**

(continued on next page)

HARDY WATER LILIES

(continued from previous page)

'Hermine'

While double flowers are voluptuous, there is a classic simplicity to singles such as pure white, long-petaled 'Hermine'. Held above the water, when fully open each flower looks almost like a snowflake with a yellow center. This cultivar blooms reliably its first year and profusely after that, always for a long season. It tolerates shade and various water depths but is restrained enough to grow in a tub, where you can more easily catch its light fragrance. **Flowers 5 inches, double, white, slightly fragrant; leaves 6 to 7 inches; spread 2½ feet.**

'James Brydon'

This longtime favorite was developed by a Philadelphia nursery at the turn of the twentieth century and named for a customer. Double rosy red flowers—cupped and peony-like, the center a range of oranges—often open several at a time. Purple-brown new foliage has darker blotches and then turns bronze. With small features and a tidy disposition, this plant makes a great water lily for a tub just a foot deep. It resists crown rot, too, but like most reds it appreciates a temperate climate. **Flowers 4 inches, double, rosy red, fragrant; leaves 7 inches, purplish to bronze; spread 3 to 4 feet.**

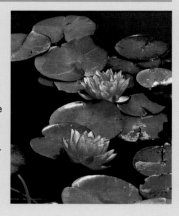

N x marliacea 'Carnea' ('Marliacea Carnea')

While many water lilies have paler sepals than petals, this one is reversed, with light pink petals and deeper pink sepals that have even darker rose markings. The central petals remain upright, embracing their yellow stamens and anthers like a flesh-colored egg cup. 'Carnea' tolerates some shade and adapts to any size pond, but it does best in medium to large ones. **Flowers 5 inches, semidouble, pale pink; leaves to 8 inches; spread 4 to 5 feet.**

'Masaniello'

This water lily is as starkly two-tone as a '57 Chevy. Rose-pink petals are dabbed with red; sepals are white. The dual colors are accentuated by the way the petals remain in a cup while the sepals spread down toward the water. Although subject to crown rot, 'Masaniello' takes some shade and adapts to small ponds. A high-contrast choice that adds flair. **Flowers to 6 inches, bright pink; leaves 9 inches; spread 4 feet.**

'Mayla'

There aren't many water lilies that can touch this fairly recent Kirk Strawn introduction for drama when it unfolds its flamboyant fuchsia flowers above the water. Inner petals have gold tips that match the stamens. Redolent of musk, 'Mayla' has bronze-maroon leaves. **Flowers 6 to 7 inches, bright pink, fragrant; leaves to 12 inches; spread 5 to 6 feet.**

'Pearl of the Pool'

Fragrant double flowers are baby-girl pink with pinkish-orange stamens and stay slightly cupped. 'Pearl' can handle fairly shallow water but needs a big container that will allow it to develop a lot of shoots. Round bronze leaves mature to deep green but often flash their coppery undersides by turning up a lobe. Aside from a classy moniker, it is a choice without disappointments. **Flowers to 6 inches, double, pink, fragrant; leaves to 10 inches; spread 4 to 5 feet.**

'Pink Sensation'

Extra hours of flowers—and a lot of them—make this intense pink Perry Slocum selection a good choice for any size pond. The fragrant flowers have long oval petals, slightly darker in the center, with both pink and yellow stamens. Leaves mature from purple to green. **Flowers 5 to 6 inches, rich pink, fragrant; leaves 10 inches; spread 4 feet.**

'Rose Arey'

Deep pink, semidouble flowers are star-shaped and smell of anise. You may notice some orange-pink along the edge of the long, narrow, pointed petals, which curve in slightly. Leaves are bronzy-green. A container 2 feet square and 1 foot deep will allow it to form a large colony. This cultivar may need a year or two to establish itself. **Flowers 7 to 8 inches, semidouble, deep pink, fragrant; leaves up to 9 inches; spread 4 to 5 feet.**

N. odorata 'Sulphurea Grandiflora'

Its flowers are among the biggest of all the hardy water lilies. Bright yellow semidouble stars, they have long narrow petals and stay open late. This is a heat lover; north of **Zone 6**, flowering is sparse and leaves can be deformed until weather warms in spring. **Flowers 9 inches, semidouble, bright yellow; leaves 11 inches, oval; spread 4 to 5 feet.**

'Texas Dawn'

This is such a new cultivar that its cold hardiness is still being tested, but it already has an award from the International Water Lily and Water Gardening Association. Semidouble, lemon-scented flowers are golden with a touch of pink on the outer petals that may become more pronounced in fall and a hint of green in the sepals. 'Texas Dawn' can produce seven or eight blooms at a time, held high above the water. It is hardy at least to **Zone 6. Flowers 7 inches, semidouble, yellow, fragrant; leaves 8 inches; spread 3 to 5 feet.**

'Virginalis'

This water lily is still considered one of the most dependable, generously blooming whites. It's a good choice for short-season gardeners because it starts blooming early and keeps blooming longer than many others. The flower is a pure white cup; its broad petals may have a faint rosy glow. Pale green

leaves are flushed with purple and have a downy covering. It needs water at least 15 inches deep. **Flowers 5 inches, white; leaves 9 inches; spread 3 to 4 feet.**

'Virginia'

Maryland water-lily expert Charles Thomas named this one after his mother. It's such a pale yellow that it's always categorized as white (most of the yellow is in the center). This buxom bloomer is a starry semidouble; long narrow petals make it look full as a pom-pom. Open later than most in the afternoon, it also has a long bloom season. Leaves start out purple and age to green, but some of the purple remains around the edges. **Flowers to 8 inches, semidouble, white to palest yellow; leaves 10 inches; spread 5 to 6 feet.**

'William Falconer'

Dark red center petals, slightly rounded at the tips, are set off by cherry pink sepals. The outer stamens have a touch of burgundy on them. Leaves, maroon at first, keep some purple veining as they mature to green. Like most red water lilies, this one does not like heat and will wilt in temperatures above 95°F. **Flowers 5 inches, deep red; leaves 8 inches; spread 4 feet.**

OTHER HARDY LILY CHOICES

- **'Vesuve'**
  Flowers 7 inches, gorgeous bright red; leaves 9 to 10 inches; spread to 4 feet.

- **'Sultan'**
  Flowers 6 to 7 inches, deep red; leaves 10 to 11 inches; spread 4 to 5 feet.

- **'Carolina Sunset'**
  Flowers to 8 inches, deep-to-light-yellow to blushed peach; leaves to 11 inches; spread 4 to 5 feet.

- **'Florida Sunset'**
  Flowers to 8 inches, yellow with a peach-color center; leaves 11½ inches; spread 4 to 5 feet.

TROPICAL LILY VARIETIES

DAY BLOOMING

'Afterglow'

Bred a half century ago, this is one of the tropical water lilies described as having "sunset" colors, in this case golden yellow toward the center, blushing to orange-pink at the tips. Wonderfully fragrant, the flower is somewhat flat and floats in the water. Leaves are nearly round with wavy edges.

'Albert Greenberg'

Similar in color to 'Afterglow', this 1969 selection has slightly smaller flowers and more of a cup shape. Leaves are much bigger, are heavily streaked with purple, and have a wavy edge and one raised lobe. It will bloom well into fall. **Flowers 6 to 7 inches, yellow with pink tips; leaves to almost 20 inches; spread 5 to 8 feet.**

'Aviator Pring'

George Pring, a hybridizer at the Missouri Botanical Garden, named this flower after a son who died in World War I. The many deep yellow, cup-shaped flowers are eye-popping semidoubles, a full foot out of the water. Mottled leaves have toothed, wavy edges. **Flowers 10 inches, semidouble, deep yellow; leaves to 12 inches; spread 6 to 8 feet.**

'Blue Beauty'

Heady-scented, semidouble flowers are blue set off by yellow stamens with violet anthers. Star-shaped, they're often 10 inches across and profusely borne 8 inches above the pond. Oval leaves are wavy edged, and flecked with brown. Wait until the water is 75°F before you set the plant out in spring. **Flowers 10 inches, semidouble, rich blue, fragrant; leaves to 15 inches;**

spread 4 to 8 feet.

N. capensis

('**Cape blue' water lily**; also sold as '**Blue Capensis**') Picture a periwinkle flower with more petals, then a yellow center, and make it the size of a dinner plate. This semidouble species is native to southern Africa. Round, speckled, mid-green leaves are toothed and have wavy margins. It thrives in water anywhere from 10 inches to 3 feet deep. **Flowers 9 inches; leaves 10 to 16 inches; spread 6 to 10 feet.**

N. colorata

Gardeners with small ponds or tubs will find several wonderful choices among blue day bloomers, and this is one of them. Even with only three to four hours of sun a day, it will be generous with its cup-shaped flowers of a violet shade similar to wisteria. It needs just 6 inches of water over its roots and will bloom well into fall—all year in frost-free areas. **Flowers 5 inches; leaves 8 to 9 inches; spread 3 to 5 feet.**

N. x daubenyana also sold as 'Daubeniana' or Dauben'

Considered the easiest of the tropical water lilies to grow, it's prolific, tough, and can grow in just 4 inches of water! Intensely fragrant, cup-shaped flowers have dark margins but overall are not as bright a blue as N. colorata and can fade to near white. It makes up for this by cranking out three and even four generations of new plants on its leaves. It needs just three to four hours of sun. Oval leaves are olive to bronze and have wavy margins. **Flowers 5 inches, pale blue, very fragrant; leaves 12 inches; spread 3 to 4 feet.**

'Director George T. Moore'

Named for a former director of the Missouri Botanical Garden, this is possibly the richest violet-blue of any water lily. Flowers are fragrant and abundant, too, with centers that are dark purple and gold. It tolerates lower light levels (5-6 hours) than other water lilies. Leaves are slightly flecked with purple. This one is happy in any size pond. **Flowers 7 to 9 inches, deep violet-blue, fragrant; leaves 10 to**

12 inches; spread 5 to 8 feet.

'Evelyn Randig'

You just have to pay attention when a breeder names a flower for his wife, as Martin Randig of San Bernardino, California, did with this water lily. The raspberry-sherbet color will have you smacking your lips. Green leaves are heavily marbled with both purple and brown. **Flowers 8 inches, deep pink; leaves up to 15 inches; spread 5 to 7 feet.**

'General Pershing'

A general arrayed in delicate lavender-pink? This double-flowered variety earns a salute with its size, strong sweet scent, and periodically dawn-to-dusk bloom. The flowers, which keep coming well into autumn, open as a cup and then are nearly flat. Wavy-edged leaves are mottled with purple. 'General Pershing' doesn't mind some shade and can adapt to any pond bigger than a tub. **Flowers up to 11 inches, double, lavender-pink, fragrant; leaves 10 inches; spread 5 to 6 feet.**

'Madame Ganna Walska'

This cultivar was named for the Polish opera singer who developed amazing Lotusland, once her home and now a public garden near Santa Barbara, California. It's considered the most profuse bloomer among pink tropical water lilies. The color is bright lavender-pink with an intense yellow center. Petals are narrow and pointed, forming star-shaped blooms. Leaves are mottled and have round sinuses. **Flowers 3 to 8 inches, lavender-pink; leaves up to 12 inches; spread 6 to 12 feet.**

'Margaret Mary'

This lady is a standout for her intensely rich blue color and ability to bloom almost nonstop in considerable shade. The cup-to-star flowers produce an appealing scent. The leaves are lightly mottled and plants are somewhat viviparous. It has a long bloom season and will adapt to small ponds and tubs. **Flowers 6 inches, rich blue, fragrant; leaves 9 inches; spread 4 to 5 feet.**

'Marian Strawn'

Texan Kirk Strawn honored his mother with this 1969 pick, a super-fragrant white star held boldly above the water's surface. Yet its big blooms are almost dwarfed by the serrated pads, which have purple blotches that radiate from the centers. **Flowers 9 inches, white, fragrant; leaves 15 inches; spread 7 to 8 feet.**

'Mrs. George H. Pring'

This Joseph Marliac pick has been on the market for almost 80 years. It earns its keep by producing up to a half dozen flowers at one time. They stay open all day as well. Star-shaped, they are cream-colored with gray-green stripes on some of the outer petals. Oval leaves usually lose most of their speckles with age. **Flowers 8 inches, cream; leaves to almost 17 inches long; spread 6 to 9 feet.**

(continued on next page)

TROPICAL LILY VARIETIES

(continued from previous page)

'Mrs. Martin E. Randig'

The flowers of this cultivar are haunting in both their fragrance and color, which deepens from a rosy purple to an intense lavender-blue. Leaves are edged in maroon. Like other viviparous tropicals, 'Mrs. Martin E. Randig' is tough and will tolerate a bit of cold weather and adapts well to water gardens of all sizes and depths. **Flowers 6 inches, violet-blue, fragrant; leaves 9 inches; spread 5 feet.**

'Pamela'

The color of these flowers is slightly more purple than an October sky, while the size can be immense. There are always a lot of them, too. The huge oval leaves are heavily mottled with chestnut and have raised lobes. **Flowers 8 to 13 inches, lilac-blue; leaves to 15 inches long; spread 6 to 8 feet.**

'Panama Pacific'

These star-shaped flowers open a claret red and deepen to a more plumy purple. Their yellow stamens are tipped with red-violet. This cultivar will be content in a tub garden and, like other viviparous tropicals, will bounce back from a slight chill. **Flowers 5 inches, red-violet; leaves to 11 inches; spread 3 to 6 feet.**

'Pink Platter'

The name reflects the way these mid-pink flowers, composed of many long, tapering petals, open almost flat. Anthers in the center are yellow touched with pink at the tips; outer anthers are pink and orange. Olive leaves have some purple mottling. 'Pink Platter' is not as viviparous as some of the tropicals, but it does share their tolerance to chills. **Flowers 10 inches, pink; leaves 10 inches; spread 5 to 6 feet.**

'Yellow Dazzler'

A clear chrome yellow with an appealing scent, these double flowers open late but stay open until dusk. The way they lie flat on the water makes these large flowers seem even larger. This can make the huge bronze-speckled oval leaves look small in comparison. **Flowers 10 inches, double, bright yellow, fragrant; leaves to 17 inches; spread 6 to 8 feet.**

NIGHT BLOOMING

'Emily Grant Hutchings'

A slightly paler center gives greater depth and sheen to this cultivar's long, slightly curved, rose-pink petals. Star-shaped flowers are semidouble and sometimes bloom in clusters. They lack the usual pungent aroma of night-blooming tropicals. Easy to please, 'Emily' has green leaves with wavy edges and a bronze sheen. **Flowers 7 inches, semidouble, rose; leaves 12 inches; spread 6 to 7 feet.**

'H.C. Haarstick'

Here's a night bloomer with an extra-long season. Its dark scarlet petals have a touch of purple at their bases, while the reddish-brown stamens shade to amber at the bottom. Leaves are burnished bronzy-red. **Flowers 12 inches, dark red, fragrant; leaves 16 inches; spread 6 to 12 feet.**

'Missouri'

White flowers will be the most visible in your pond at night, especially in moonlight or under artificial light. This broad-petaled beauty is a great choice for a big pond. With an ample container and regular feeding, it will develop creamy white flowers the same size as its toothed and fluted leaves. **Flowers to 14 inches, white, fragrant; leaves 14 inches; spread from 6 to 10 feet.**

'Mrs. George C. Hitchcock'

The narrow petals on this reliable bloomer are a soft pink. 'Mrs. George C. Hitchcock' should keep blooming late into the summer. The stamens are burnt-orange, and the copper-green foliage is specked with darker green. **Flowers 10 to 12 inches, pink, fragrant; leaves up to 15 inches; spread 7 to 8 feet.**

'Red Flare'

When this cultivar rises a full foot above the water and opens its glowing red petals wide, the effect is a lot like a tumultuous Fourth of July fireworks. Maroon leaves, which retain their reddish tinge, have a toothed, crimped edge and open sinuses. 'Red Flare' turns up the temperature in any pond. **Flowers 10 inches, deep red; leaves 12 inches; spread 5 to 6 feet.**

'Wood's White Night'

A fragrant, semidouble, star-shaped, creamy-white flower touched lightly with yellow on the tips of its stamens. The scalloped leaves grow large, but the plant stays compact enough for a medium-size pond. **Flowers 12 inches, semidouble, white, fragrant; leaves up to 16 inches; spread 8 to 10 feet.**

OTHER TROPICAL LILY CHOICES

- **'Bagdad'**
  Flowers 8 inches, light-blue petals with lavender sepals, day-blooming; leaves 10 to 12 inches; spread 6 to 7 feet.

- **'August Koch'**
  Flowers 4½ to 5½ inches, blue petals with purple sepals, day-blooming; leaves 12 inches; spread 4 to 6 feet.

- **'Midnight'**
  Flowers 6 to 8 inches, dark violet-blue, dayblooming; leaves 9 to 10 inches; spread from 4 to 6 feet.

- **'Antares'**
  Flowers 6 to 10 inches, deep red petals and sepals, night-blooming; leaves 10 to 12 inches; spread 5 to 7 feet.

- **'Trudy Slocum'**
  Flowers 6 to 8 inches, flat white, night-blooming; leaves 13 inches; spread 5 to 6 feet.

Lotuses

The history and lore surrounding lotuses have left a lot of people with the impression that they are tropical or at least hard to grow. While it's true that they are showstoppers and may overwhelm a small pond, they don't need any more care than a water lily once they're established. All they absolutely require is two to three months of daytime temperatures over 80°F. All lotuses are hardy to Zone 4, and some will survive in Zone 3.

There are only two species: the sacred East Indian lotus (*Nelumbo nucifera*), which can be pink or white, and our native American lotus (*N. lutea*), which is yellow. But hybridizers have wrung vast variety from the genes of these two, so lotuses can range in height from less than 2 feet to more than 8 feet.

Lotus flowers are fragrant and can be as big as a basketball. Most bloom for only three days, many of them changing color each day. These are flowers for early birds. The first day, they open before dawn and close again by the time most of us are at work. The second day, they are open from midmorning to noon, and on the last day the petals fall by midafternoon.

The show still isn't over, though. The cone-shaped seedpod, which during bloom has gone from yellow to green, expands and turns brown—offering itself for dried arrangements. And lotuses remain impressive when not in

Plant or transplant lotus tubers as early in spring as possible, before they turn into a maze of runners.

bloom, with both floating leaves and upright leaves that look like parasols. Up to 2 feet across, the leaves have a waxy coating that catches raindrops and holds them for hours.

Lotus seeds and tubers are edible. This fact is reflected in one of the older names for American lotus: pond nuts. Another of its names is water chinquapin, chinquapins being nuts related to chestnuts.

ANATOMY OF A LOTUS

Petal
Stigmas
Stamens
Seed Pod
Sepal

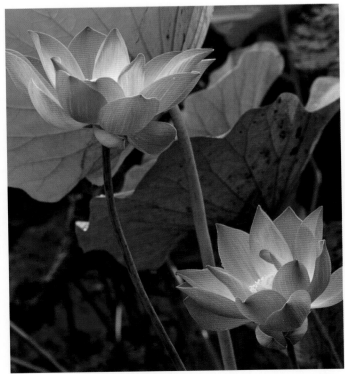

The roots of this lotus are planted in the soil at the bottom of the pond; the leaves float on the surface of the water.

GROWING LOTUSES

For each lotus tuber, you will need a round planting tub about 18 inches in diameter and at least 9 inches deep. One 3 feet in diameter and 1 foot deep is even better. When you receive your lotus tuber, you'll probably notice one or more buds, or growing tips. Be careful not to break them. In fact, most experts recommend against planting lotuses in square containers because the buds are so delicate that they can break just by jamming into a corner as they grow. You can plant lotuses in March in Zone 9, but wait until May in Zone 4. Gardeners in between should plant in April.

Fill your tub to within 2 to 3 inches from the top with heavy garden soil. Lay the rhizome on the soil horizontally, and add a couple more inches of soil, leaving about ½ inch of the lotus's growing tip above the surface. Add ½ inch or so of clean gravel to hold the soil down, keeping it away from the bud. Lotuses are heavy feeders; add four to six fertilizer pellets at this point to ensure a good display. Fertilize once or twice a month after planting, until a month before your first frost date.

Place your tub in the pond with just 2 to 3 inches of water above the growing tip. Lotuses can handle about 1 foot of water over their tips, but less is better. You should see your first floating leaves three to four weeks after the water has reached 80°F.

If your pond will freeze in winter, store your lotus container in a plastic bag in a cool, frost-free place (ideally around 55°F). Lotuses grown in tubs may be overwintered if you can bury the tub in the ground.

To start your own lotuses, collect seeds when the pod has turned brown; dry them; and save them until early spring. Then nick a hole in the hard seed covering and drop the seeds in water, where they should germinate in 10 to 20 days. Transplant the seedlings to soil once the third leaf has appeared. Move the container to a sunny location for several days prior to moving the container into the pond water. Avoid burning the tuber with too much fertilizer when planting initially.

Lotuses

Dramatic and relatively shade tolerant, lotuses make a wonderful addition to a pond. They are cold-hardy throughout much of the United States and southern Canada, but require two to three months of 80° temperature in order to flower. You will need to rise early to see their flowers.

READILY AVAILABLE LOTUSES

(*Nelumbo* species and cultivars)

American lotus, water chinquapin
(*N. lutea*)
This American native is easy to grow. Its sunny yellow flowers usually bloom 10 inches above the water. Round blue-green leaves can reach 2 feet. It likes shallow water and can adapt to fairly small ponds. **Flowers 7 to 11 inches, yellow; leaves 12-18 inches; height 2½ to 5 feet.**

Sacred lotus (Egyptian)
(*N. nucifera*)
This Asian species is bigger all around than our native species. The flowers, most typically a rose-pink but sometimes red or white, have an arresting aroma, especially when they first open. **Flowers 12 inches, usually rose, fragrant; leaves to 3 feet; height to 6 feet.**

Asiatic lotus ('Alba grandiflora')
This classic and vigorous lotus is sometimes called the "magnolia lotus" because of its flower's resemblance to that tree's substantial white blossom. The frill of anthers around the seedpod is especially showy. Bluish green leaves

have wavy edges and can sometimes hide the flowers. **Flowers 12 inches, white; leaves 16 to 23 inches; height to 6 feet.**

'Angel Wings'
You may imagine a band of angels in these white, pointed petals, which curl in slightly. As each flower first opens, the central seed capsule is chartreuse with a green rim. The wavy, concave leaves may expand to 2 feet wide, but

the plant itself rarely reaches 4 feet tall. **Flowers 9 inches, white; leaves 18 to 24 inches; height under 4 feet.**

'Baby Doll'
You'd be hard-pressed to find a better choice for a tub than this miniature lotus: dainty flowers that look like white tulips, seedpods not much bigger than a thumbnail, and petite in stature. In a bigger pond it will show off with a dozen flowers at once. **Flowers 5 inches; leaves 9 to 11 inches; height 2½ feet.**

'Charles Thomas'
Just a bit bigger than 'Baby Doll' but still adaptable to a small pond, this selection is unique for the lavender-pink color of its flowers, which smell sweetly of anise. **Flowers 6 to 8 inches, lavender-pink, fragrant; leaves 14 to 22 inches; height 2 to 3 feet.**

'Momo Botan'
The rosy pink flowers have yellow at their base and a yellow center. With more than 100 petals, each looks like a double peony and that's what its name means. But 'Momo Botan' is most famous for blooming for a week, twice as long as other lotuses. The fragrant flowers may stay open all night and are produced over a long season. It's another cultivar that will be happy in a small pond. **Flowers 6 inches, rose-pink; leaves 12 to 15 inches; height 2 to 4 feet.**

'Mrs. Perry D. Slocum'
This has become America's favorite lotus. Its colors are often compared to those of a favorite rose, 'Peace'. First yellow blushed with pink, the flowers fade to equally lovely cream and pink. Each bloom is subtly different, and a single plant can have several differently tinted blossoms at once. The flowers have more than 80 petals and a strong anise scent. Felty leaves grow large and the plant is over 4 feet tall, so it will need a medium to large pond. **Flowers to 12 inches, pink with yellow or cream, fragrant; leaves to 23 inches; height 4 to 5 feet.**

'Red Lotus'
(*N. nucifera var. rosea*)
A naturally occurring variety in China and Japan, this is among the bigger lotuses. Its medium-size, anise-scented flowers are a rosy pink similar to 'Rosea Plena' (below) but with fewer petals, so that on the first day each looks like an unfolding rose. The leaves are held more than 4 feet over the water. **Flowers 8 to 10 inches, rose-pink, fragrant; leaves 18 inches; height to 6 feet.**

Double rose lotus ('Rosea plena')
The flowers of this cultivar resemble a peony or a full, open rose with up to 100 deep rose-red petals, which are yellow at their base. Its 1-inch seed capsules almost disappear inside the blossom. If well fertilized, this cultivar can grow shoulder high to most gardeners. **Flowers to 13 inches, deep rose; leaves 18 inches; height to 5 feet.**

Tulip lotus ('Shirokunshi')
This pure white flower looks even more delicate because it has a mere 16 petals. This one is a good patio choice, since it stays relatively petite. **Flowers 8 inches, white; leaves 18 inches; height 30 inches.**

'Shiroman' ('Alba Plena')
Here's a peony look-alike for those who want a pale lotus. The blossoms are fluffy and cream colored. It will spread rapidly, so choose this lotus only for a medium to large pond. **Flowers 10 inches, cream; leaves 24 inches; height to 5 feet.**

Marginal Plants

Marginal plants occur naturally along the edge of ponds and streams, and they usually like their roots covered in water at least part of the growing season. These are plants you can use inside the edge of your pond. They generally make excellent plants for tub gardens and can be planted in containers set on pond shelves or blocks under water. Some species thrive in soil outside the pond's edge if the soil contains organic matter and is kept moist.

A few grasses and grasslike plants are good for marginal planting. Soft rush (*Juncus effusus*), bulrush (*Schoenoplectus*), and woolgrass bulrush (*Scirpus cyperinus*) can grow in water up to six inches deep (either in containers or planted in a natural or earthen pond) as well as in constantly moist soil. Spiky plants such as sweet flag or true irises provide a strong vertical interest at the pond's edge.

The are many beautiful rises that will grow in shallow water or moist soil. While the flamboyantly flowered bearded irises are typically grown in very well-drained soil with their tubers slightly exposed above the ground, there's no reason you can't plant them in well-drained soil along the edge of a lined pond. The irises most closely associated with ponds are beardless irises in the category called "Laevigatae irises." They need moist, acidic soil, or even a couple of inches of standing water. They will be happiest in a wetland garden, or in a bed that is heavily amended with peat moss and watered frequently. These species differ from bearded irises, and each other, in the shape of their upright petals (called "standards") and their horizontal or drooping petals (called "falls").

Using plants with vertical leaves and flowering stems along with mounding plants creates visual interest. Look for interesting leaf shapes, such as those of the aptly named arrow arum and arrowhead. While the colors of some marginal flowers are subtle, they have interesting shapes, as well. Some, such as skunk cabbage and golden club, have a hoodlike modified leaf called a spathe that encloses a flower spike or spadix, similar to the woodland flower called "jack-in-the-pulpit."

RECOMMENDED MARGINALS

Sweet flag (*Acorus calamus*)
The strap-shaped foliage of this perennial looks for all the world like that of an iris, or "flag," but its midsummer flowers are underwhelming 2-inch horns. The leaves smell like cinnamon if you crush them, and can be 4 feet tall. The cultivar 'Variegatus' is striped from top to bottom with white or cream. Grow sweet flag in water up to 9 inches deep or a well-watered flower bed. **Zones 4–11.**

Water plantain, mad-dog weed
(*Alisma plantago-aquatica*)
The baby's breath of marginals, water plantain will self-seed and is too vigorous for all but large ponds. Lance-shaped, gray-green leaves about 1 foot long form spiky rosettes, which are topped with frothy sprays of tiny pink or white flowers that reach up to 30 inches. Plants do best in water 6 inches deep. **Zones 5–8.**

Flowering rush
(*Butomus umbellatus*)
Native to North America, Europe, and western Asia, this 3 to 5 footer has twisted, strongly vertical leaves ½ inch wide, which are bronzy purple when they're new. Fragrant, cup-shaped, rose-pink flowers appear in 4-inch-wide clusters in late summer. It can grow in water up to 5 inches deep. Divide it frequently if you're growing it in a container. **Zones 5–11.**

Bog arum, wild calla
(*Calla palustris*)
Bog arum, in the same family as jack-in-the-pulpit, has a flower similar to that of the South African calla lily. A nearly round spathe cups the green-and-yellow club of the spadix; after a long season of bloom, flowers are followed by red-orange berries. Its 6- to 20-inch rhizome (modified stem) creeps along the soil surface with shiny, leathery, heart-shaped leaves, spreading to about 2 feet. Give it full sun and water to a couple of inches deep, or plant it in wet pondside soil heavily amended with peat moss to increase its acidity. **Zones 3–8.**

Marsh marigold
(*Caltha palustris*)
The bright yellow flowers of this spreading native look more like buttercups than what we usually call marigolds. Growing from rhizomes to about a foot tall, it has toothed kidney-shaped leaves. The cultivar 'Flore Plena' (also sold as 'Multiplex') has double flowers. Marsh marigold likes water only a few inches deep. **Zones 3–7.**

Green taro
(*Colocasia esculenta*)
Every water garden deserves at least one elephant-leaved perennial, even though most can be challenging. Cultivated as a root vegetable in Southeast Asia, taro has 2-foot arrow-shaped leaves on 3-foot stalks. Look for the cultivar 'Fontanesii', which has violet stalks and leaves that glow with dark red veins and margins. 'Hilo Beauty' has white mottling; 'Illustris' has dark purple mottling and stalks. All like high humidity and filtered sun and can be planted 12 inches under water. In **Zone 8** and north, store the tubers (dry) over winter in a place where they won't freeze. **Zones 9–11.**

Umbrella sedge
(*Cyperus* species)
These grasslike plants are topped with tufts of brownish flowers, some radiating like the ribs of an umbrella. You can grow the smaller ones in containers and enjoy them indoors in winter. Giant papyrus or Egyptian paper reed (*C. papyrus*) is an African native that can grow 12 to 15 feet tall. Long thin leaves sprouting from the top look like green dust mops. It needs a huge container (20-gallon), lots of sun, and protection from wind. **Zones 10–11.**
Dwarf papyrus (*C. profiler*, formerly *C. isocladus*), from South Africa, is at the other end of the spectrum at only about a foot tall. Grow it in 2 inches of water. **Zones 9–10.**
Umbrella palm (*C. alternifolius*), from Madagascar, which is often sold as a houseplant, grows 1 to 3 feet tall; it has a daintier cultivar, 'Gracilis', and one with lengthwise stripes, 'Variegatus'. It tolerates a bit of shade and thrives in up to 6 inches of water. **Zones 9-11.**

Spike rush
(*Eleocharis montevidensis*,
also sold as *E. palustris*)
This plant also goes by the name of fiber-optic plant (as do a couple of completely different plants with a similar shape). Spike rush occurs naturally over much of the United States and grows a foot high, producing a quill of little brown tufts. It

likes 2 to 4 inches of water. **Zones 6–11.**
If you enjoy Asian cuisine, try related Chinese water chestnut (*E. dulcis* or *E. tuberosa*) for its edible tubers. It also offers graceful stems up to 3 feet tall and can grow in water up to 1 foot deep. **Zones 9–10.** (Another species, *E. acicularis*, grows completely underneath the water.)

Horsetail
(*Equisetum* species)
These grasslike plants have jointed hollow stems and brown cones at the tip. Common horsetail (*E. hyemale*) is also called scouring rush. It usually grows 3 to 4 feet tall. Dwarf horsetail (*E. scirpoides*) may stop at 6 inches and is less hardy. Other species range to more than 6 feet. Grow them in containers in up to 8 inches of water or in a wetland area. **Zones 3–11.**

Cotton grass
(*Eriophorum* species)
A field of cotton grass looks almost surreal when it opens its 2-inch balls in midspring. The plant is about 18 inches tall; height doubles with the flowering spike. Two widespread and similar species are common cotton grass (*E. angustifolium*) and the aptly named broad-leaved cotton grass (*E. latifolium*). Both will grow in up to 2 inches of water in full sun but don't like hot summers. **Zones 4–7.**

Chameleon plant
(*Houttuynia cordata*)
Like many ground covers, this native of eastern Asia can be invasive, but it is useful for wet shade. Heart-shaped leaves exude an orange scent if bruised. The true flowers are tiny yellow-green knobs, with four white petal-like bracts (modified leaves). Look for the cultivar 'Chameleon', which has yellow and red mixed with the green on its leaves and is less invasive. Grow it in a container under 1 to 2 inches of water in sun or partial shade. **Zones 5–11.**

Japanese iris
(*Iris ensata* and cultivars)
Many people consider these the most beautiful of irises. These plants have been bred over centuries so that their standards have all but disappeared, but the almost horizontal falls are huge and often double. This makes them look somewhat flat, best viewed from above. The many selections, 2 to 3 feet tall and in almost every color but green, frequently bear Japanese names. They can grow in an inch of standing water and should not be allowed to dry out during the growing season. **Zones 4–9.**

Rabbit-ear iris
(*I. laevigata* and cultivars)
This Asian native is similar to the Japanese iris in its rather flattened flower, which is 2 to 3 inches across and lavender. Flowers are larger when grown in a few inches of water than when grown in moist soil. Cultivars are available in white and shades of violet, blue, or rose; one variety has variegated leaves. Soil for these also should be constantly wet but can be more alkaline than for other water irises. **Zones 4–9.**

Louisiana hybrids
You're more likely to find hybrids for sale than any of the species, which are becoming rare. The five species (*I. brevicaulis, I. fulva, I. nelsonii, I. giganticaerulea,* and *I. hexagona*) are always grouped together because they have the same habitat and requirements. Their flowers have no beards, and both species and hybrids tend to have drooping standards and narrow falls. Hybrids offer larger flowers than the species and are unusual among irises in the fact they come in reds as well as blues, purples, yellows, and white. They thrive in hot summers, but breeders have made them adaptable much farther north than the state for which they're named. **Zones 4–9.**

Yellow flag
(*I. pseudacorus*)
It's hard to imagine this graceful perennial as a pest, but it has escaped and run roughshod over natives in the Mid-Atlantic states. As with all such plants, a gardener may end up loving it for its toughness or detesting it for its rambunctiousness. Yellow flag averages 3 feet tall, has ribbed gray-green leaves, and in early to midsummer bears 3- to 4-inch yellow flowers with slightly darker falls and brown or violet markings. It can grow in up to a foot of water. **Zones 4–9.**

Siberian iris
(*I. sibirica* and hybrids)
In May or June, this elegant flower bears small flowers of a dark, rich lavender-blue. Slender leaves up to 4 feet tall continue to provide a punctuation mark after the flowers are gone. There are innumerable cultivars in many colors, including bi-colors. Disease-free Siberian irises can survive with average moisture and go several years without being divided. While they bloom well in a few inches of water, they'll overwinter better if the pots are removed and buried in well-drained garden soil until spring. **Zones 4–9.**

(continued on next page)

RECOMMENDED MARGINALS

(continued from previous page)

Blue flag
(I. versicolor)
Native to the United States from New York to Texas, blue flag has dramatically narrow falls of lavender-blue, each with a white splotch veined with purple. A few cultivars in other colors are available. Similar to yellow flag in shape but only 2 feet tall, it blooms in late spring or early summer. Unlike the other species described here, it doesn't grow in standing water. **Zones 3–8.**

Western skunk cabbage
(Lysichiton americanus)
Musky-smelling skunk cabbages are a favorite harbinger of spring. This western native produces rosettes of glossy, heavily textured leaves 2 to 4 feet long. A banana yellow spathe forms a vertical dish 16 inches long around a club (spadix) of tiny yellow-green flowers. It will tolerate moving water, but no deeper than an inch over its crown. It will also thrive in deep, rich, moist soil. **Zones 7–9.**

Moneywort, creeping Jennie
(Lysimachia nummularia)
This central European creeper can grow in or out of the water; it usually ends up right on the edge. It has escaped into the wild in much of eastern North America. Moneywort has small round leaves and bears bright yellow, cup-shaped flowers with dark red spots. The yellow-leaved cultivar 'Aurea' is less likely to get out of bounds. **Zones 4–8.**

Water mint
(Mentha aquatica)
The leaves are much like those of dry-land mints—slightly hairy, serrated, and aromatic—and have reddish stems. In summer, tiny tubular lavender flowers appear in globes. Native to Eurasia, it will grow 3 feet high and wide and can be useful for stabilizing a bank, but like other mints it can gallop all over the garden. Grow it in a container in 6 inches of water. **Zones 5–9.**

Parrot's-feather
(Myriophyllum aquaticum)
This versatile plant from the Southern Hemisphere is sometimes categorized with submerged plants. (It's related to the milfoils described under "Submerged Plants" on page 207.) But it will creep from the water's edge to make itself at home on a muddy bank; even in the middle of a pond, it waves its brushy whorls of blue-green leaves high above the water surface. The underwater leaves are yellow-green, and its stems can grow up to 5 feet long. It can sometimes overwinter beneath the ice in frozen ponds north of its usual hardiness range. **Zones 7–11.**

Golden club
(Orontium aquaticum)
"Odd but endearing" describes this flower, a 7-inch skinny white spadix tipped with yellow, like a miniature club or poker, blooming from late spring to midsummer. Its 18-inch lance-shaped leaves are blue-green and velvety. You can plant it as deep as 12 inches under water or on a muddy bank. **Zones 6–11.**

Arrow arum
(Peltandra species)
These native marsh dwellers can become invasive, but it's hard to resist their arrowhead-shaped foliage. White arrow arum (*P. sagittifolia*) has white spathes that open wide, followed by red berries. **Zones 7–11.**
Green arrow arum (*P. virginica*) is twice as big, at 3 feet tall, and produces green, nearly closed spathes and green berries. Grow them in containers in up to 8 inches of water. **Zones 5–9.**

Pickerel weed
(Pontederia cordata)
If you love blue flowers, you'll want to have several plants of this wonderful native growing on the edges of your pond. Its tiny baby blue flowers are clustered on spikes up to 6 inches long, blooming from late spring to autumn. Plants can grow to more than 4 feet tall and spread to 2 feet and offer shiny, upright, lance-shaped leaves. Grow it successfully in full sun in water up to 5 inches deep or along the sides of a wetland garden or pond. **Zones 4–11.**

Arrowhead, swamp potato
(*Sagittaria* species)
These plants have even more dramatically arrow-shaped leaves than arrow arums and look poised to be shot into space. Three-petaled white flowers have yellow centers. A common native is the vigorous duck potato (*S. latifolia*), which grows 1½ to 3 feet tall and offers 1½-inch flowers and variously shaped leaves 4 to 12 inches long. Waterfowl love to snack on its walnut-size tubers. **Zones 4–11.**

Also native is the smaller-flowered awl-leaf arrowhead (*S. subulata*), which is 2 feet tall and has 3-foot submerged leaves and egg-shaped floating leaves. **Zones 5–11.**
Japanese arrowhead (*S. sagittifolia*) has 18-inch leaves and purple-blotched flowers on 3-foot stems, but it can spread too eagerly; its double-flowering form, 'Flora Pleno', is better behaved. **Zones 5–11.**
Giant arrowhead (*S. montevidensis*), a tropical species, reaches to 30 inches; they are marked with red at the base of each petal. **Zones 9–11.**

Lizard's tail
(*Saururus cernuus*)
Despite the common name, the spikes of tiny fragrant white flowers look more like big caterpillars standing on end. One fan compares them to swans' necks. A southeastern U.S. native, it grows 1 to 2 feet tall and has bright green, heart-shaped leaves. The species name means "nodding"; if you give lizard's tail moisture and shade, it will reward you by romping about and producing hundreds of these bobbing "tails" more than 6 inches long. **Zones 4–9.**

Hardy canna
(*Thalia dealbata*)
This plant will be the showpiece of a water garden. It has long fishing-pole flower stalks topped with 8-inch panicles of violet flowers. The leaves grow on stalks, too: oval or more lance shaped, 20 inches long, and gray-green with a white powdery coating. Sometimes called "hardy canna," the plant can reach 10 feet tall and spread 6 feet wide. Give it an appropriately large container (at least 5-gallon) and grow it in 6 inches of water along the margin of a sunny pond. **Zones 6–11.**

Eastern skunk cabbage
(*Symplocarpus foetidus*)
The eastern skunk cabbage has a purple-brown spathe, fatter than that of its western counterpart, enveloping the spadix like a monk's hood. The flower generates heat to protect it when it emerges from pondside ice or snow as early as February. Despite its name, it only smells unpleasant if you handle it. The "cabbage leaves" emerge when the flower is gone. Give it a bog or shallow water. **Zones 4–8.**

Cattail
(*Typha* species)
Cattails are aggressive, but their flower spikes and long pointed leaves are invaluable for waterfowl. Two common native species are narrow-leaved cattail (*T. angustifolia*), which grows to 5 feet tall, and common cattail (*T. latifolia*), which reaches 10 feet. Both can be planted in water 6 to 12 inches deep and need at least a half day of sun.
A variegated form of *T. latifolia* with stripes, called 'Variegata', is less vigorous and half as tall. Graceful cattail (*T. laxmanii*) has narrow leaves and grows 4 feet tall. The male (tan) and female (dark brown) "tails" are separated on its stem. **Zones 3-11.**
Dwarf cattail (*T. minima*) is less than 2 feet tall. Its leaves are slender and itsspikes are short. It can take lots of water but likes full sun. Flowers may be non-existent in warm climates. **Zones 4–9**

Calla lily
(*Zantedeschia aethiopica*)
Beloved by florists (and their customers), this 2- to 3-foot-tall bulbous plant from Africa can be grown as a marginal aquatic in warm climates—although it's almost too beautiful to look at home in an informal pond. Its shiny leaves are arrow-shaped. The cup-shaped fragrant white flower (spathe) surrounds a club, or spadix. Grow calla lilies in a container of heavy soil under a foot of water. They can also be grown in garden beds; they tolerate a wide range of soils provided the soil is moist or they get regular watering. **Zones 8–10.**

Plants for the Periphery

A pond that's placed in the middle of a large lawn may look artificial. Use some of the plants described in this section to dress up the surroundings. Add some perennial borders or use shrubs to define a seating area. Larger shrubs and trees can serve as a pleasant backdrop to frame the pond, or they can mask views of property fences or a neighbor's house.

Scale. Plantings around the pond should blend with the style of the rest of your garden and even the architecture of your home. For example, tightly clipped evergreens will only look good next to the most formal pool, while a mix of plants is best for an informal pond. The easiest way to make an informal pond look as though it belongs in its setting is to surround it with plants that occur naturally. That's why many of the perennials, shrubs, and trees described in this section are species native to North America.

The plants described here like moisture, but they also need soil that drains well. In their natural setting, you would find them on the banks above a stream or a pond, not right at the water's edge. If you're looking for plants to grow in constantly soggy soil, look at the Marginal Plants section.

Well-chosen shrubs and trees can draw attention to your water garden, providing a lush border around it, or they can mask or draw attention away from a less-than pleasant view.

MOISTURE-LOVING PERENNIALS

All the herbaceous perennials featured here prefer moist soil, but some can tolerate more average garden soil. As a rule, moisture lovers in shade can survive with less watering, but most will produce fewer flowers in those conditions. To create a more hospitable environment for moisture-loving perennials, dig in a generous helping of peat moss, compost, or leaf mulch that will retain more moisture. A layer of organic mulch (shredded bark, chopped leaves, or compost) will also help keep soil moist.

Moisture-loving plants may be perfect around a natural, earth-bottom pond in a low spot, but they may be totally inappropriate for ponds with liners. If you are siting your pond in the middle of a lawn or otherwise naturally dry area, rather than in a zone of constantly wet soil, you'll need to amend the soil. Moisture-loving plants that prefer shade won't thrive next to a pond that's situated in full sun.

The good news is that many wetland plants adjust to drier conditions. Some of these plants have "look-alike" relatives that don't require as much water. Look in standard garden catalogs and at nurseries for other plants in the same genus (indicated by the first word of a plant's botanical name.)

Bulbs. These are nature's clever way of helping plants survive difficult periods: too wet, too dry, too hot, or too much root competition. Because they can remain dormant for so long, planting them always seems a huge leap of faith, and their eventual appearance something of a miracle. A few of the bulbs described here have adapted to wet soils, but most require good drainage. If the soil where you want to grow them doesn't drain well (especially during the bulbs' dormant season), you'll need to plant the bulbs in raised beds to prevent rot. Corms, tubers, and rhizomes are always included in discussions about bulbs because they are handled in a similar fashion, although technically they're not bulbs but different types of underground storage organs.

Ferns. Ferns add wonderful texture to any garden. Tucked in among rocks surrounding a pond or a waterfall, their featherweight fronds make a particularly refreshing contrast to stones and boulders. While some can prosper in full sun or slightly dry soil, none of them will live long in both. Most ferns benefit from some wind protection. Once in a happy home, ferns rarely need attention. Some, like ostrich ferns, can spread rapidly, so choose a clump-forming species if you don't want to control them.

RECOMMENDED PERENNIALS

Jack-in-the-pulpit
(*Arisaema triphyllum*)
Jack is the flower (a tiny knob called the spadix) and the pulpit is the hooded spathe that surrounds him. The spathe is green, sometimes streaked with dark purple, and about 5 inches long; the spadix gives way to a stalk of bright scarlet berries. Either flower or berry is a delightful surprise to find in eastern woodlands. The leaves, which follow the "flowers," have three parts and reach 6 to 24 inches tall. Give this plant a cool, shady place with moist but well-drained soil. **Zones 4–9.**

Goatsbeard
(*Aruncus dioicus*)
Goatsbeard grows 4 to 6 feet tall and in rich soil can spread 6 feet, but it's surprisingly delicate for such a large plant. Its five-part leaves are toothed and ferny, and in late spring plants develop flowing, creamy white "beards." Give goatsbeard afternoon shade if you live south of **Zone 5.**
The popular cultivar 'Kneiffii', at 3 feet tall, is more manageable for smaller ponds and its foliage is more threadlike. **Zones 3–8.**

Swamp milkweed
(*Asclepias incarnata*)
Like other milkweeds, this has tough stems, a lot of branches which make it almost shrublike, and narrow elliptical leaves. Plants are topped by flat clusters of small flowers, each purple-pink with paler little upright "horns" and slightly fragrant. 'Ice Ballet', developed as a long-lasting cut flower, offers white blooms. Flowers give way to spiky pods that pop open to release dark brown seeds on silky threads. The pods work well in dried arrangements. Despite its common name, swamp milkweed can grow in fairly dry soil. Milkweeds are slow to emerge in spring. **Zones 3–8.**

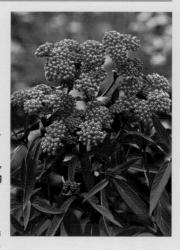

Astilbe, false spirea
(*Astilbe* species)
Some astilbes are native to North America, but most sold for gardens are *A.* x *arendsii,* hybrids of Asian species bred in Germany by Georg Arends. The plants' fuzzy plumes are usually in the white-pink-red range, with a few salmons and lavenders; the leaves are divided and lacy. Plants range in height from about 1 to 4 feet. Astilbes will turn to toast before summer's end if they don't have fluffy, moist, neutral to slightly acid soil. **Zones 4–8.**

Astilboides
Astilboides tabularis; formerly *Rodgersia tabularis*)
The off-white plumy flowers are astilbe look-alikes, but most gardeners plant this for its bold leaves, which are round and slightly lobed and can be 3 feet across. Stems attach to leaves in the center, like umbrellas. Plants are about 5 feet tall and 4 feet wide. They demand cool summers and moist but not soggy soil. **Zones 4–7.**

Black cohosh, black snakeroot
(*Cimicifuga racemosa*)
This perennial grows naturally in damp places in the eastern U.S. Although black cohosh grows 4 to 7 feet tall and 2 feet across, its much-divided leaves give it an airy quality. Because side branches flower late, the long wands of little white flowers keep coming for weeks. 'Atropurpurea' has purple foliage, and the flowers of American bugbane (*C. americana*) flaunt a touch of pink. Native Americans used black cohosh to treat a variety of ills; hence one of its common names. These plants like some shade, especially in the South, but are not fussy about moisture. **Zones 3–8.**

Umbrella plant
(*Darmera peltata*, formerly *Peltiphyllum peltatum*)
Round-topped clusters of pink or white flowers appear in spring on 6-foot stalks. In autumn, leaves turn copper. Umbrella plant forms mats that stabilize banks, in exchange for some shade and constant moisture. **Zones 5–8.**

Joe-Pye weed
(*Eupatorium* species)

Joe-Pye was once used for medicinal purposes, but today it's planted to attract butterflies, which flock to its big frizz of flowers in mid- to late summer. Most common is spotted Joe-Pye weed (*E. maculatum*), which grows 2 to 6 feet with pink flowers; 'Gateway' is especially colorful. Similar E. purpureum is the biggest, at 9 feet tall. Sometimes called boneset, *E. perfoliatum* has white flowers and grows to about 5 feet. All prefer slightly alkaline soil that retains moisture but isn't soggy during the winter. Spotted Joe-Pye weed is the most cold hardy and may survive in **Zone 3**. Otherwise, **Zones 4–8.**

Queen-of-the-prairie
(*Filipendula rubra*)

Related to spirea, this native, with five-fingered leaves and fuzzy spires of peachy pink flowers grows 6 to 8 feet tall and spreads 4 feet across in **Zones 3-9.** 'Venusta' has more intense color. A Japanese relative, meadowsweet (*F. purpurea*), is usually pink but can be white. It's about 4 feet tall and grows in **Zones 4-9.** Both like moist, well-drained soil and will take some shade. A shorter relative is dropwort (*F. vulgaris*). It has white flowers. **Zones 4–9.**

Bog avens, Indian chocolate
(*Geum rivale*)

Bog avens, native to wet meadows and marshes, has strawberrylike leaves, but its flowers are usually a dusky pink. Cultivars include 'Leonard's Variety', having pink flowers flushed with orange; 'Lionel Cox', a yellow-orange; and bright orange 'Tangerine'. Give Bog Avens full sun and moist soil. It may take some hunting to find these. **Zones 3–8.**

Gunnera
(*Gunnera manicata*)

Toothed leaves can grow 6 feet across, and the stalks to 8 feet tall. It will spread to the size of a small bedroom. Tiny red-green flowers appear in early summer on a 3-foot 'cob', followed by little round fruits. Gunnera needs protection from winds and dislikes heat. **Zones 7–10.**

Swamp sunflower
(*Helianthus angustifolius*)

This is one of those swamp plants with many handsome cousins that can substitute in a drier pond margin. The sunflowers that most people know are annuals that require well-drained soil. Swamp sunflower is a perennial native to the eastern United States that produces rather sparse, 8-inch-long, narrow leaves on plants 5 to 8 feet tall. Its late-summer flowers are 3 inches across and have little dark purple centers. Like all sunflowers, it provides late-summer seeds for birds. Its natural habitat is moist and shady. It can grow in partial shade but will get tall and floppy; in full sun, it will be sturdier and produce more flowers. **Zones 6–9.**

Common rose mallow
(*Hibiscus moscheutos*)

The first time you see one of these growing in an eastern United States swamp, you may have trouble believing that some gardener didn't plant it. Lobed leaves 3 to 9 inches across give it a decidedly tropical look, as do the 8-inch funnel flowers in white, pink, or red. It grows 4 to 8 feet tall. Bright red 'Lord Baltimore' is a popular cultivar. Rose mallow needs full sun and consistently moist soil. **Zones 5–11.**

Swamp hibiscus (*H. coccineus*), which bears red flowers and has more finely divided leaves, is hardy only to **Zone 7**. It doesn't attract Japanese beetles like most mallows do.

Blazing star, gayfeather
(*Liatris spicata* and *L. pycnostachya*)

These wet-meadow natives have relatives that take drier conditions. All are recommended as a substitute for invasive purple loosestrife (*Lythrum salicaria*), which is banned in some states. Blazing star and gayfeather have a similar magenta color and upright shape, but the flower spikes are bottlebrushes, about 1½ feet long. The foliage is a grassy clump. Compact 'Kobold' is one of the best cultivars. All like full sun. **Zones 3–9.**

(continued on next page)

RECOMMENDED PERENNIALS

(continued from previous page)

Ligularia
(*Ligularia* species)
These imposing perennials can be difficult, but if you have a moist site with some afternoon shade, you may want to give them a try. Most people grow ligularia primarily for the big leaves, but some species also bear

showy yellow flowers. *L. dentata* has heart-shaped leaves a foot across, and the plant can reach 5 feet tall with a 3-foot spread. The leaves of *L. stenocephala* are toothed; a popular cultivar is 'The Rocket', which produces dramatic 2-foot spires of yellow flowers. Both are hardy to **Zone 4**, but wilt quickly in the unrelenting heat of southern states. **Zones 4–8.**

Lobelia
(*Lobelia* species)
The screaming red cardinal flower (*L. cardinalis*), a spike clustered with tiny three-lipped tubes, is astonishing to spot in an otherwise drab woodland. The shape and color (even brighter than the bird it was named for) make it a hummingbird magnet. A short-lived perennial, it can grow

to more than 4 feet tall and produce dozens of flowers in the right conditions, namely unceasing moisture. **Zones 3–9.**
Big blue lobelia (*L. siphilitica*) isn't really any bigger than its relative; it's sometimes called "blue cardinal flower." It bears bright blue flowers and will tolerate somewhat drier conditions. It got its unfortunate species name because it was once thought to cure venereal disease. Look for new cultivars with magenta or dark purple blooms. **Zones 5–9.** You'll need to divide any of these every two to three years to keep them from dying out.

Water forget-me-not
(*Myosotis scorpioides*)
Like most other forget-me-nots, the aquatic version bears flat little sky blue flowers, each with an eye of yellow, white, or pink. It starts blooming in spring or early summer and will rebloom throughout the growing season. Creeping along the ground on stems as

long as 18 inches, it will droop over the edge of a pond or waterfall. Grow it on a bank or in shallow water with afternoon shade. **Zones 4–9.**

Primrose
(*Primula* species)
Among the moisture-lovers in this genus are the dramatic candelabra types, with several tiers of flowers whorled around their stems and rosettes of semievergreen leaves. *P. beesiana*, from damp mountain meadows of China, is 2 feet tall and wide and bears up to eight whorls of rosy red flowers. **Zones 4–8.**

P. japonica has purple flowers and is easier to grow, even in moving water. Cultivars with red or white flowers are available. **Zones 5–8.**
Drumstick primrose (*P. denticulata*) unspools both leaves and flowers in March or April. The leaves, eventually a foot long, are toothed and spoon-shaped. The round flowers that inspired its common name are purple with a yellow center. Many primroses loathe the hot dry summers common to much of the United States, but they can perform beautifully as long as they have partial shade or never dry out. They'll suffer without winter mulch in snow-free areas. **Zones 4–8.**

Chinese rhubarb
(*Rheum palmatum*)
This brawny perennial gives you the same satisfaction as Gunnera or Ligularia and is easier to grow. Dark-green, lobed leaves are 2 to 3 feet across; deep-red flower panicles look like 6-foot feather dusters. It spreads to 6 feet.

'Atrosanguineum' has leaves that are bright reddish-purple before they mature. Plant it in the fall, feed it in spring, and don't let its soil dry out. **Zones 5–9.**

Rodgersia
(*Rodgersia* species)
One of these Asian plants will add drama to a pondside. They average 3 feet wide and up to 5 feet tall. They're easier to grow than some other big-leaved moisture lovers. Flower clusters, 2 feet tall, are like an astilbe's. Fingerleaf rodgersia (*R. aesculifolia*) gets its species name from textured leaves, with large "fin-

gers" radiating from a central point. Its flowers are white, while those of featherleaf rodgersia (*R. pinnata*) are often pink or red. Leaves of the latter are more closely attached and look bronze in spring. R. sambucifolia usually grows only 3 feet tall; it has white or pink flowers. **Zones 5–8.**

RECOMMENDED BULBS

Chinese ground orchid
(*Bletilla striata*)
Even if you tremble at the thought of growing fussy hothouse orchids, you can succeed with this temperate species. Plants have dark-green strappy leaves about a foot long and tuberous rootstocks. The bell-shaped magenta flowers last for a long time. Give plants a sheltered spot with rich, moist, well-drained soil, plus some shade in summer. **Zones 6–9.**

Quamash
(*Camassia* species)
More and more gardeners are including these blue beauties in their gardens. The spring flowers are six-petaled stars on tall spires. Cusick camas (*C. cusickii*) bears 2 to 3 feet tall with spires of steely blue flowers, while the flowers of common camass (*C. quamash*) are cup-shaped, brighter blue, and from 1 to 2 feet tall. Native to moist meadows, both do best with full sun and good drainage, and want ample moisture in spring. **Zones 4–10.**

Water canna
(*Canna glauca*)
Cannas, once associated with Victorian-style flower beds, are making a big comeback. Unlike garden cannas, this species is a Brazilian native that has been bred to thrive in 6 to 12 inches of water. Plants will grow to 6 feet and produce gray, white-margined, lance-shaped leaves. Yellow flowers reappear throughout the summer. Cultivars include 'Endeavor' (flaming red), 'Erebus' (salmon), 'Ra' (yellow), and 'Taney' (orange-brown). Give cannas a sunny location in containers of fertile soil. **Zones 9–11**; north of **Zone 9**, unearth and dry the rhizomes in fall and overwinter them in slightly damp peat moss.

Bog lily
(*Crinum* species)
These bulbs make striking specimens for a pond margin. Southern swamp lily (*C. americanum*), a native of Florida and the Gulf Coast, has leaves 2 inches wide and up to 2 feet long plus long-petaled, pungent white flowers. It will grow in 12 inches of water but prefers half as much. Plant so the neck of the bulb sits just above ground. The bulbs need to be overwintered indoors in all but frost-free areas. **Zones 10–11.**

Crocosmia 'Lucifer'
This increasingly popular bulb is native to South African grasslands. Its arching lance-shaped leaves and stems add a grace note to any pondside planting, and the flaming red flowers make a striking reflection on the water's sucrface. It grows 3 to 4 feet tall and tolerates partial shade. If you get tired of red, there are other cultivars with orange, yellow, or bicolored flowers. All need moderately rich, moist, and well-drained soil in full sun or partial shade. **Zones 5–8**; to **Zone 10** in the West.

Angel's fishing rods
(*Dierama* species)
It's hard to imagine any flowers that would look more appropriate beside a pond than these 2 to 3 foot African natives, related to irises. Long, thin leaves are topped in summer by drooping wands of bell-shaped flowers, most often pink. Plant them in spring 2 to 3 inches below the soil surface. Zones vary with the species, either **Zones 7–9** or **8–10.**

Spider lily
(*Hymenocallis* species)
White with six long petals, *H. caroliniana* is hardy. Its leaves grow about 18 inches tall and the flowers are up to 5 inches across. **Zones 6–9.** The evergreen *H. liriosome* has 8-inch flowers that smell lemony. Plant in moist soil. **Zones 7–11.**

RECOMMENDED FERNS

Maidenhair fern
(*Adiantum* species)
These lacy ferns are tougher than they look as long as they have moist soil with good drainage. They grow naturally on cliffs along waterfalls, so they will look especially appropriate tucked into some soil pockets next to your pond. Both American maidenhair fern (*A. pedatum*; **Zones 3–8**) and southern maidenhair fern (*A. capillus-veneris*; **Zones 8–10**)

grow about 1 to 1½ feet tall and have black stalks. The former is deciduous and has triangular frond segments; the latter is evergreen, has fan-shaped frond segments, and needs consistently moist, alkaline soil.

Lady fern
(*Athyrium filix-femina*)
Not demure in stature at 3 feet—even 5 feet in a marshy spot—this deciduous fern earns its common name with finely divided, light green triangular fronds, delicate enough for a lace curtain. It's easy to grow, too, provided it has some shade. It will survive drier soil conditions than many other ferns. **Zones 3–9.**

Wood fern
(*Dryopteris* species)
Members of this tough genus are common in eastern American woodlands. Crested wood fern (*D. cristata*) is the most moisture-loving; it grows 2 to 3 feet tall and has leathery blue-green fronds and leaflets that march up the stem horizontally. This species doesn't like heat, so give it cool shade. **Zones 4–8.**
Goldie's wood fern (*D. goldiana*) is an attention getter at 4 feet tall. Its

deciduous pointed fronds are widest at the center and pointed at the tip. Its color is a light green verging on gold that glows in the shade that this fern needs. **Zones 4–8.**

Ostrich fern
(*Matteuccia struthiopteris*)
This is a giant of the fern world at up to 5 feet tall. It has horizontal rhizomes and is a very aggressive spreader—so beware. Brown spore-bearing fronds appear in late summer and last through the winter. Ostrich fern will tolerate some sun in northerly zones if it has consistently moist, well-drained, acidic soil. **Zones 2–8.**

Sensitive fern
(*Onoclea sensibilis*)
The common name of this eastern native derives from its reaction to cold: it goes dormant at the first whisper of autumn. Its smooth broad leaflets are reddish in spring; the spore-bearing fronds appear in summer as a row of dark beads and often last through winter. Unlike most ferns, it can grow in shallow, still water. If your soil is wet enough, sensitive fern can take a lot of sun. **Zones 3–9.**

Osmunda **species**
These deciduous native ferns will grow at least 3 feet tall and wide. Cinnamon fern (*O. cinnamomea*) has spore-producing fronds in spring. They fade away once the spores are shed, leaving green fronds up to 5 feet tall. **Zones 3–7.**
The green fronds of interrupted fern (*O. claytonia*) are interspersed with brown spore cases that fall. Fronds are often white in spring and gold in fall. **Zones 3–6.**
Royal fern (*O. regalis*) reaches 6 feet tall. Its brown spore cases form at the tips of the fronds. It's a moisture lover that can take sun. **Zones 3–8.**

Christmas fern
(*Polystichum acrostichoides*)
Widespread in eastern forests, this fern forms a nest of dark-green 2-foot fronds that earn their common name by remaining green right through December. Each leaf segment has a little "boot" (think of Santa Claus) near where it

branches from the main stem. A cinch to grow, Christmas fern will spread rapidly in fertile, moist soil and even take some sun. **Zones 3–9.** Western sword fern (*P. munitum*) is the western equivalent. **Zones 5–9.**

Marsh fern
(*Thelypteris palustris*)
On a sunny, never-dry patch of ground, marsh fern will spread 3 feet a year. The deciduous fronds are delicate and somewhat twisted, on black stems up to 2 feet or longer; they turn an appealing yellow in fall. **Zones 5–8.**

Chain fern
(*Woodwardia* species)
These deciduous ferns creep assertively along the ground instead of forming clumps. The East is home to the 2-foot-tall netted chain fern (*W. areolata*; **Zones 4–8**) and slightly larger swamp-dwelling Virginia chain fern (*W. virginica*; **Zones 4–10**). Giant chain fern (*W. fimbriata*, also sold as *W. radicans*; **Zones 8–10**), which has fronds up to 7 feet long, forms large colonies in our western redwood forests. It needs constant moisture and protection from wind.

OTHER FERN CHOICES

■ **Brittle Maidenhair Fern** (*Adiantum tenerum*)
Evergreen fern; mid-green fronds; height to 2 feet; width to 3 feet. **Zones 9–10.**

■ **Male Fern** (*Dryopteris filix-mas*)
Deciduous fern; mid-green fronds; height 3 to 4 feet; width 3 feet. **Zones 4–8.**

■ **Marginal Wood Fern** (*Dryopteris marginalis*)
Evergreen fern; grayish-green fronds; height 2 feet; width 2 feet. **Zones 3–8.**

■ **Licorice Fern** (*Polypodium glycyrrhiza*)
Evergreen fern; mid- to dark-green fronds; height 1 foot; width 1 foot. **Zones 4–9.**

Grasses and Grasslike Plants. Grasses, like water, can add two powerful dimensions to your garden: movement and sound. All year, grasses sway in the breeze, helping you hear the wind if not see it and accompanying the music of your pond. In fall, when everything else is winding down, their iridescent flower heads catch the setting sun and provide food for migrating birds. Grasses make good hiding places for small animals, but also can create a barrier against predators such as raccoons and herons in search of fish. And the best news is that grasses need almost no care except for a crewcut back to the ground in spring and division every three years or so.

To make the mounds that you've created for waterfalls look more natural, plant them with broad sweeps of smaller grasses; include more broad sweeps around your pond. Taller grasses work best as one-clump specimens and make a good counterpoint to broad-leaved plants such as lotuses.

Although most grasses need well-drained soil, some grasslike plants grow well in standing water. You'll find the following species described in the section on marginal plants: spike rush (*Eleocharis montevidensis*), cotton grass (*Eriophorum* species), and cattail (*Typha* species). Soft rush (*Juncus effusus*), bulrush (*Schoenoplectus* species), and woolgrass bulrush (*Scirpus cyperinus*) can grow in water up to 6 inches deep, but they also grow well in moist soil, so they're included here.

Grasses and ferns add color and texture to your pond but require very little maintenance.

RECOMMENDED GRASSES

Giant reed
(*Arundo donax*)
This hulking, bamboolike, eastern European plant, the reeds of which are used in reed instruments, is a noxious weed in California and other warm states. You might want to take a chance on it in colder areas, though. It will form pondside clumps 15 feet high and 5 feet wide

of broad, cornlike leaves up to 2 feet long. The fluffy light green or purple flower heads can also be up to 2 feet long, but giant reed won't flower or set seed in the northern part of its range. 'Variegata' is a striped form. Giant reed will grow anywhere in wet soil; you may elect to slow it down by letting it go a bit dry. **Zones 6–10.**

Common quaking grass
(*Briza media*)
A knee-high grass with blue-green blades, quaking grass doubles in height when its flower stalks appear in spring. The tiny seedpods are slightly heart-shaped and remind some people of rattlesnake tails, others of puffed oats. This plant's

charm lies in the way it nods, bobs, and shivers in a slight breeze. Native to wet meadows of the Mediterranean region, it tolerates a wide range of soil moisture, texture, and pH. **Zones 4–10.**

Feather reed grass
(*Calamagrostis* x *acutiflora*)
The 1-foot flower heads of this upright, graceful grass emerge narrow and bronzy purple, becoming more open and airy as they fade to tan. They bring the height of the clump to 6 feet. A popular selection is sold as 'Stricta' or 'Karl Foerster'. **Zones 4–9.**

Smaller 'Overdam', which has longitudinal creamy stripes, doesn't like heat. **Zones 5–8.**

A native wetland relative, Canada bluejoint (*C. canadensis*), is often burgundy in autumn; it tends to spread by rhizomes rather than clumping as feather reed grass does. You won't find this native for sale in ordinary garden catalogs; you'll need to seek out a nursery that specializes in prairie plants. **Zones 3–7.**

All like moist, well-drained soil, but feather reed grass shows its ability to please by tolerating less desirable conditions found in clay soil.

Sedge
(*Carex* species)
There are some 1,000 species of sedges; as a general rule, if a grasslike plant reminds you of a mop head or the hairdo of the early Beatles, it's a sedge. Most sedges form tussocks rather than being strongly vertical like grasses. Since nearly all grow in damp places, there are many choices for pondside. Two cultivars of *C. elata* will brighten a shady area or cast a glowing reflection: 'Bowles Golden' has bright

yellow leaves narrowly edged in green; 'Aurea' has yellow margins. About 2 feet tall and wide, both will grow in 2 to 3 inches of water. They like high humidity and a half day of sun. **Zones 5–9.** Another multicolored selection of similar size is silver-variegated Japanese sedge (*C. morrowii* 'Variegata'). The white-margined blades are stiff, making it appropriate for a more formal pool. Its soil should be moist, not wet, but like 'Aurea' it sulks with exposure to hot drying winds and too much sun. **Zones 5–9.**

Palm branch sedge
(*C. muskingumensis*)
From the north-central states, it gets its common name from the palmlike way its leaves radiate from the 2-foot stems. Somewhat floppy, it can look appealing over the edge of a pot or a pond. If it has shade, it can tolerate drier soil. **Zones 3–8.**

Drooping sedge
C. pendula is unusual among sedges in that it is grown for its flowers. The leaves form a grassy fountain up to 5 feet tall, and then in midsummer the flower stems jut out another 2 feet, arching almost horizontally and seeming to drip with dark brown, catkinlike flowers up to 7 inches long. Give it light shade unless you can provide steady moisture. It may self-sow. Hard-to-find *C. crinita* is similar but tolerates drier soil in partial shade. **Zones 5–9.**

Tufted hair grass
(*Deschampsia caespitosa*)
On stems that arch 2 to 3 feet out of the foliage, flowers glisten and catch early spring light, opening green and then changing to gold, bronze, or purple. A few cultivars offer flowers with different colors. Hair grass will survive wet, heavy soil. Buy plants locally. Northern plants don't like southern heat. **Zones 4–9.**

Manna grass
(*Glyceria* species)
The most widely available manna grass is *G. maxima var. variegata*, the 2 to 3 foot blades of which emerge pinkish in spring and then turn cream-colored with green stripes. It will spread eagerly along your stream bank and take on a pink tinge again before disappearing in fall. **Zones 5–9.**

Rush
(*Juncus* species)
Rushes, like sedges, are generally residents of wet places, so they look and feel right at home next to a pond. They differ in having round stems with six-petaled, sometimes inconspicuous flowers at the end of the stems. Common or soft rush (*J. effusus*) grows 18 to 30 inches tall and bears round flower clusters that complement its vertical lines.

Switchgrass
(*Panicum virgatum*)
Switchgrass sends up stems to 7 feet tall with 18 to 24 inch leaves. Flowers have a reddish cast that turn pale brown and continue to provide airy grace most of the winter. Leaves turn yellow in fall. The cultivar 'Haense Herms' is reddish-orange in fall; 'Heavy Metal' is straight and has blue-green leaves that turn yellow. Switchgrass will put up with almost any abuse. **Zones 5–9.**

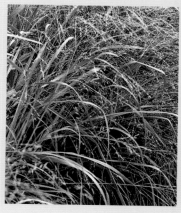

Bulrush
(*Schoenoplectus* species, still generally known by the earlier name *Scirpus*). If bulrushes make you recall the biblical story of Baby Moses, remember that he got big and went afar: these plants need to be restrained. *S. lacustris ssp. tabernaemontani* grows 4 to 9 feet tall and has brown terminal spikes; it will thrive in up to a foot of water. There are two popular, smaller cultivars: 'Albescens' is white with vertical green stripes; 'Zebrinus', also sold as zebra rush or zebra bulrush, has striking horizontal cream-colored bands. Both grow 3 to 6 feet tall. **Zones 5–9.**

Prairie cordgrass
(*Spartina pectinata*)
Another constituent of our tallgrass prairies, cordgrass grows to 6 feet in moist situations, less in drier ones. The leaves, which arch gracefully, turn gold in fall. The cultivar 'Aureomarginata' has the thinnest of gold margins on its summer foliage. Cordgrass tolerates brackish water, wind, and both heavy and sandy soils. But it doesn't do well in dry conditions and spreads too eagerly in moist ones, so confine it in a wet garden. **Zones 4–9. Zones 3–9.**

OTHER GRASS CHOICES

- **Flowering Rush** (*Butomus umbellatus*)
  Long dark-green leaves; likes water no deeper than 3-5 inches. **Zones 3–11.**

- **Star Grass** (*Dichromena colorata*, also sold as *Rhynchospora colorata*)
  An evergreen sedge; arresting star-shaped flowers at the stem tips; 1 to 1½ feet tall. **Zones 9–10.**

- **Jointed Rush** (*Juncus articulatus*)
  Jointed, deep-green leaves; clusters of dark-brown flowers; height to 2½ feet; width 2 feet. **Zones 5–8.**

- **Hard Rush** (*Juncus inflexus* 'Afro')
  Spiraled blue-green stems; brown flowers; height to 2 feet; width to 2 feet. **Zones 4–8**

Shrubs

Shrubs will give shape and texture to your garden throughout the seasons, even after perennial plants have died to the ground and your pond is skimmed with ice. Although you may decide to keep trees well away from your pond—to give water lilies plenty of sun or to avoid having leaves and twigs fall into the water—consider planting some shrubs nearby to define a path, to create a nice backdrop, or to serve as a wind barrier. If you want wildlife to visit your pond, plant shrubs where birds can perch, build nests, and steal berries. Many of the species listed bear showy flowers, and most offer interest when out of bloom, sporting fragrant summer leaves, colorful fall foliage, interesting seedpods or berries, or eye-catching bark.

Most of the shrubs in this section prefer moist soil. To encourage them to thrive, dig plenty of compost or other organic matter into the entire planting area. After you plant them, spread at least an inch of compost or leaf mold over the soil. Keep the soil mulched throughout the year so it won't dry out. (You'll still need to water them during dry spells.)

'Blue Pacific' juniper has dense foloiage that provides a blue-green carpet near this pond year-round.

RECOMMENDED SHRUBS

Bog rosemary
(*Andromeda polifolia*)

Here's a little evergreen shrub for northern pond gardens. Native to sphagnum bogs in Canada and the northern United States as well as in Europe and Asia, this slow grower bears bell-shaped, pale pink flowers in late spring. The long, stiff, leathery leaves (like those of rosemary) are dark green and curve downward. Give it partial shade, work lots of peat moss into the soil, and make sure its soil stays cool and damp; moisture is especially crucial in spring. Only 1 to 2 feet tall, it's a spreading plant that works well between rocks used to create a waterfall or edging. **Zones 2–6.**

Sweetshrub
(*Calycanthus floridus*)

The main reason people grow this shrub (which also goes by the name of sweet bubby) is for the scent of its red-brown flowers: fruity fading to spicy. Two inches across, the pinwheel-shaped flowers appear first in May and then on and off through fall. Urn-shaped seed capsules follow the flowers. Stems are fragrant when crushed; the bark was once used as a cinnamon substitute. It grows 6 to 8 feet tall and up to 12 feet wide. Native from southern Pennsylvania to Florida, it prefers acidic soil, but is adaptable. **Zones 4–9.** For western gardeners, there's California allspice (*C. occidentalis*). **Zones 6–9.**

Buttonbush
(*Cephalanthus occidentalis*)

This is not a shrub that will adapt to dry soils, but it's worth looking for if you have a naturalistic swampy area. From Canada to Florida, through the Upper Midwest and into New Mexico and California, its natural home is wetland edges and shallow water. Unusual creamy-white, 1 inch flowers look more like prickly little golf balls than buttons; they appear in midsummer and last for several weeks. Pruning it to the ground every two to three years keeps it shapely and flowering heavily. The glossy leaves are slow to emerge in spring, so be patient. **Zones 5–11.**

Summersweet, sweet pepperbush
(*Clethra alnifolia*)

Walking in a woodland in midsummer, you may detect summersweet's dreamy scent before you see the bush. The flowers are white to pink bottlebrushes 2 to 6 inches long. Growing 3 to 8 feet tall, summersweet spreads by suckers and makes a good hedge or windbreak. The leaves turn yellow in fall, leaving spikes of round seed capsules. This shrub will tolerate salt spray and dry soil, but needs acidity and some shade. There are several cultivars chosen for smaller size, such as 'Hummingbird', or for pinker flowers, such as 'Rosea'. **Zones 4–9.**

Dogwood
(*Cornus* species)

Most people are familiar with the native flowering dogwood tree that produces white bracts each spring. Its smaller cousins work well for a naturalistic pond planting. The most eye-catching of these may be red-twig dogwood (*C. stolonifera*). Most people buy it for its blood-red stems, arranged in a V, which brighten the garden in winter. Averaging 7 to 9 feet in height and spreading even wider, it produces late-spring clusters of whitish flowers. You can heighten the stem color by cutting off old branches that are fading to brown. This species is somewhat adaptable but does not like drought or heat. **Zones 2–7.**
Another dogwood for naturalizing is Tartarian dogwood (*C. alba*), which also has red twigs and offers variegated cultivars for more formal plantings. **Zones 3–7.**
Silky dogwood (*C. amomum*) grows 8 to 10 feet tall, tolerates poor drainage, and helps prevent erosion on banks. In nature, dogwoods grow under taller trees, so they can take some shade. **Zones 4–8.**

Titi, leatherwood
(*Cyrilla racemiflora*)

Gardeners and landscapers, especially those who admire native plants, seem to have discovered titi (pronounced TY-ty) in a big way. Its merits include 3 to 6 inch dangling tails of flowers that appear in groups in midsummer, lustrous leaves that turn flaming red and orange, and twisted stems for the winter garden. Growing 10 to 15 feet tall, it spreads equally wide and puts out suckers, so it needs lots of room and full sun. It will tolerate poor drainage—but not drought—and is evergreen south of **Zone 7. Zones 6–11.**

Fothergilla
(*Fothergilla* species)

A relative of the witch hazel, it has similarly veined leaves. Dwarf fothergilla or witch alder (*F. gardenii*) grows 2 to 3 feet tall. Large fothergilla (*F. major*), as its common and botanical names hint, is 6 to 10 feet tall and bears larger flowers; it may also be a little more cold tolerant. Both require acid soil that is moist but fast draining and can prosper in sun or shade. **Zones 5–8.**

Winterberry
(*Ilex verticillata*)

This deciduous holly is a must if you like both winter color and birds. Low-key all summer, it houts for attention in late summer or early fall when its berries turn icrimson. It likes slightly acid soil but tolerates dry or damp soil, sun or shade. Ask your nursery for both male and female plants in order to get berries. The usual height is 6 to 10 feet. There are hybrids and cultivars that grow faster and larger; 'Sparkleberry' (female) and 'Apollo' (male) are a top-rated pair. **Zones 4–9.**

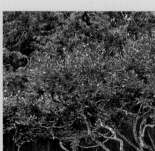

Anise tree
(*Illicium* species)

Among Southern gardeners, the anise tree is hot—no pun intended. Native to Florida, Louisiana, and Georgia, it will flourish in moist shade farther north. The Florida or purple anise tree (*I. floridanum*) has pungent foliage and maroon, starburst flowers in spring. It needs damp to wet conditions and shade. The small anise tree (*I. parviflorum*) gets just as big—8 to 10 feet—but is more amenable to both sun and dry conditions. **Zones 6–9.**

Sweetspire
(*Itea virginica*)

Here's a small shrub to choose for a site in deep shade, or for spectacular fall color. Native from New Jersey to Florida and west to Missouri, it grows 3 to 5 feet tall and bears fragrant white flowers, 2½ to 6 inches long in May or June. Sweetspire makes a great low hedge or edging. It prefers moist fertile soil but is fairly adaptable. 'Henry's Garnet', is a popular cultivar. **Zones 5–9.**

(continued on next page)

RECOMMENDED SHRUBS

(continued from previous page)

Spicebush
(Lindera benzoin)

Most people love spice-bush for the clovelike scent the leaves give off when crushed. In the spring, fragrant little yellow-green flowers light up the woods for three to four weeks before the leaves appear. In fall, it often has yellow leaves and, if you have both male and female shrubs, bright red berries that birds appreciate. (Folks have used the berries as a substitute for allspice, and the stems and leaves to make tea.) It tolerates dry soil and deep shade, but

performs better with some sun and moisture. Spicebush grows 6 to 12 feet tall and spreads up to 15 feet wide. **Zones 4–9.**

Sweet gale
(Myrica gale)

This is a moisture-loving relative of the bayberry, and its deciduous leaves share the scent that many people associate with bayberry candles. Leaves are dense, glossy, and dark green; the lower limbs can be removed to show off the plant's almost white bark. Sweet gale

bears yellow fruits that dangle in catkins. Growing 5 feet tall or less, it's a good choice for small gardens. It grows naturally at the edge of woods with sandy, acid soil, so it can take sun or part shade. **Zones 2–7.**

Swamp redbay
(Persea palustris)

You might want to try this 6- to 18-foot, broad-leaved evergreen if you have a water garden near the coast, since it's a salt-tolerant native of the Atlantic seaboard. A hardy relative of the avocado, redbay grows naturally in swamps but adapts to drier, sandy soils. Aromatic leaves have a rusty brown fuzz on the underside. The plants develop blue-black, powdery-looking berries. This species

is not available from standard nurseries; you'll have to track it down from regional plant specialists. **Zones 7–9.**

Azalea
(Rhododendron species)

There are several native azaleas that like damp conditions. All need acid soil and protection from intense sun (but well-drained). Most are deciduous but make graceful and often fragrant additions to a garden, contributing flowers in spring or early summer. Sweet azalea (*R. arborescens*) produces white flowers (sometimes with a hint of deep pink) with a powerful heliotrope scent in late May or June. It can get 20 feet tall and will adapt to relatively dry soil. **Zones 4–7.**

Coast azalea (*R. atlanticum*) is only 2 feet tall and bears sweetly fragrant blossoms in midspring. **Zones 5–8.**

Rosebay rhododendron (*R. maximum*), an evergreen, is the state flower of West Virginia. It tolerates deep shade and earns its botanical name by growing 30 feet tall where it is protected from winds in the southern part of its range. Its late-spring to early-winter flowers are white with a pink blush. **Zones 4–7.**

Swamp azalea (*R. viscosum*) unfolds spicy-sweet white to pink flowers in late June. It averages 5 feet tall and wide. **Zones 4–9.**

Willow
(Salix species)

Most people find the sight of a weeping willow near a pond an irresistible combination. But weeping willow roots will make a beeline for a water source and can tear through a pond liner, plus willow trees also get too large for most gardens and then tend to drop litter and large branches. Here are a few small species to try with caution; install a root barrier between pond and willow to teach the plant its place. All of them like sun.

Most of us know pussy willow (*S. discolor*)—either in the garden or in flower arrangements—as a first sign of spring. It isn't beautiful, but it may be worth tucking away in an unobtrusive corner. It reaches 12 to 15 feet in height. **Zones 4–8.**

S. caprea is another species sold as pussy willow; it's a bit larger. **Zones 6–8.** A showier little shrub that likes moist soil is rosegold pussy willow (*S. gracilistyla*), which gets big, pinkish catkins in spring. It likes full sun, will tolerate clay soil, and grows 3 to 9 feet tall. **Zones 5–8.**

Black catkin willow (*S. gracilistyla var.*) has purple stems in winter and black catkins with touches of red and yellow. It will grow in any soil and may be useful in controlling erosion. This species grows 10 feet tall. **Zones 5–7.**

Elderberry

(Sambucus canadensis)
You may want this eastern native near your pond if your interests include edibles, herbs, or birds. The flat white flower heads are used for fritters and herbal medicine and the fruits for jams, jellies, and wine. Butterflies are drawn to the flowers and birds to the purple-black fruits, which can sometimes bow the bush toward the ground. Severe pruning will help keep it in shape. Elderberry tolerates a wide range of soils and likes sun. **Zones 4–9.**

Snowbell

(Styrax americanum)
This 6 to 8 foot shrub will grow with its roots in water; they at least need to be both cool and moist. If you can give it those conditions, it will reward you in late spring with lightly scented white flowers, the petals of which are bent back (reflexed) like those of a tiger lily. Japanese snowbell *(S. japonicum)* is three times as big, but there are cultivars of this species that are the same size as the American snowbell; some of these are variegated. All snowbells appreciate some shade and moist soil. **Zones 5–9.**

Viburnum

(Viburnum species)
Once you get hooked on viburnums, you may want them everywhere in your garden for their flowers, fruits, fall color, or all three. There are many wonderful cultivars for ordinary soil. Those called double-files—for the way their white flowers march down the branches—are particularly beautiful. Wide-spreading 'Shasta' (6 feet tall by 11 feet wide) or 'Shoshoni' (which gets only half

as big) would look beautiful reflected in a pond.

There are also several underused native species that are adapted to moist soils. Denizens of woodland edges, they will grow in shade but need some sun to flower well. Most of these species bear flat to rounded clusters of white flowers, followed by berries that are either dramatically colored or attractive to birds.

Hobblebush (*V. lantanoides*, formerly *V. alnifolium*), which grows 6 to 9 feet high, has veined and toothed leaves and white hydrangea-like flowers. Late in the season red fruits turn black against deep red leaves. **Zones 4–7.**

The 6-foot withe-rod (*V. cassinoides*) is the most moisture loving of the group. Its fruits start out hot pink and turn red, blue, and then black. Some clusters can have all these colors at the same time. Fall foliage is orange-red or purple. **Zones 4–8.**

Arrowwood (*V. dentatum*), a 10- to 12-footer, has toothed leaves that turn bright red in fall where it gets moderate sun. **Zones 3–8.**

American cranberry bush (*V. trilobum*) gets its common name from its edible, translucent orange-red berries. Leaves, shaped like a maple's, turn scarlet to purple-red in autumn. It grows 8 to 12 feet tall. **Zones 2–7.**

The similar European cranberry bush, *V. opulus*, is easier to find but somewhat susceptible to pests and diseases. Tough southern black haw (*V. rufidulum*) isn't quite as good looking as some of the others but will tolerate a slew of conditions, including heat, clay soil, and sun or shade. It bears 4-inch clusters of white flowers in May or June and then dark blue fruits. The leathery leaves on this 10- to 12-foot shrub turn burgundy in fall. **Zones 5–9.**

OTHER SHRUB CHOICES

- **Beautyberry** (*Callicarpa americana*)
Deciduous native to 8 feet with small pink flowers followed by bright magenta berries. Tolerates some shade. **Zones 5–9.**

- **Winterhazel** (*Corylopsis* species)
These deciduous species range from 6 to 12 feet tall and bear fragrant yellow flowers in early spring. **Zones 6–8.**

- **Ornamental Cherry** (*Prunus* species)
Pink spring flowers, a tree associated with Japanese gardens. Look for small cultivars. **Zones 5–7.**

- **Snowbell** (*Styrax* species)
Japanese silverbell (*S. japonicum*) grows to 30 feet. American species (*S. americanum*) to 10. Both have bell-shaped white flowers. **Zones 5–8.**

- **Bald Cypress** (*Taxodium distichum*)
Deciduous native conifer that develops "knees" in standing water. Grows slowly to 70 feet. **Zones 4–11.**

- **Eastern Arborvitae** (*Thuja occidentalis*)
Flat, scalelike evergreen leaves are fragrant. Grows slowly to 30 feet. Useful for windbreak or formal pool. **Zones 3–7.**

Trees

Large or small, trees offer shade and other orna-mental qualities like flowers or good fall color. If you plan on having water lilies and other sun-loving plants, small flowering trees are a better choice than large trees that will shade the pond and drop leaves, twigs, seeds, or fruit into the water.

There are many lovely small trees that reflect beautifully in ponds and can fit into almost any space. There are many moisture-loving native trees to consider, as well, for shading a bench or a patio or attracting wildlife. If you have room, you can plant several trees to create an inviting grove near the pond, or an allée (double row) to line a path toward a formal pool. A single dramatic specimen can be perfect in a formal garden as well.

The smallest trees can be grown in large contain-ers. When you buy a tree, leave it in its container or burlap for a day or two and try it in several differ-ent locations to find the most effective spot. Many homeowners don't pay attention to the ultimate size of tree. Like baby raccoons, they are cute when they're small, in a nursery container. But a maple tree or an oak grow quickly the first 10 years and can reach staggering heights over time. Consider the mature height and spread and where you'll plant it before buying. Tree roots trees don't go straight down like a carrot; they spread along the surface, generally to the edge of the canopy or drip-line—the outermost branches. The roots are typically in the top 24 to 30 inches of soil. Plant the tree far enough from the pond that the roots won't eventually pierce the liner, and so the canopy won't hang over and drop leaves, twigs, and other debris.

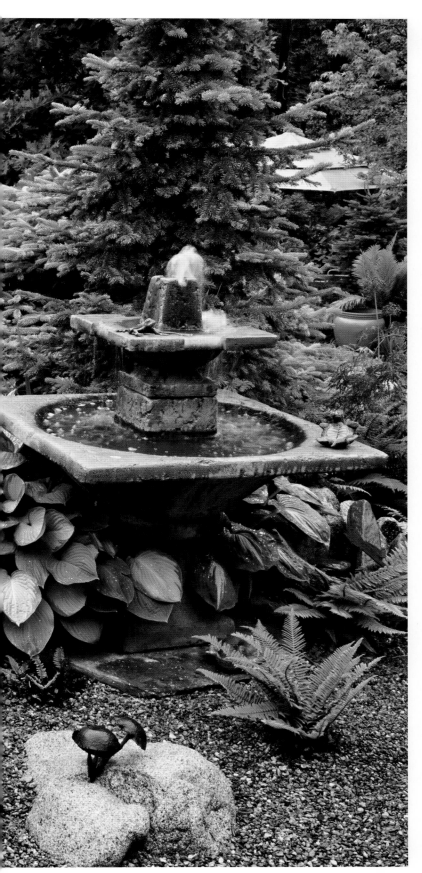

The deep red leaves of a Japanese maple tree provide visual contrast to the evergreens that surround this landscape.

RECOMMENDED TREES

Japanese maple
(*Acer palmatum*)
A Japanese-style garden isn't complete without one of these exquisite small trees. The biggest problem with them is choosing one. You can have leaves that are almost threadlike, variegated foliage, leaves that are burgundy in spring and fall, and types that grow

upright to 25 feet or others that stay small and weep almost to the ground. Many will suffer in hot sun, so some high shade is helpful. Height varies with the cultivar, but these trees generally spread equal to or greater than their height. **Zones 5–8,** depending on the cultivar.

Red maple
(*Acer rubrum*)
This maple grows naturally in low, wet areas. Red maples vary a lot in heat tolerance and fall color, but they can provide some of the earliest and most intense autumn color for reflections in your pond. Fall color is generally not as good in the Southeast. Try to buy a tree grown in your area and plant it when dormant.

There are many cultivars chosen for greater tolerance to cold or wind, or richer fall color. Two of the most widely available are 'October Glory' and 'Red Sunset'. Usually 40 to 60 feet tall and 50 feet wide, these are not for small landscapes. **Zones 3–9.**

Shadbush, serviceberry
(*Amelanchier* species)
The delicate white flowers of shadbush appear on the edges of woods in spring before dogwoods bloom. Several native species and hybrids offer subtle differences in growth habit or fall color, which can range from burgundy to orange or

yellow. Flowers are followed by tiny, sweet, blue-black berries. As with other plants in the rose family, its leaves can be magnets for Japanese beetles. 'Autumn Brilliance', 'Ballerina', and 'Princess Diana' are cultivars of downy serviceberry (*A. arborea*) that get high marks. Most serviceberries grow with multiple trunks, about 25 feet tall, but some can be single-trunked and taller; the spread is roughly half the height. **Zones 4–9** (a few other species are even hardier).

Pawpaw
(*Asimina triloba*)
All of our native pawpaw's close relatives are semitropical fruit trees, and the pawpaw's foot-long leaves make it look tropical as well. Its spring flowers are dark red bells, not flashy but fascinating. You need more than one tree to get the custardy

fruits. These trees grow naturally in deep shade, but need sun for better fruiting. With ample moisture they have bright yellow leaves in fall. Buy container-grown plants for more successful transplanting. Pawpaws rarely get more than 20 feet high and wide. **Zones 5–8.**

River birch
(*Betula nigra*)
Birches are usually grown for their striking bark and their frequently multitrunked form. These are some of the most effective trees for clustering in groves or planting in rows for an allée toward your pond. The popular

cultivar 'Heritage' has good disease resistance and showy peeling bark. In autumn, river birches have yellow leaves and in spring, little catkins. They'll take either wet or dry soil, as long as it isn't alkaline, and adapt to heavy clay soil. They grow quickly, up to 70 feet high and spreading to 50 feet; some new compact forms grow more slowly. **Zones 4–10.**

Redbud
(Cercis canadensis)
Native to woodland edges, the redbud has early-spring magenta flowers that will glow in a pond reflection. It's not a wetland plant, but it will thrive in well-drained soil of any type. It rarely grows more than 25 feet tall and wide. **Zones 4–9.**

Atlantic white cedar
(*Chamaecyparis thyoides*)
This eastern native is a water lover. Atlantic white cedar grows slowly to about 45 feet high and 15 feet wide. Give it moist, sandy soil and full sun. **Zones 4–8.**
Two West Coast natives like moist well-drained soil: Lawson

false cypress, also known as Port Orford cedar (*C. lawsoniana*), and Nootka false cypress (*C. nootkatensis*). These reach about 30 to 50 feet in cultivation and about a third as wide. Nootka needs moist air to thrive and has a weeping cultivar, 'Pendula'. **Zones 4–8,** but Lawson false cypress is subject to winter burn (browning caused by winter winds or sun) in **Zones 4-5** and doesn't like areas of **Zone 8** with hot summers.

Dogwood

(*Cornus* species)
There are many native dogwoods worth growing, but undoubtedly the best known is the eastern flowering dogwood (*C. florida*). Its horizontal branching pattern and upturned white flowers (actually bracts) make it an inspiring sight in spring. It offers wonderful reflections in fall as well, with red

foliage and berries that birds love and can reach 30 feet high and wide. **Zones 5–9.**

Pagoda dogwood (*C. alternifolia*) has horizontal branches in a pagoda-like form and grows 15 to 25 feet tall; it produces flat-topped clusters of small white flowers and blue-black fruits. **Zones 3–7.**

Ginkgo, maidenhair tree

(*Ginkgo biloba*)
This ancient Asian tree offers some of the most striking yellow fall foliage imaginable, made even more stunning by the leaves' unusual fan shape. It prefers sandy yet slightly moist soil, but is adaptable. Ask for a male tree, as females drop copious bad-smelling fruits. The mature height can be 50 feet or more and the spread half as much; if space is at all limited, look for 'Princeton Sentry', which grows upright rather than spreading. **Zones 4–8.**

Silverbell

(*Halesia* species)
These are among the best trees for a patio or a container because they really stay small and tolerate either sun or shade. One catalog aptly describes the hanging white bell flowers as "magical." Little silverbell (*H. parviflora*) is probably the smallest, tending to form a shrub (with several main stems) less than 12 feet tall.
Zones 6–9.
The easiest to find is most likely Carolina silverbell (*H. tetraptera*), which can get relatively large at 30 feet or

more high and wide. Becoming more popular is the award-winning American snowdrop tree (*H. diptera* var. *magniflora*), which generally stays under 30 feet high and wide. **Zones 4–8.**

Witch hazel

(*Hamamelis* species and cultivars)
Every landscape with ample room should have at least one witch hazel for the delightful surprise the spidery fragrant flowers bring when everything else seems dead or dying. The witch hazel's natural habitat is high up on riverbanks; give it moist but well-drained soil. Most of

these trees grow only 15 to 20 feet tall but will spread almost as wide. Birds enjoy the exploding seeds. Vernal witch hazel (*H. vernalis*), a native with yellow, red, or orange flowers, is probably the smallest, averaging 6 to 10 feet. **Zones 4–8.**
Common witch hazel (*H. virginiana*), the largest at up to 30 feet tall and more than 20 feet wide, bears yellow flowers in mid- to late fall. **Zones 4–8.**
Cultivars developed from Asian species (*H. x intermedia*) can have reddish ('Diane'), copper ('Jelena'), or paler yellow ('Palida') flowers in late winter. **Zones 5–8.**

Sweet bay, swamp magnolia

(*Magnolia virginiana*)
Native to wetlands from New England to Florida, sweet bay is more demure than the more familiar southern magnolia, rarely growing as tall as 30 feet. It spreads 10 to 20 feet wide. Plant it near a resting spot where you can enjoy

the delicate lemon scent of its 3-inch creamy flowers. The leaves, spicily fragrant when crushed, have silver undersides that flash in a breeze. Sweet bay will shed its leaves north of **Zone 8** (a natural variety, *M. virginiana* var. *australis*, is evergreen farther north). It wants moist, acid soil and some shade. Several cultivars are available.

Tupelo, black gum

(*Nyssa sylvatica*)
You won't beat this Ontario-to-Florida native for brilliant red fall color, intensified by glossy leaves. When young, it has a handsome pyramidal shape, but may become irregular later, reaching 30 feet or more high, and almost as wide. Clusters of navy-bean-size, dark blue fruits are a hit with birds, and bees like the tiny early flowers. Salt resis-

tance makes it good for seaside plantings, and it will tolerate wet or dry acid soil. **Zones 4–9.**

About the Technical Editor

An award-winning gardening expert, Nina Koziol has been an adjunct faculty member at the Chicago Botanic Garden and an instructor at The Morton Arboretum since 1998. She is a frequent writer and contributor for Chicago Botanic Garden's website, and she has also written for *Aquascape Lifestyles, Organic Gardening, Chicagoland Gardening, Old House Journal, Fine Gardening, Country Garden*, and *The American Gardener*. From 1995 to 2016, Nina was a garden writer and contest judge for the *Chicago Tribune*, and she currently writes for Illinois Landscape Contractors Association's *The Landscape Contractor* magazine and teaches educational classes at their annual conference. The Garden Writers of America (now GardenComm) awarded Nina "Musings of an Everyday Gardener" in the *Chicago Tribune's* Home & Garden section. She has also presented a variety of programs for the Illinois State Master Gardener conference, the Perennial Plant Association, and other organizations.

Glossary

Aeration. The infusion of oxygen into water, usually through a fountain, waterfall, or bubbling device.

Algal bloom. Sudden rapid growth of microscopic, free-floating algae, usually as weather warms in spring. The situation usually corrects itself in a well-balanced pond.

Algicide. A chemical treatment that controls algae growth. This should be used only after natural and mechanical controls have failed.

Allée. A double row of trees, intended to create a path.

Ammonia. A compound of hydrogen and nitrogen. Sometimes found in municipal water supplies, its presence in pond water is usually due to fish waste. High levels of ammonia are stressful and even fatal to fish but can be controlled with biological filters.

Anthers. The part of a plant's stamen, or male reproductive organ, that produces pollen. Anthers in water lilies are sometimes showy by virtue of being a different color than the stamen.

Backfill. Earth, sand, or gravel used to fill the excavated space under a pond shell or liner.

Bell fountain. A spray fountain that falls in a semispherical pattern.

Bentonite. Powdered clay made from volcanic ash, used to make dirt-bottomed ponds more watertight. You can also buy sheets of bentonite sandwiched between landscape fabric.

Berm. A mound of earth used in landscaping designs to help control the flow of water or improve drainage for plants.

Biological filter. A device that converts organic pollutants (primarily ammonia from fish wastes) into relatively harmless substances by utilizing large concentrations of beneficial bacteria.

Bog. A wetland in which soil is highly acidic and low in oxygen and nutrients.

Bubbler. A geyser-type fountain, usually less than a foot high, used in small water features or to mimic a spring in a natural-style pond.

Butyl. A type of rubber sometimes used as a pond liner.

Canopy. The overhanging branches of a tree that create shade around its trunk.

Carnivorous. Said of plants that obtain nutrition by trapping insects and other tiny creatures. Most are bog dwellers.

Cascade. The vertical part of a waterfall or stream, at which point the water drops to the next level.

Catch basin. The horizontal part of a waterfall or stream, where the water current slows briefly before reaching the next cascade.

Chicken wire. Flexible wire mesh used to reinforce thin concrete structures.

Chloramine. A mix of chlorine and ammonia, frequently added to public water supplies. It is toxic to fish and requires removal with chemicals.

Chlorine. A common additive to public water supplies. It is harmful to fish but dissipates after water has stood for 24 to 48 hours.

Coping. The individual stones, bricks, or other units that constitute the finished edging of a pond or pool.

Crown. In a piece of lumber, the edge that has a slightly convex curve. In a plant, the point at which plant stems meet the roots.

Daphnia. Water fleas, often used as high-protein fish food. They also help control algae.

Diverter valve. A device that allows outflow from a pump to be switched on or off, so that one pump can operate more than one water feature.

Ecological balance. In a pond, the situation attained when an ideal ratio of plants, animals, and water serve to prevent an excess of harmful chemicals. Oxygen levels are high, and both flora and fauna are healthy.

Ethylene propylene diene monomer (EPDM). A synthetic rubber. Flexible sheets of EPDM of varying thicknesses are formulated for lining ponds and waterfalls.

Fall. In an iris, one of the petals or petal-like structures that droop, or are held horizontally.

Float valve. A device that triggers automatic topping off of a pond when the water falls below a certain level.

Flow control valve. A device that allows control of the amount of water flowing through a pump to be turned up or down so that the height of a fountain or current of a stream or waterfall can be adjusted.

Footing. A poured concrete foundation for a heavy, more upright structure like a wall, statue, or stepping-stone.

Frost line. The maximum depth to which soil freezes in winter.

Fry. Newly hatched fish. Fry are vulnerable to predators, including the parent fish.

Geyser. A type of spray fountain having just a single jet of water.

Grotto. An artificial recess or structure made to resemble a natural cave, sometimes including water spouts, sculpture, and inlaid crystals.

Ground-fault circuit interrupter (GFCI). A safety circuit breaker that compares the amount of current entering a receptacle with the amount leaving it. If there is a discrepancy, the GFCI breaks the circuit and stops the current. The device is required by the National Electrical Code in areas that are subject to dampness.

Hard water. Water containing an excess of minerals. While not harmful in itself, it is usually associated with alkalinity in water and suggests the need to check pH.

Hardscape. The portion of a landscape that is made of non-living material, such as cement, stones, or lumber.

Head. Also sometimes called "lift." The vertical distance between a pump and water outlet, used to determine pump performance. Pumps are sized by how many gallons per hour they can deliver at different heads.

Jet. The outlet of a spray fountain.

Kakehi. A bamboo pipe used as a simple fountain in Japanese gardens.

Liner. A plastic or rubber sheet used to create a watertight foundation for a pond or pool.

Marginal plants. Those plants that grow along the edge of a pond or stream, with their roots under shallow water for at least part of the growing season.

Mechanical filter. A device for removing large particles of suspended matter from a pond.

Microclimate. A portion of a landscape with different growing conditions caused by variance in the amount of sunlight received, wind currents, topography, and other factors.

Milt. Sperm of a male fish.

Nitrate. A nitrogen compound that results in a pond from the breakdown of ammonia or nitrites. Nitrates are harmless and serve as nutrients for plants, although an excess may encourage algae.

Nitrite. A nitrogen compound that results in a pond from the chemical breakdown of ammonia. If not further broken down into nitrates, nitrites will be toxic to fish.

Ozone generator. A device that breaks down pollutants into gases that escape the pond. It also promotes clumping of other particles so they are more easily removed by filters.

Oxygenators. Submerged plants used in ponds primarily to aerate the water.

Parterre. A level area of low-growing ornamental plants and/or formal pools, usually enclosed with dwarf or closely cropped hedges.

pH (potential hydrogen). A measure of alkalinity/acidity of soil or water in a range from 1 to 14, where 7 is neutral, above 7 is alkaline, and below 7 is acidic.

Photosynthesis. A process by which plants use sunlight, carbon dioxide, water, and their own chlorophyll to produce carbohydrates, which are needed in order for growth.

Plastic cement. A dry cement mixture with a powdered latex additive to make it more waterproof and resistant to cracking.

Polyvinyl chloride (PVC). A plastic formulation. Flexible sheets of PVC are used for inexpensive pond liners. Rigid PVC is used for water supply lines to ponds, streams, and waterfalls.

Pool sweep. A device used to clean algae and debris from ponds by suction created when attached to a garden hose.

Preformed shell. A rigid structure made of molded plastic or fiberglass and used as a pond foundation.

Rhizome. A specialized underground stem, usually horizontal, that acts as a storage organ and produces vertical stems at its ends and along its length. Water lilies grow from rhizomes.

Runoff. Surface water moving downhill after rain or irrigation. Runoff can wash dirt, organic matter, and pollutants into a pond.

Sinus. The area between the lobes of a water lily leaf, often used to distinguish one variety from that of another.

Skimmer. A type of mechanical filter that removes debris from the surface of a pond before it can fall to the bottom and begin to decay.

Spawn. The mating process of fish; also used to refer to their eggs.

Spray fountain. A fountain in which water spouts up from a jet or nozzle.

Stamen. A plant's male reproductive organ, which includes the pollen-producing anther. The size or color of the stamens often makes plants more showy.

Stand-alone fountain. A fountain that has its own reservoir and does not require a pond. (Also called a "self- contained" fountain.)

Statuary fountain. A fountain in which water issues from a sculpture such as a stone fish.

Subsoil. The layers of soil under topsoil, usually of poorer structure and texture than the topsoil.

Sump hole. A small depression created in the bottom of a pond for placement of a pump and to make draining and cleaning easier.

Shishi odoshi. A bamboo fountain, sometimes called a "stag scarer," designed to fill and refill accompanied by a clacking noise.

Standard. In an iris, one of three inner petals or petallike structures, usually erect.

Tamper. A hand tool or power device that is used to compact soil so that it is less likely to shift or crumble.

Topsoil. The uppermost layer of soil, which is the most fertile and workable for gardeners.

Tsukubai. A stone basin, used in the traditional Japanese tea ceremony.

Turion. A bud of certain water plants, which falls to the pond bottom over winter.

Underlayment. A thick fabric placed under a liner to protect it from sharp objects in the pond excavation. Some liners have underlayment attached.

Ultraviolet sterilizer. A device that kills microscopic organisms harmful to fish by causing their cell content to explode. It causes other particles to clump so that they can be more easily removed by filtration equipment.

Wall fountain. A fountain that spills water from a decorative plaque mounted on a wall or other vertical surface.

Water table. The highest level at which the ground is completely saturated with water.

Zeolite. A silicate often used to soften water, it comes in gravel or rock sizes. Water gardeners sometimes use it in an emergency to absorb pollutants such as ammonia.

Index

Numbers in *bold italic* indicate pages with photos or illustrations of the subject.

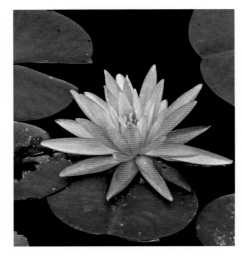

Credits

Front cover: *left* Brian Vanden Brink *top right* Jerry Pavia *right center* carolynbates.com *bottom right* Elena Elisseeva/Dreamstime. com **Page 4:** John Magyar/ Universal Aquatics LLC; **page 5:** *top* Mary Allen/ Plandscape, Inc.; *bottom* Elena Elisseeva/ Dreamstime.com **page 6:** Jan Kranendonk/ Dreamstime.com **page 7:** Jerry Pavia **pages 8–9:** courtesy of the USDA **pages 10–11:** Tom Dowd/ Dreamstime.com **pages 12–13:** *top center* & *bottom left* Northwind Pictures; *center* Redeyed/ Dreamstime.com; *bottom right* Brian Vanden Brink **page 14:** P. Berger/ Photo Researchers **page 15:** Steve Allen/ Dreamstime.com **page 16:** Osaka Museum/ Bridgeman Art Library **page 17:** Aryu/ Dreamstime **page 18:** Stapleton Collection/ Bridgeman Art Library **page 19:** *left* Derek Fell; *right* Villa Lante della Rovere/ Bridge-man Art Library **page 20:** Derek Fell **page 21:** *top* Stapleton Collection/ Bridgeman Art Library: *bottom* Jose I. Soto/ Dreamstime.com **page 22:** *top* Eric Crichton/ Bruce Coleman; *bottom* Derek Fell **page 23:** *left* Steve Solum/ Bruce Coleman; *right* Derek Fell **page 24:** Brian Vanden Brink **page 25:** Jerry Pavia **page 26:** *left* Jason Lenox/ Ponds, Inc. of Illinois; *right* Bob Hursthouse/ Hursthouse, Inc. **page 27:** Jason Lenox/ Ponds, Inc. of Illinois **pages 28–29:** Nastiakru/ Dreamstime.com **page 30:** *left* Larry Carnes/ Caplan Studios; *right* Bob Hursthouse/ Hursthouse, Inc. **page 31:** *left* Saxon Holt; *right* Ken Druse **page 33:** Elena Elisseeva/ Dreamstime.com **page 34:** Brian Vanden Brink **page 37:** *left* Walter Chandoha; *right* Nina Koziol **page 38:** *bottom left* Jane Grushow/ Grant Heilman Photography, Inc.; *top right* Roger Foley **page 39:** *top left* and *bottom right* Larry Carnes/ Caplan Studios; *bottom left* judywhite/ New Leaf Images; **page 40:** Ron Sutherland/ Garden Picture Library **page 41:** *top* Jane Grushow/ Grant Heilman Photography, Inc; *bottom right* Bob Hurst-house/ Hursthouse, Inc. **page 42:** John Magyar/ Universal Aquatics LLC **page 43:** *top* Walter Chandoha; *bottom* Larry Carnes/ Caplan Studios **page 44:** Fabio Cardano/ Dreamstime.com **page 45:** Eric Crichton/ Bruce Coleman **page 46:** *left* Larry Lefever/ Grant Heilman Photography, Inc. **page 47:** *top* judywhite/ New Leaf Images; *bottom* Photos Horticultural **page 48:** Brian Vanden Brink **page 49:** Larry Carnes/ Caplan Studios **page 50:** *all* courtesy of Beckett Corp. **page 51:** Brian Vanden Brink **page 52:** *top* Ashley Marrin/ Bret-Mar Landscape; *bottom both* Derek Fell **page 53:** Jerry Pavia **page 54–55:** Larry Carnes/ Caplan Studios **page 56:** Jason

Lenox/ Ponds, Inc. of Illinois **page 57:** Saxon Holt **page 59:** *top* Brian Vanden Brink design; *bottom* Jason Lenox/ Ponds, Inc. of Illinois; **page 61:** Larry Carnes/ Caplan Studios **page 62:** Nina Koziol **page 63:** Bob Hursthouse/ Hursthouse, Inc. **page 64–65:** Larry Carnes/ Caplan Studios **page 66:** Jerry Pavia **page 67:** Mark Lohman **page 68:** *left* Derek Fell; *right both* John Parsekian **page 69:** Jerry Pavia **pages 70–71:** *all* Derek Fell **pages 73–75:** *all* Jerry Pavia **page 76:** Derek Fell **pages 77–79:** Jerry Pavia **page 81:** *top* courtesy of Beckett Corp.; *bottom* Mary Allen/ Plandscape, Inc. **page 82:** Jerry Pavia **page 83:** *all* Derek Fell **page 85:** *top* Alan & Linda Detrick; *center* & *bottom* Jerry Pavia **page 87:** *top* Photos Horticultural; *bottom right* Jerry Pavia; *bottom left* Ron Sutherland/ Garden Picture Library **page 88:** *top* judywhite/ New Leaf Images; *bottom* John Magyar/ Universal Aquatics LLC **pages 90–91:** Jerry Pavia **page 93:** Photos Horticultural **page 94:** *all* courtesy of Danner Mfg. **page 95:** Brian Nieves/ CH, products courtesy of Waterford Gardens **page 96–103:** *all* Jerry Pavia **pages 104–107:** *all* Harry Heit/ Steve Katona's North Hill Water Gardens **page 108:** Jerry Pavia **page 110:** Jerry Pavia **page 111:** *both* Bob Hursthouse/ Hursthouse, Inc **page 113:** Walter Chandoha **page 114:** John Glover **pages 116–119:** *both* Mark Lohman **page 120:** Bob Hursthouse/ Hursthouse, Inc. **page 121:** Tim Wood/ Aquatic Edge Ponds & Landscaping **page 123:** Jerry Pavia **page 124:** Dean MacMorris/

Night Light, Inc. **page 126:** Jan Kranendonk/ Dreamstime.com **page 127:** Jerry Pavia **pages 130–131:** Nina Koziol **pages 132–135:** *all* Jerry Pavia **page 136** Steven Wooster/ Garden Picture Library, design: Anthony Paul; **page 137:** *left* Steven Wooster/ Garden Picture Library, design: Anthony Paul; *right* Nina Koziol; **page 138:** Larry Carnes/ Caplan Studios **page 141:** *top* Larry Carnes/ Caplan Studios; *bottom* Jason Lenox/ Ponds, Inc. of Illinois **page 143:** Photo Horticultural, design **page 144:** Larry MellicHamp, University of North Carolina **page 145:** John Glover **pages 146–147:** Jerry Pavia **page 148:** M.L. Dembinski/ Dembinsky Photo Associates **page 149:** *top left* Jeff Lepore/ Photo Researchers; *bottom left* Dick Scott/ Dembinsky Photo Associates; *right* Larry Mellichamp, University of North Carolina **page 150:** Brigitte Thomas/ Garden Picture Library **page 151:** *left* Larry Mellichamp, University of North Carolina; *right* Tamara Kulikova/ Dreamstime.com **page 152:** Nina Koziol **page 153:** *top* Nina Koziol; *bottom* Mary Allen/ Plandscape, Inc. **page 154:** Elena Elisseeva/ Dreamstime.com **page 155:** *all* Hanson Man **page 156:** *left* Crandall & Crandall; *right* Michael Elliott/ Dreamstime. com **page 157:** *all* Hans Reinhard/ Bruce Coleman **page 158:** *top* Gary Meszaros/ Dembinsky Photo Associates; *middle* E.R. Degginger/ Bruce Coleman; *bottom* Kim Taylor/ Bruce Coleman **page 159:** Bob Hursthouse/ Hursthouse, Inc. **page 160:**

Mary Allen/ Plandscape, Inc. **page 161**: Brian Nieves/ CH, products courtesy of Waterford Gardens **page 162**: Photos Horticultural **page 163**: *top* Jerry Pavia; *bottom* courtesy of Danner Mfg. **page 164**: Linda Z. Ryan/ Dreamstime.com **page 165**: Webitect/ Dreamstime.com **page 166**: Stan Osolinski/ Dembinsky Photo Associates **page 167**: *top left* Anthony Merciera/ Dembinsky Photo Associates; *top right* Dr. Eckhart Pott/ Bruce Coleman; *bottom right* Tom Brakerfield/ Bruce Coleman **page 168**: *left* Jane Burton/ Bruce Coleman; *right* Gary Maszaros/ Dembinsky Photo Associates **page 169**: *top left* Michael Gadomski/ Photo Researchers; *top right* Ken Druse; *bottom right* Gregory Scott/ Photo Researchers; *bottom left* E.R. Degginger/ Bruce Coleman **page 170**: *top left* David Cavagnaro; *bottom left & right* E.R. Degginger/ Dembinsky Photo Associates **page 171**: *top left* Photos Horticultural; *bottom left* Larry Miller/ Photo Researchers; *bottom right* Jack Dermid/ Photo Researchers **page 172**: *both* Nina Koziol **page 173**: *top* Lee Rentz/ Bruce Coleman; *bottom* Carl Sams/ Dembinsky Photo Associates **pages 174–175**: Mary Allen/ Plandscape, Inc. **page 176**: John Magyar/ Universal Aquatics LLC **page 177**: *both* Larry Carnes/ Caplan Studios **page 178**: Alex Rakovsky/ Dembinsky Photo Associates **pages 179–180**: *both* Jane Legate/ Garden Picture Library **page 181**: Joyce Michaud/ Dreamstime.com **page 182**: courtesy of Beckett Corp. **page 183**: courtesy of Danner Mfg. **page 184**: Gary Wittstock/ Pond Supplies of America **page 185**: Venkatesan Parkunan/ Dreamstime.com **page 186**: *top* Photos Horticultural; *bottom* Mary Allen/ Plandscape, Inc. **page 187**: Mary Allen/ Plandscape, Inc. **page 188**: John Glover/ Garden Picture Library **page 189**: *left* Gary Wittstock/ Pond Supplies of America; *right* Michael Howes/ Garden Picture Library **page 190**: Michael Howes/ Garden Picture Library **page 191**: *left* Nina Koziol; *right* John Glover/ Garden Picture Library **page 193**: K. Rice/ H. Armstrong Roberts **page 196**: Jerry Pavia **pages 198–199**: Jerry Pavia **page 200**: Lbarn/ Dreamstime.com **page 201**: Tim Wood/ Aquatic Edge Ponds & Landscaping **page 202**: *left* Jerry Pavia; *right* Ken Druse **page 203**: Brian Vanden Brink **page 204**: *top* Bob Gossington/ Bruce Coleman; *top middle* Will & Deni McIntyre/ Photo Researchers; *bottom middle* Derek Fell; *bottom* Robert Pelham/ Bruce Coleman **page 205**: *top left* Roger Foley; *top right* M. O'Keefe/ Bruce Coleman; *middle* Derek Fell; *bottom* John Bova/ Photo Researchers **page 207**: clockwise from *top left* Bio-Photo Services; Jerry Pavia; Derek Fell; Crystal Palace Perennials; Bio-Photo Services; E.R. Degginger/ Photo Researchers;

Bio-Photo Services **page 208**: *top* John Glover; *top middle* Runk/ Schoenberger/ Grant Heilman Photography, Inc.; *bottom middle* David Cavagnaro; *bottom* H. Reinhard/ Okapia/ Photo Researchers **page 209**: clockwise from *top left* Albert Squillace/ Positive Images; Photos Horticultural; John Glover; Derek Fell; Crystal Palace Perennials; Howard Rice/ Garden Picture Library; David Cavagnaro; Crystal Palace Perennials; Barry Runk/ Grant Heilman Photography, Inc. **page 213**: Jerry Pavia **page 214**: clockwise from *top left* Allan Mandell; Photos Horticultural; Roger Foley; Ken Druse; Derek Fell; Runk/ Schoenberger/ Grant Heilman Photography, Inc.; David Cavagnaro **page 215**: clockwise from *top left* Liz Ball; Elizabeth Crowe/ Garden Picture Library; Ken Druse; Bill Heritage/ courtesy of Lilypons Water Gardens; Jerry Pavia; John Glover; Jerry Pavia; Derek Fell **page 216**: clockwise from *top left* courtesy of Lilypons Water Gardens; Photos Horticultural; Derek Fell; Perry D. Slocum; Dick Keen/ Visuals Unlimited; Michael Thompson; Ken Druse **page 217**: clockwise from *top left* Runk/ Schoenberger/ Grant Heilman Photography, Inc.; Kjell B. Sandved/ Photo Researchers; Derek Fell; judywhite/ New Leaf Images; John Glover; Perry D. Slocum **page 218**: clockwise from *top left* courtesy of Lilypons Water Gardens; Photos Horticultural; Photos Horticultural; Rex Butcher/ Garden Picture Library; Ken Druse; Perry D. Slocum; Albert Squillace/ Positive Images; Alan & Linda Detrick **page 219**: top left Roger Foley; middle left Dency Kane; all others Perry D. Slocum **page 220**: *top left* Pam Spaulding/ Positive Images; *middle left* Michael Thompson; all others Albert Squillace/ Positive Images **page 221**: clockwise from *top left* Dency Kane; Alan & Linda Detrick; Ken Druse; Perry D. Slocum; Dency Kane; Van Ness Water Gardens **page 222**: *top* J. Paul Moore; *bottom* Jerry Pavia **page 224**: clockwise from *top left* Byron Jorjoran/ Bruce Coleman; Perry D. Slocum; Perry D. Slocum; J. Paul Moore; Perry D. Slocum; Perry D. Slocum; Crystal Palace Perennials; Jerry Howard/ Positive Images **page 225**: *top* Perry D. Slocum; *top middle* J. Paul Moore; bottom both Crystal Palace Perennials **page 226**: clockwise from *top left* David Cavagnaro; David Cavagnaro; Francois Gohler/ Photo Researchers; Derek Fell; Michael Gadomski/ Photo Researchers; Alvin Staffen/ Photo Researchers; Howard Rice/ Garden Picture Library; David Cavagnaro **page 227**: clockwise from *top left* David Cavagnaro; Ken Druse; judywhite/ New Leaf Images; David Cavagnaro; David Cavagnaro; David Cavagnaro; Jerry Pavia; Kim Francisco/ Visuals Unlimited **page 228**: clockwise from

top left Skip Moody/ Dembinsky Photo Associates; Derek Fell; Liz Ball; Crystal Palace Perennials; David Cavagnaro; Perry D. Slocum; David Cavagnaro; Liz Ball **page 229**: clockwise from *top left* Crystal Palace Perennials; Neil Soderstrom; Michael Thompson; Photos Horticultural; Derek Fell; David Cavagnaro **page 231**: Jerry Pavia **page 232**: clockwise from *top left* David Cavagnaro; David Cavagnaro; Galen Gates; Dency Kane; Derek Fell; David Cavagnaro; David Cavagnaro **page 233**: clockwise from *top left* David Cavagnaro; Jim Strawser/ Grant Heilman Photography, Inc.; Michael Thompson; Michael Thompson; David Cavagnaro; Michael Thompson; David Cavagnaro **page 234**: clockwise from *top left* David Cavagnaro; Lefever/ Grushow/ Grant Heilman Photography, Inc.; Jerry Pavia; Derek Fell; David Cavagnaro; David Cavagnaro **page 235**: clockwise from *top left* Saxon Holt; Crystal Palace Perennials; Dency Kane; David Cavagnaro; Grant Heilman/ Grant Heilman Photography, Inc.; David Cavagnaro; Derek Fell **page 236**: clockwise from *top left* Rod Planck/ Dembinsky Photo Associates; Galen Gates; Saxon Holt; David Cavagnaro; Dency Kane; Michael Thompson; David Cavagnaro **page 237**: *top* Galen Gates; *bottom left & right* Jerry Pavia **page 238**: clockwise from *top left* Dick Keen/ Visuals Unlimited; Robert Lyons/ Visuals Unlimited; Ben Phillips/ Positive Images; Derek Fell; judywhite/ New Leaf Images **page 239**: clockwise from *top left* Dick Keen/ Visuals Unlimited; Michael Dirr; Arthur Gurmankin & Mary Morina/ Visuals Unlimited; David Cavagnaro; Paul Grecian/ Visuals Unlimited; Dick Keen/ Visuals Unlimited **page 240**: *left & middle right* Jerry Pavia; *top right* David Cavagnaro; *bottom right* Joseph Strauch **page 241**: clockwise from *top left* Dency Kane; Catriona Tudor Erler; Michael Dirr; David Cavagnaro; Jerry Pavia; Jerry Pavia; David Cavagnaro **page 242**: clockwise from *top left* Galen Gates; Joseph Strauch; Skip Moody/ Dembinsky Photo Associates; Joseph Strauch; Galen Gates **page 243**: *top* David Cavagnaro; *middle & bottom* Jerry Pavia pages 244–245: Jerry Pavia **page 246**: clockwise from *top left* Photos Horticultural; Lucy Jones/ Visuals Unlimited; Ken Druse; Jeff Lepore/ Photo Researchers; Mark Bolton/ Garden Picture Library; Michael Dirr; Jeff Lepore/ Photo Researchers **page 247**: clockwise from *top left* Derek Fell; Galen Gates; Galen Gates; Galen Gates; Howard Rice/ Garden Picture Library; J.C. Carton/ Bruce Coleman **page 251**: Bob Hursthouse/ Hursthouse, Inc. **page 254**: Jerry Pavia **page 255**: Elena Elisseeva/ Dreamstime.com back cover: *top* right Jerry Pavia *bottom left* Photo Horticultural, design